BEHIND CLOSED DOORS

----------Book One----------

THE AWAKENING SERIES

> **Book Two: Journey to the Heart**
> Available for order at
> www.ElizaAnneMcDaniel.com

By ELIZA ANNE McDANIEL

Copyright © 2018

All Rights Reserved.

No content of this book whatsoever may be copied, excerpted or replicated without permission from the author.

Published by SuburbanBuzz.com LLC

ISBN-13: 978-1986873536
ISBN-10: 1986873536

Dedication

In memory of my mother:

In my younger years
An emotional mess,
Mental, sexual, physical abuse,
How could I be blessed?
A loving daddy
I thought I knew,
But the love he gave
Was not so true.
So many crossed signals of affection,
Shattered my being,
Becoming disconnected.
I created a world of happiness
Locking away all the pain
But at times it would rear its ugly head,
Until the tears fell down like rain.
I always felt so all alone,
No one could ever see,
The fear of footsteps at my door,
And no one to rescue me.
I closed my eyes as the door slowly opened,
Knowing who was there,
Praying real hard it would soon be over
It was more than I could bear.
My voice is muffled
By pain and fear,
Tears fill up my eyes,
Do daddies do this to all little girls?
And do they ever hear their cries?
Life goes on, and I'm older now
My dad is in his grave,
But God has never forgotten me,
My life He wants to save!
He put me through fiery trials
One that burned for many years,
To bring me out as pure as gold,

And wash away my fears.
The dysfunction that was in my life
Was the major key,
To bring me where I am today
To finally set me free.
So now I look back in time
Not seeing such a mess,
For when I learned to love myself,
I saw that I was blessed!

I wrote this book through the lens of my parents' childhoods and their marriage, which ultimately affected the trajectory of my life. But I also want to let readers know that my dad was married previously and had three children—two daughters and a son. I love them very much, and even though they did not grow up with me, I had a close relationship with them (especially my brother). I'm sorry to say that one sister passed away from pancreatic cancer in 1998 and the other from bone cancer in 2000. Even though my brother lives a long way from me, we are still very close. I dedicate this book to them as well, because they, too, suffered abuse at the hands of our father. Much love to each one, and they will forever be in my heart!

Acknowledgments

I want to thank everyone who helped me through my journey from abuse to awakening. From the kindness of those in the ministry, to friends who experienced similar trauma, to experts who shared the Reiki philosophy with me—all had a profound impact on who I am today as a Reiki Master and healer.

Special thanks to my editor, Melanie Saxton, who worked diligently through difficult subject matter, went above and beyond, and became a friend in the process.

Table of Contents

Introduction 1

About this book 7

Primary Characters 9

Chapter 1: Faith and Hope 11

Chapter 2: Richard 19

Chapter 3: In and Out of Jail 25

Chapter 4: News 29

Chapter 5: The Move 35

Chapter 6: Road Trip 51

Chapter 7: Daddy's Nap 63

Chapter 8: Candy Spree 75

Chapter 9: Hot Stove 79

Chapter 10: The Slide 85

Chapter 11: Another Move 101

Chapter 12: Pothead 113

Chapter 13: New Set of Wheels 121

Chapter 14: Layers of Betrayal 129

Chapter 15: More Dysfunction 139

Chapter 16: Out of Town Escape 145

Chapter 17: Never Again 153

Chapter 18: Independence Day 163

Chapter 19: A Home of Her Own 185

Chapter 20: A Second and Third Home 203

Chapter 21: Diagnosis and Loss 225

Chapter 22: Life Goes On 233

Chapter 23: A New Start 243

Chapter 24: Revelation 257

Chapter 25: An Answered Prayer 267

Chapter 26: Two Baby Girls 273

Chapter 27: Loss and a Long Lost Sister 287

Chapter 28: Ministry 301

Chapter 29: Messages 315

Chapter 30: Divorce 325

Chapter 31: Turning Their Backs 333

Chapter 32: Special Purpose 339

Chapter 33: An Uncertain Future 355

Chapter 34: Nowhere to Go 369

Epilogue 375

Introduction

"We all have the ability to heal ourselves; I know, I've done so …In the morning, know that you are Loved, You Are Love, and You Love."
~ Lisa Bellini

This was not an easy book to write, especially as the first in a series. I call it The Awakening Series because that's precisely what happens when child victims heal from years of abuse. They awaken to self-love, self-respect, and self-dignity, which enables them to lead a full and functional life.

The years of writing took me back to the suffering of my childhood, which I laid out in a family narrative in this book, Behind Closed Doors. The journey toward my awakening is addressed in Book Two, Journey to the Heart.

Child abuse—especially sexual abuse—is considered an unspeakable act … and the "unspeakable" nature of it is part of the problem. Victims have a hard time coping with the layers of betrayal, let alone speaking of it. The shame, repressed memories, and shattered self-worth are isolating and often result in silence. But society, too, silences victims by looking the other way or refusing to believe that this awful crime exists in almost every city and nation.

We should continue to push for investigations, convictions, harsher penalties, and justice for victims. Many prison systems have built special units to house, treat, and rehabilitate pedophiles and sexual offenders. However, in light of the incredibly high recidivism rate, the reality is that these crimes will continue to occur all around the globe. They always have, and they always will.

Therefore, my mission is to provide "aftercare"—a means to cope and heal. It begins with learning to love oneself. Yes, you have to learn to love who you are no matter what you've endured. Quite possibly, that's the most difficult thing to do, considering children often blame themselves for events they have no control over. But when self-blame, self-doubt, and self-hatred are replaced with self-love, the paradigm shifts. It becomes possible to achieve a healed mindset and move forward into a life of dignity—a life you deserve. I'm not saying it's easy. More often than not, it's extremely difficult to process the past. But it can, and has, and continues to be done. People do heal.

Sometimes victims find their voices, and that's certainly true in my case. The contents of this book are true and unflinchingly told, but I've changed names and locations to protect identities. This book—Book One—involves a story that spans generations and begins with the narrative of my parents' childhoods. It extends well into my life as a wife and mother before I was healed, and ends on a cliffhanger… simply because there is too much content to contain in one book. I wrote it decades after my healing, and it lays out the "first half of my life" to show the reader how child sexual abuse affects the body, mind, and spirit. This horrific abuse affects a child's ability to learn in school, socialize appropriately, choose friends wisely, trust or distrust, and make positive life choices. The building blocks of "normalcy" are simply missing, and must be rebuilt.

***

The truth is, I'm much more a survivor than a victim at this point in my life. Just as important, I'm now in a position to help others. By stepping forward and sharing my truth, book-by-book, I hope to encourage fellow survivors to do the same. As terrifying as that sounds, it's also liberating. From my perspective, it's necessary because thousands—perhaps hundreds of thousands—are still struggling with the emotional, spiritual and physical trauma. Simply talking about it sheds light on deep secrets, and it has been said that light is a great disinfectant.

Of course, we each deal with our childhood atrocities in our own way. Healing is a highly personal journey, and my healing occurred over time. That journey includes one extraordinarily uncomfortable encounter as my father—and abuser—lay dying in a hospital room. It is always difficult to watch as someone nears death, especially if that person gave you life. I really did not want to be there, for this man did so much to harm me. Yet there he lay helpless—a human being whose life was nearly extinguished.

He motioned for me to sit next to him on the bed. The thought of being anywhere near him on a bed brought back involuntary and horrifying flashbacks, so I perched on the very edge. At this moment, it was safer for me if I didn't have to look directly into his eyes. I just needed this moment to be over. Looking down and away, I felt that old fright of a helpless child who had endured years of physical, emotional, and sexual abuse. I was also overwhelmed with the intense love I had for my father, who could also be kind, caring, and generous. There were two sides to him, and I was raised by both sides of him. This partially explains the terrible conflicting mix of love and loathing, not to mention the scars on my soul that defined my relationship with my dad, and others throughout my life. Suddenly, his hand took mine, and I felt a little squeeze. *Oh my God!* I remember thinking. *I can't believe he's holding my hand!* It caused an involuntary reaction, and my eyes shifted to his.

I can access that memory as if it had occurred only five minutes ago, although it happened thirty years ago. That day, I summoned all my strength and forced myself to maintain eye contact. I remember the shame of it—a shame so intense that it took everything in me not to hang my head and cry. On top of that was the shock of his physical appearance. He looked like a frail old man filled with remorse, yet he was only 59 years old. His countenance relayed broken-hearted sorrow and the ravages of pancreatic cancer.

"Can you ever forgive me for all that I've done to you?" He asked, tears welling up in his eyes. More old feelings of unworthiness crept up at the sound of his voice. Soon those feelings were running rampant throughout my body, mind, and soul, bombarding me with the force of a tornado. It was all returning to me in a flash.

And yet, out of my mouth flew the words, "Yes, I forgive you." I'm not sure how those words were even possible after enduring things no child should ever have to endure. *How is it that I felt so very sorry and sad for him?* The truth is, I knew he had also endured the same in his own childhood, and that molestation is often generational.

Did I believe that this master groomer, who had preyed on my innocence and exploited my sister and our childhood friends, was truly sorry for the awful acts he had committed—the rapes, the beatings, and the psychological coercion? The answer was yes. Yes, I believed he was sorry, for a faint smile of relief crossed his face at this undeserved forgiveness. He thanked me and somehow, still holding it all together, I told him that it was okay. He drifted off to sleep, and I quietly slipped out of the room. Now I was alone with my thoughts—long ago thoughts— swirling in a backstory of horrific dysfunction.

Through a blur of terrible, clashing emotions, I remember wishing my pain would die with him. But that would not happen because the child inside me was still traumatized, and my adult soul had not yet awakened. In other words, it would be a few more years before I could fully process all that transpired. So much of it had to do with flashbacks, humiliation, outrage and the feeling of helplessness, all of which I had to overcome. For years, my birth and the events that followed made no sense until I was healed enough to deal with it all.

***

He passed away decades ago, during which time I became healed enough to present both sides of my father. I awakened. What I'm about to share could not be possible without that awakening. I know I've focused on the abuser side of my father, but there was certainly another side to my dad. You see, there's often "another side" to an abuser that makes them likable, lovable, and able to "fit in."

If my father ever saw someone stranded on the road with car problems, he turned around and helped. He also donated toys to the children's hospital a couple of times a year. They all knew him there and loved seeing him walk through the doors. Almost every single person who ever met him for the first time really liked him. There were also many fun-filled times growing up as well. My thoughts are that he was a child once. He was innocent once.

I think of these things when I hear any type of abuse today. When I see someone or hear of someone being abusive, whether it is physical, emotional or sexual, I wonder what happened to them when they were little. I wonder how and when will they ever break that chain. Most will carry on to the next generation or their girlfriends/boyfriends/husbands/wives if they do not get help during the early years. I know that back in my dad's day, everything was kept secret, and it still does today to an extent.

If my dad had received the help he needed when he was younger, would he have been able to break the chain? I don't know. I'm the only one healed out of six full-and-half siblings. It wasn't until I was healed that I could look back and see why my siblings and I did the things we did. With healing comes understanding. Wisdom. Self-love. Dignity.

You can always tell by the words that come out of people's mouths whether or not they are healed. If they are still hurting inside, chances are they'll belittle people to the point of tears. They'll have control issues and deep-seated anger. They'll hurt others because they hurt.

If there were some way that any of us could have sought help when we were younger, I wonder what the outcome would be. So, this is what I believe with my whole heart—during care and aftercare is life changing. And by walking hand and hand with me through this book, which is my journey, my hope is that you will begin or continue the healing process … until you are awakened.

About this Book

I wrote this manuscript with an "omniscient" point of view, meaning most of the people in the book have their own point of view. I do my best to tell their stories while telling my own. It was almost a stream of consciousness process, for I had to delve into my innermost recollections, some excruciatingly painful, and then write about it.

Most of these points of view are shared through dialogue, with the storyteller (me) filling in some blanks. After all, it's all intertwined and interrelated and generational, which makes each point of view part of the bigger picture. A primary cast of characters is included below.

There is no way to make heads or tails of a story like this without understanding the "why's"— why people behave the way they do and why they are compelled to use and abuse others. So you'll get a glimpse of that, which in no way excuses the behavior. It simply helps us understand and heal from it.

Primary Characters

Emily: Wife of Tom and mother to [Erin], Richard, Faith, and Hope, and later known as Nanny to her grandchildren.

Tom: Husband of Emily and father to [Erin], Richard, Faith, and Hope, and also father to three older children from a previous marriage.

Erin: Oldest daughter of Emily and Tom, given up at birth for adoption and appearing in their lives many decades later. Mentioned fleetingly in the latter part of the book.

Richard: Son of Emily and Tom who was physically and emotionally abused by Tom, and brother to [Erin], Faith, and Hope.

Faith: Daughter of Emily and Tom, sister of [Erin] and Richard, twin of Hope, wife of Kenny, and mother of Mark and Julie—and the one character who healed from sexual, physical, and emotional abuse.

Kenny: Husband to Faith, father to Mark and Julie

Hope: Daughter of Emily and Tom, sister of [Erin] and Richard, twin of Faith, wife to Jason, and mother of Matthew and Angelica

Brandi: Faith's lifelong best friend

Granny: Brandi's mother (eventually referred to as Granny)

Aunt Jennifer: Emily's sister and aunt to [Erin], Richard, Faith, and Hope

Greg: Tom's brother, Claudia's husband, and father to Rachel

Claudia: Greg's wife, sister-in-law of Tom and Emily, and mother to Rachel

Rachel: Greg and Claudia's adopted daughter, and cousin and dear friend of Faith and Hope

Monty: A preacher who involves himself in Faith's life, eventually alienating her from her family and friends

Sylvia: Faith's best friend and mentor

Chapter 1: Faith and Hope

> *"A healer's power stems not from any special ability, but from maintaining the courage and awareness to embody and express the universal healing power that every human being naturally possesses."*
> ~ Eric Micha'el Leventhal

They named me Faith. Believe me; the name is no mistake. I've needed every drop of faith to make it through to my adulthood. The story has been told so many times that it unfolds in my mind like an old familiar movie. There they were, my parents Tom and Emily, sitting nervously in an attorney's office. Each lost in thoughts; they waited for the owner of the law firm to enter the room. It was all to finalize the documents required for an adoption.

We were our parents' third pregnancy—unborn twins they could neither afford nor raise properly. They had already adopted out their first baby girl. My mother's sister Jennifer, along with her husband Bill, had taken over most of the responsibility of raising our five-year-old brother Richard.

But this only skimmed the surface of my parents' story. The "Emily and Tom Saga" was awash in questionable decisions, bad behavior, and ultimately tragic abuse.

***

Poor Emily. She was worn out, so weary from the life choices she had made with Tom. Both knew they could not afford more children, financially or emotionally. It all became too real for them a few days earlier when Emily's water broke. Tom drove her to the hospital, and only a few short hours later, a new baby girl arrived. Tom ran out to buy a new pink blanket. While he was gone, and much to Emily's surprise, the doctor told her to hang on tight—another baby was about to arrive!

Emily cried out, "I can't afford one baby, much less two!" Seven minutes later I made my debut into what would eventually become a scary, chaotic world.

Tom returned, blanket in tow, to find out he had become a father the second time that day. The doctor announced that Tom should go back to the store and buy another pink blanket. Back in the car, Tom recalled that he had always daydreamed of what it would be like to have twins of his own. His thoughts drifted back to the twin girls his mother had delivered. They lived to be only three months old.

Now his dream had come to pass, and he rushed back to the hospital with the second blanket. Emily had named the babies Hope and Faith. He was overjoyed, but the reality was grim. There was no way he and Emily could keep one baby, let alone twins.

And so they ended up in the attorney's office on a December morning in 1960, dazed, conflicted, and saddened. Emotions bombarded Emily, who did her best to keep those feelings at bay. But as she sat, numb and still, she couldn't help but recall the past ten years. Anxiety haunted her over the fate of her firstborn daughter, who now lived with an adoptive family. The child's happiness, quality of life, and even what she looked like was a mystery. To cope, she reminded herself that adoption had been the best decision then … and now. Still, she had to fight against the shame and pain of what she was about to do.

The attorney, himself, would now be raising her babies as his own. Surely her daughters would be well cared for in a good, decent, normal family. It only reminded her of what a mistake it was to be with Tom. She felt caught in a trap and out of options—lost with him and hopeless without him, for she had nowhere else to go. And so she stayed. They were poor and struggled daily. It was hard on them both, and she really did not know what else to do.

They'll have a better life, she inwardly reasoned, looking around the attorney's office. At that moment the door finally opened, and in walked the attorney, jolting Emily back from inside her head. They shook hands, and the attorney spoke casually for a few moments to ease their discomfort, knowing everyone just wanted to get this over with and put it behind them. Then he called a witness into the room and opened his folder. The attorney presented a paper for Tom and Emily to sign. Both were handed a pen and told to read and place their signatures on the document.

Each did as instructed. Tom signed first, then handed it to Emily. With trembling hands, she quickly penned her name. Unable to hold back tears, she handed the paper and her rights as a mother over to the attorney. *It's too late now. It's done. I cannot reverse this,* she thought.

It was the attorney's turn to sign. Sliding his glasses over the bridge of his nose, he picked up his pen…which slipped out of his hand as he grabbed his chest and fell forward. Tom and Emily jumped up in shock and disbelief. The witness screamed for help and attempted to assist the attorney, but the poor man—the very man who was about to adopt Tom and Emily's twin baby girls—was already dead of a massive heart attack.

The secretary called the hospital to send an ambulance. In the commotion, Tom grabbed the paper they had just signed and tucked it under his arm. Under his breath, he instructed Emily to scoop up one baby as he grabbed the other, and they casually walked out of the office.

This part of the story, as it was repeated to me time and again throughout my childhood, sounded almost idyllic—two parents struggling with an enormous decision and fate intervening to save the day. How I wish this story was true! The complicated reality was that my mother was co-dependent and my father was unstable in a disturbing way. And that's putting it charitably.

As our family narrative unfolded, it turned out that adoption would have been much more humane. For years, I questioned why the Spiritual Gavel came down that day in favor of my parents. I questioned why my sister and I faced such a fate. It wasn't until I had a healed mindset that I realized my destiny was tied to my parents for a reason. I could help others survive similar ordeals only by living it myself.

***

The drive home was quiet. Emily and Tom kept their thoughts to themselves, as usual. She was relieved that they were keeping the twins, but had no idea how she and Tom could provide for them. Tom's first thoughts were that he had rescued the twins—he had fallen in love with his baby girls and didn't want to give them up in the first place.

Now the challenge of feeding, clothing, and keeping a roof over their heads loomed. One obstacle was a police record that followed Tom like a shadow. With a deep, silent sigh, he breathed a prayer: *Dear God, I hope I can do right by these little girls. You know I'm not the greatest father material in the world.* Still lost in these thoughts, they arrived home and in silence carried the babies inside. Without a word between them, Tom left the house.

It felt as though they had already lived a full day, but it was not yet noon. Emily knew Tom would not return before dinner. Accustomed to this behavior, she silently warmed the bottles and laid the babies in their crib. Still feeling dizzy from all that had occurred, she sat in her rocker and fed them one at a time. Then she watched in wonderment as they drifted into sleep. Staring blankly through the window, her thoughts still swirled with the events of the day. It had all happened so quickly. She had left home that morning, prepared as anyone can be to give her babies up, and now was back home with them, wondering what she was going to do and how she was going to care for them.

Emily's son Richard was already being raised by her sister Jennifer, who lived a short distance away. *Maybe she'll help with the babies while I work,* Emily thought, with a bit of hope. *Maybe I can work more hours at the restaurant.* The thoughts dashed through her mind, one after the other, until she leaned over in the rocking chair with her hands on her face and began to weep. *How did my life ever come to this? Where did I go wrong?*

Recalling memories of her childhood in a poor family, Emily struggled again with feelings of hopelessness. She was the youngest of five children, and her mother and father had great difficulty finding work in the 1930s. All they had ever known was struggle and strife. One day while the other children were in school, she watched her mother empty bags of potatoes into a basket. In those days, potatoes came in large burlap sacks.

"What are you doing?" five-year-old Emily asked.

"Well, honey, Mama has to get the potatoes out and wash these bags so I can make dresses for you and your sisters."

The wide-eyed youngster tried to imagine wearing a burlap potato sack as a dress, but her mother had already read her mind.

"Don't you worry about a thing, because Mama is good at sewing. By the time I'm finished, you'll be the prettiest girl on the block!"

Emily, leaning her head back on the rocking chair, wished, *If only I could have one of those moments back with my mother.* She recalled the excitement she had felt over helping Mama wash those burlap sacks—hands in that soapy water, making bubbles, smelling of the green grass and the warmth of the sun as she watched Mama hung the potato sacks on the clothesline to dry. She remembered the wonder of feeling like the prettiest little girl on the block in her new dress.

How clever Mama was, using potato sacks! she mused. Emily had no idea that they were dirt poor, although times were tough. On a few occasions, they went to bed hungry. Potatoes and beans were pretty much all they ate because they were so cheap.

Eventually, her parents decided that they could no longer take care of their children and wanted better lives for them. They distributed them among family members and neighbors who were willing and had the means to take better care of them. Emily was too young to know what was actually occurring. She only knew that she felt lonely and that her family was no longer together.

She recalled lying in bed at night, wondering where Mama and Daddy were and why they didn't come get her. She remembered feeling as though she must have done something to make Mama and Daddy angry at her and cried herself to sleep at night until there were no more tears left. She always hoped that someday she would be reunited with her parents, but Emily never saw them again.

To make matters worse, Emily's brother Jimmy died about a year later at the age of fourteen from pneumonia. She could not be consoled over Jimmy's death. "It just isn't fair!" she screamed. She loved her brother and clung to him, as he had been placed with her in the same family. Playing hide and seek with him had been one of her favorite games. Jimmy always let her find him.

Emily wondered what life would be like today if her family hadn't unraveled. A tear streamed down her face, and she gently wiped it away. She had lost contact with her oldest sister Karen, but her other two sisters, Diana and Jennifer, had always lived close by. They saw each other from time to time and took long walks in the neighborhood. When they approached the huge patch of honeysuckle growing alongside the street, they took off running to pluck the fragrant blossoms from the vines. Diana always seemed to get the first one. They slowly pulled the little threads inside the blossoms to gather up the "honey" on the end of the strands. It was always so tasty and sweet!

Of course, they also shared bittersweet memories of Mama and Daddy. Sometimes they cried together over the pain of being left with neighbors. A big three-way hug brought comfort and reminded them that they were blessed to be together, and they vowed to remain close. That brought much comfort to the siblings as they walked home. Their parting words were always "Can't wait 'til our next adventure!"

Suddenly the memories struck a painful nerve, for five years ago she was eight and a half months pregnant with Richard. Tom was serving an eighteen-month jail sentence for some illegal business deals. Diana asked her to go along for an afternoon ride on the warm, sunny day. Fortunately, Emily listened to the uneasy feeling inside and told Diana she'd rather stay home. Diana understood since Emily was getting closer to her delivery date. They sat outside and chatted for a short while, and hugged when Diana was ready to leave.

Emily had no way of knowing she would never see her sister again. Later that afternoon, a knock on her door changed her life forever. A policeman delivered news that Diana had been in a terrible head-on collision. Another car entered her lane as she was rounding the bend on a mountain road, and Diana did not survive. Emily shook from the news, and the policeman did his best to console her, knowing that she was traumatized in her condition. He guided her to the couch and stayed long enough to be certain there was no need of medical attention. Emily assured the officer she was fine. Closing the door, her body shook which forced her back to the couch.

***

The babies stirred and drew her back to the present. Still, she couldn't help feeling her sister's presence in the room. *I love you and miss you so much, Diana, and I'm so sorry that I didn't ask you to stay with me that day.* Certain that Diana could hear her, she continued, *I know you're with God now and watching over me and my children. I'll always remember the good times we shared. Do you remember, Diana, the day when we were little, and you stayed home from school sick? Remember, I sat beside you on the bed and held your hand and told you that you would feel better? Remember, Diana?*

At this moment, Emily realized just how lonely she was. The sweet memories and the sense that Diana was listening opened the floodgate. *Hey Diana, do you remember when Mama sent you to the store to buy some bread, and I wanted to go with you? Mama said no at first, but gave in when you promised to hold my hand all the way there and all the way back. I just wanted you to know I had so much fun that day. I remember we both loved looking at all the candy in those jars, even though we couldn't have any. Still, it was fun looking, wasn't it? I used to think that maybe next time we could buy a piece. Well, Diana, you're with our brother Jimmy now. Please hug him and tell him I love and miss him dearly.*

The mix of happy and sad memories faded, and Emily wiped her tears. Looking over at her sleeping babies somehow brought a warm and other-worldly peace, and she held out hope that everything would work out … somehow … some way. Assured that her babies were sound asleep, she left her post and began preparing dinner. She heard the sound of Tom's car door shutting and marveled that she had been lost in her thoughts for so long. She wiped her face again and reached deep to cover her emotions. She never knew what kind of mood Tom might be in, and had learned to play it safe. She had been blindsided by his violent outbursts too many times, and the stress of today's events might have negatively impacted him. She had to be ready for anything.

Tom came through the door, and Emily feigned cheerfulness, announcing that she was fixing his favorite dinner. He smiled, kissed her cheek, and went off to shower. Her heart felt relieved. There was very little conversation at the dinner table, but occasional glances revealed that they were both wondering the same thing: *How will it all turn out?*

While clearing the dishes and preparing new bottles, Emily was grateful to feel kindness—even a sense of family—from Tom, who offered to help feed the babies this time. As he reached into the crib to pick up one of the twins, he looked at Emily and said, "I'm so glad we're able to keep them." She smiled and handed him a bottle. They had a few moments of togetherness as they each fed one of the babies, then out the door he went. As usual, he was gone until the wee hours of the morning.

Chapter 2: Richard

"Give yourself permission to let it hurt, but also allow yourself the permission to let it heal."
~ Nikki Rowe

With Tom away from the house, Emily could breathe easier. No tiptoeing around his anger issues. *Was it really only just this morning?* Emily thought as she picked up the phone to call Jennifer. The events at the attorney's office were almost unbelievable, and she wanted to catch up on news of Richard. It was both a relief and a shame that her son spent most of his time with Aunt Jennifer and Uncle Bill.

"Good morning, Jennifer," began Emily.

"Well, good morning to you. How did it go with the attorney?"

Emily recounted the drama of thwarted adoption, with Jennifer adding occasional words like "Oh my," and "Wow!" and "You've got to be kidding!" The conversation brought up a flood of emotions in Emily, who felt like a failure as a mom all the way around—first Richard's being raised by relatives, a daughter adopted out, and now two newborns she tried but failed to give away.

Emily shared how jarring it was to witness the attorney's death. That event became even more difficult to process, considering he was minutes away from becoming the adoptive father of her children. And then came the escape from the office with the ill-fated adoption paperwork tucked under Tom's arm ... the whole story sounded like something out of a novel.

"Okay, Emily, how are you going to make this work?" Jennifer asked.

"I'll just have to put in longer hours, Jennifer. Is there any way you can help me out with the twins? I know it's asking a lot, but I don't know what ..."

Jennifer interrupted with an ecstatic, "YES! Of course, Emily! You KNOW how I love the little ones, and you know that yours are the same to me as my own!"

Relief flooded through Emily's heart. "How can I ever repay you?" she asked through her tears.

"Oh Emily, I'm so happy that you're keeping your twins! I'm over the moon in love with them already and can't wait to meet them!"

Jennifer trailed on in her excitement, but for Emily, hearing "Yes" was all that was needed to lift a heavy load. It felt like a physical release off her shoulders. And the babysitting money would help Jennifer and Bill, at least in a small way. They, too, struggled with finances.

***

It so happened that Emily did get more hours as a waitress at the restaurant down the street. Jennifer took over full-time responsibility for the twins that year, while Richard spent most weekends at home with his parents. Tom and Emily saw the babies when they visited, and over time, it proved to be the best arrangement for everyone. On visits, Tom tended to pay more attention to the twins, while Emily focused on Richard.

Tom always projected the appearance of a loving, caring father, and never left any other impression. He seemed almost too perfect—especially for a father whose children lived with other family members. If one looked further, Bill seemed just as perfect—so willing to take in the children of his wife's sister and her husband. The reality was not as perfect.

One weekend Emily and Tom had the luxury of staying home and brought Richard over to spend the weekend. Monday morning, Emily prepared to leave for work. Gathering Richard's belongings, she planned to drop him back with Jennifer on her way. Richard became unusually quiet and more withdrawn as the moments passed.

Although her son spent more time away from her than with her, her love was still protective. She did her best to lighten his mood and asked Richard if he was excited to see his sisters, aunt, and uncle.

Richard blurted out, "I don't want to go back to Aunt Jennifer and Uncle Bill!"

There was something disconcerting in his voice—more than just not wanting to end the weekend. Emily stopped everything and sat down on the floor next to her boy.

"Why don't you want to go, Honey?" she asked.

"Uncle Bill is mean to me, and so are Hope and Faith!"

Emily was puzzled because the twins were not yet two years old, and Richard was nearly seven. She asked him with deep concern, "What do they do that is so mean, Richard?"

"Well..." Richard looked down at his shoes and started kicking at the floor.

Emily put her face close to his and cupped her hands around his cheeks. "Tell me what you mean, Richard," she spoke, almost sternly, although she did not mean for it to sound that way. The sick feeling in her stomach grew, and she wanted the truth about what was happening.

Richard, speaking reluctantly in a near-inaudible tone, began telling Emily why he no longer wanted to stay with his aunt and uncle. He looked at his feet.

"Bill holds me down and tells Hope and Faith to spit on me," he said.

"Oh Richard!" exclaimed Emily.

"And he tells them it's a game. And then Uncle Bill makes them jump on me and pull my hair!"

Emily had always suspected that that Bill might have some mental issues, but there was never the slightest hint that he would ever bully a child, especially Richard. Bill seemed to dote on her son each time she was present. She wracked her brain to recall even the slightest indication, but could not recall one red flag of concern over leaving any of her children with Bill.

Richard continued, "Uncle Bill tells Hope and Faith to hit me too. I can't move because Uncle Bill is real strong and he holds me down hard!"

Emily hugged Richard and told him how much she loved him. "Honey, when I get off work today, I'll come by Aunt Jennifer's to talk with her about all of this, okay?"

Richard, still hanging his head said, "Okay, Mommy."

Completely taken aback by Richard's revelation, Emily did her best to act with composure. "Okay, honey. Mommy has to finish getting ready for work. Go get your things ready to take over to Aunt Jennifer's. We'll be leaving shortly."

As Emily finished getting ready, she couldn't help but wonder whether Richard was telling the truth or making things up. After all, the babies were just learning to walk, let alone kick. She did note that he seemed reluctant about returning to Jennifer's during the past few months. *I'll ask Jennifer about it,* Emily told herself. Of course, the question about how to handle the situation stuck in her mind all day. *Just what I need, another problem to deal with! And what will I do if this is all true?*

Arriving at her sister's house, Emily hid her feelings of despair in the same masterful way she had always done and walked Richard to the door. Jennifer, who was already on her way out to greet them, met Emily with a cheery "Hello!" and affectionately tousled Richard's hair.

"Hi there, Buddy! Did you have a great weekend?"

Richard gave his mother a quick, dutiful hug and grunted, "Yeah…" and "Bye Mom" in his seven-year-old "boy-speak." Then he went inside.

"Don't wake up your sisters, Richard!" Jennifer called after him.

"Thanks for all you do for my kids," said Emily with a bit of strain in her voice. "Can I talk with you after work?"

"Sure. Swing by around dinner time," Jennifer invited with a sideways tilt of the head, inwardly wondering *what's up?* "Is everything okay?" she asked.

"I hope so," answered Emily, and gave her sister a hug before leaving for work.

***

It was a slow day at work, which meant that a head full of thoughts and worries built up in Emily's mind. While she wanted to settle the issue, there was still a twinge of worry over hashing it out with her sister. Emily never liked conflict, and as the clock ticked closer, she began dreading it. Still, she knew that it was up to her to work this out. She knew it could not be left in Tom's hands!

The pit in her stomach grew as she pulled into Jennifer and Bill's driveway. Richard was playing in the yard like any normal kid. "Mommy's here!" he yelled with excitement. Richard nearly knocked Emily over as he barreled into her with big hugs. Hand in hand they walked into the house, and Emily called out, "Jennifer! I'm here!"

Jennifer rounded the corner into her living room with a smile. "Hi Emily, How about a cup of coffee? I just made a fresh pot!"

"Oh good! It was a slow day at work, and that wears me out more than the busy days. So I can sure use a cup of coffee right now!" Emily responded with genuine gratitude.

Jennifer poured the coffee and Emily told Richard to go play. He disappeared down the hallway, and Jennifer brought the coffee into her favorite little room and took a seat across from Emily.

"So, what's up, sis? You seemed pretty serious this morning," Jennifer opened.

"Well …" Emily began, "Richard came to me this morning with some disturbing news, and I really need your help sorting out …" She hesitated, feeling the tension building. It seemed to indicate that Jennifer must know something. Emily decided to spill the whole pot of beans without sugar coating any of it. "Jennifer, Richard told me that Bill holds him down and tells the twins to pull his hair and to spit on him."

"Oh," said Jennifer. "Well, I did once hear some ruckus going on in the playroom. I checked on the kids and saw Richard getting up off the floor. Richard seemed somewhat upset, so I asked what was going on. He said, 'Nothing.' Bill was there in the room and explained that the kids were just roughhousing."

"Jennifer, Richard is scared of Bill. I'm asking, please, can you keep a more watchful eye on what's going on when Richard is here?" It was a balancing act. She had to keep the peace because there was no one else to take care of the kids. *I really have to work this out,* she thought.

Jennifer apologized and reassured her that she would keep a watchful eye on what was going on between Bill and Richard. Emily felt better, and the sisters chatted over their coffee a bit longer, both relieved that the tension had dissipated. Emily hugged her sister and the children goodbye, telling them she would be back to see them tomorrow after work.

Richard walked his mom to the car. *He is growing so big,* she thought as he opened the car door for her. Hesitating, she bent down to his eye level and told Richard that he didn't need to worry anymore. "Aunt Jennifer will make sure you're safe, and this won't happen again," she promised.

"Thanks, Mom," Richard said, trusting that his mother and Aunt Jennifer had fixed the problem for him.

"I'll see you tomorrow, son. I love you." Emily hugged him again.

"I love you too, Mom!" Richard hollered as she started the engine in the car.

"Now run back into Aunt Jennifer's house!" Emily called through the car window. She waited until he was inside, and with a deep sigh and teary eyes backed out of the driveway. All the way home she wished her life was different and that she could make her children's lives better. By the time she pulled into her own driveway, she had put back on the face that concealed all her emotions.

Richard still complained from time to time that Uncle Bill was holding him down and letting the twins jump on him and be mean to him. Emily continued to ask Jennifer to keep a watchful eye on Richard, and Jennifer continued to make the promise that she would. Over time, Richard built a wall of anger and resentment—even hatred—toward the twins. The little boy's emotions could not allow him to see that they were just innocent little girls doing what they were taught. The separation between him and his siblings prevailed well into their adulthood.

Chapter 3: In and Out of Jail

"No one saves us but ourselves. No one can and no one may. We ourselves must walk the path."
~ Buddha

Life with Tom was an "adventure," to say the least. Emily knew he involved himself in underhanded dealings, but he never told her what they were. Both of their lives could be in danger if he said too much, and he kept his business to himself. Tom was financially rewarded for that loyalty, and Emily told herself not be too inquisitive.

Once she was in the car with Tom on their way home from a visit with Bill, Jennifer, and the children. Police sirens suddenly blared behind them. Emily didn't know Tom carried a gun in the car until he reached for it and emptied the bullets into his hand.

"Put these bullets in the cuff of your jeans!" he yelled frantically.

Emily quickly grabbed the bullets and placed them carefully, one by one, into her Capri pant cuffs. Tom pulled over, and the police asked them both to step out of the car. While they searched and found the gun, the bullets were not found—they were free to leave. Tom never told her the reason they had been pulled over, and Emily knew better than to ask. When they returned home, she handed him the bullets. There was no further mention of the incident.

Tom always seemed to be in some sort of trouble with the law, and it began to take its toll on Emily. She spent most of her life working, worrying about her children, and wondering when Tom would be arrested. She resigned herself to her fate—being poor with three children. *Where else would I go?* she wondered. *What else can I do?*

Because Tom always presented himself to the outside world as a loving, caring man, no one suspected him of domestic violence. Emily felt hopeless. No one knew what happened behind closed doors, and she didn't dare report it. He always knew exactly what to say and could win an academy award for his acting skills. He also had a way with the ladies that rivaled any leading man in the movies. This was the charm that Emily fell in love with. By the time his true colors began to show, she was in over her head with no way out.

One early morning as she got ready for work, Emily heard police sirens in front of her house. They had finally come for Tom. When all was said and done, he was incarcerated because he would not give up the names of his associates involved in dozens of scams. He adhered to the doctrine that no one likes snitches, and kept his word to his boss about never snitching.

***

Emily worked long hours trying to make ends meet. It was a struggle, and she greatly appreciated her sister for taking care of her children. Each time Tom was released from jail, he returned to the same line of work. She loved him and hated him all at the same time. This was her trap.

Tom knew exactly how to control her and used extreme passive-aggressive measures to do so. He romanced her and told her she was beautiful. When she let down her guard, he got out his camera and took photos of her, all the while building her self-esteem. Emily loved the attention from her husband—positive attention that didn't involve violence. Soon he coaxed her into unbuttoning her blouse. Soon she was posing in lingerie, which in those days was considered risqué. But Tom complimented the photos and said the intimate images were just for him.

Compliance meant peace, at least temporarily, and soon involved her best friend, Annie. Tom suggested "photo sessions" of the ladies baking in the kitchen or sitting on the porch swing. He told them how pretty they were and what great pictures they took. As Annie became more comfortable, Tom made subtle suggestions, and soon both women were involved in the risqué photographs. Annie was willing, and of course, if Annie was willing, then Emily was also willing. Tom told Emily and Annie how pretty they were, building up their confidence until he had them where he wanted them.

The "photo sessions" seemed to be a "passion" of Tom's over the years, and involved more friends and even Emily's sister. They all gloated over how pretty they were, and none saw any harm. Besides, it was always a lot of fun! Good-natured Tom laughed and carried on, snapping more and more risqué photos that he sold to his "work associates." Of course, the women had no clue he was using them to make money.

After a while, Annie mentioned to Emily that Tom seemed to be flirting with her. Being best friends meant something to Annie, and Tom's behavior made her uncomfortable. Emily's heart was broken when she heard the news, especially when Annie mentioned she had seen Tom flirting with younger girls over the years, but had really never considered it much until now.

Emily knew better. She also knew that other "ideas" were going through Tom's head. Although she never blatantly caught him, there was always a feeling that he was capable of anything. She just didn't know exactly what it was but was beginning to imagine. Of course, bringing it up caused fights, and Tom threw accusations back at her. Then he'd tell her how much he loved her and how pretty she was. To keep his terrible anger from resurfacing, Emily dropped the matter. It was better just to leave it alone.

Annie told Emily that she was no longer interested in the photo shoots because of her discomfort over Tom's flirting. Emily held Annie's hand and apologized for her husband's behavior. It seemed she spent her life covering for Tom and excusing his behavior.

Chapter 4: News

Everything you need, your courage, strength, compassion and love: everything you need is already within you.
~ Anonymous

By the spring of 1964, Tom had finished serving his final prison sentence. Law enforcement agencies of both Ohio and Pennsylvania made it very clear that his only option was to relocate to a different state, or face constant police "harassment." Tom's luck seemed to have run out, and he knew that breaking the news to Emily would require some delicate handling. After all, he had already put her through a great deal of stress, not to mention how the move would affect the three children. He faced the situation head-on, and for the first time in a long time felt genuine concern for his family.

Emily met Tom at the front door and could see that he was visibly shaken. His words were filled with gentleness as he asked her to sit down to talk about their circumstances.

Seeing Tom in such a serious demeanor frightened Emily, who nearly fell backward onto the couch, her heart pounding in her ears with worry. Her past experiences with Tom proved that when he was sweet, it never meant good news. His level of sweetness now was off the charts, and she was terrified.

He spoke slowly and concisely, detailing all that had transpired.

"Emily, I need you to hear me out. I've just come from the police station and was informed we'll have to move out of the state of Ohio. And we're not welcome in Pennsylvania, either."

It was now Emily's turn to be visibly distraught. "What will we do? Where will we go? How will we ever afford a move, and what will become of us?" she wailed.

Tom, doing his best to console her, gave her all the time she needed to process the news. He said he'd put in a call to his brother Greg in

North Carolina to ask him for assistance. "I'll call him first thing tomorrow," he promised.

***

Tom and Greg had been closer to each other than with their other siblings. They had come from a very poor family with five children—four boys and one girl. Debbie was the oldest, and Tom was the youngest. His brother, Greg, was two years older than Tom. Growing up in the late 1920's was difficult. They lived in a broken-down cabin off the road with no inside plumbing. Everyone shared an outhouse. The children walked to school through the snow with holes in their shoes. In the cold winters, they doubled up on socks, hoping their feet stayed dry. Of course, their feet were always wet when they arrived, so they removed their socks to warm their feet by the school's wood stove, hanging their socks to dry. They had no car and walked everywhere. Once in a while, the neighbor down the road offered them rides in the winter.

Their grandfather lived with them and took care of the children while their parents looked for work. Tom rarely spoke of his grandfather, who was hated and feared by all the boys. When their parents were away, which seemed to be quite often, their grandfather would bring one of the boys back into his bedroom. It was never spoken of by any of them.

Debbie, the oldest child, did her best to help take care of the boys, cooking, cleaning and washing their clothes. Neither she nor their parents were aware of what transpired behind Grandpa's closed bedroom door. By Tom's fourteenth birthday, he had run away from home. Lying about his age, he joined the Army. During those years, he disconnected from his family. Later, in his thirties, he re-opened communications with Debbie and Greg, who had both moved to North Carolina in the late 1950's.

Greg, who was married with a good-paying job, seemed to have escaped the poverty and the damage of their childhood. The brothers never spoke much of it. Tom never spoke of it even with Emily. However, the feelings of unworthiness, anger, bitterness, and fear were still what seemed to drive Tom's life. Although he was aware of his own bad temper, he could not gain control over it. As his feelings built into a rage, the anger would take over and then had to run its course. He was always remorseful, vowing it would not happen again. But, of course, it always did.

Despite his lack of control, Tom did have a good heart buried beneath the unseen pain. When he felt the goodness of his own heart emerging, it gave him a hope that he would overcome his impulses. But the "black dog" followed him. He'd default to doing unspeakable things—things he regretted but sometimes enjoyed, despite knowing how wrong it was.

Tom had no awareness that the root of all his problems stemmed from what he had suffered as a child. He believed the bad temper and his hateful actions just "ran in the family." Nor did he know that it would essentially eat him from the inside out one day.

His mood could change in an instant. One moment he was happy, and all was well. Then something—the least little thing—would set him off. He hated himself, but it seemed there was nothing he could do to change. His demons always got the better of him. No one saw the many times when Tom, alone with himself, cried out, asking, *Why? Why? Why do I do the things I do?* Yet a few days later, he would let it get the best of him again. It was like he was caught among the debris of a whirling tornado, tumbling through a vicious cycle with no possibility of escaping it. Then the whirlwind would die down, leaving a wake of devastation behind him.

***

Promising once again to call his brother Greg for help, Tom kissed Emily and told her that everything would work out. He knew that Emily didn't quite believe it, but he did his best to convince her. As always, Emily's concern was about the kids.

"Tom, Jennifer has been taking care of our kids since they were born. That's four and a half years for the twins! You know how she loves those twins, just like they were her own! How will I ever tell her that we're moving and taking all of the children with us?"

Her stomach was in knots, but there they were, between a rock and a hard place. She would, like always, suck it up and face what had to be faced. Tom, knowing that he was responsible for all of it, was very understanding and tried his best to comfort Emily, promising that he would do better.

The next day, Tom called his brother in North Carolina with the news. Greg was really happy that Tom wanted to bring his family to live near him, and vowed to help in any way he could. "Don't worry, Tom," Greg assured him. "I'll begin looking to find you a house, and I'll help you pay for it too. Give me a week, and I'll call you as soon as I have some news."

Greg's voice was so positive and reassuring that Tom felt a flicker of hope. Maybe life could really change and be good for once. He loved the idea of being close to his brother, who was welcoming him and his family with open arms.

"Thanks so much, Greg. I'll make this up to you!" Tom vowed.

The difficult part, as usual, fell on Emily's shoulders. Once again, at Jennifer's house, she asked her sister to sit down.

"I have some news, and it won't be easy for either of us, Jennifer," Emily began. She took her sister's hand and broke down. For the first time in ages, she was unable to hide her own emotional state.

Jennifer's face turned white, her hand involuntarily reaching for her heart, "What's wrong, Emily? Tell me what's happened!" She had not seen her sister this emotional since Diana's death. All she could imagine was that someone had died.

Emily, gulping deep breaths, composed herself. "Jennifer, there is no other way. I've spent hours going over it in my mind, and there is just no other way," she said.

"Tell me," said Jennifer, squeezing her hand.

Emily explained all that Tom had told her, and how they were being forced to leave the state. "Thank God for Tom's brother in North Carolina. He is helping us and looking for a house. We expect to hear from him by the weekend, and then we'll begin the plan to move to North Carolina."

"What? North Carolina!" exclaimed Jennifer, her eyes wide with shock. "How will you bear to be so far away from the children?"

"Oh, Jennifer. This is so difficult. Tom and I will take all three children with us. We're so grateful that you've been there for Richard and the twins, but we have to leave as a family—that means the twins will be coming with us."

Jennifer burst into tears, crying so hysterically that she grabbed a kitchen towel and held it to her face. It truly was as though someone had died.

"No!" she sobbed. "Please don't take the twins from me! I've loved them like my own! They know me as their mama. Please! There must be another way!"

Emily cried with her, but a reserve of unseen strength kept her resolve intact.

"Jennifer, I truly am sorry, but there is no other way. The police have already warned us to leave the state, and it must be soon. I'm truly, truly grateful that we have had these years together, and I'm going to miss you terribly. But it must be this way."

They sat together for a while longer, quietly talking and processing the changes ahead. *This may be one of the last times we have coffee together,* Emily thought to herself, knowing Jennifer had the same thought. She watched as Jennifer's gaze moved in slow motion to the children playing across the room. Tears again flowed down her cheeks. Emily felt Jennifer's broken heart and wavered ever so slightly. She had a fleeting thought of leaving the twins behind, but then again, knew that it was time for her and Tom to begin a new life as a united family in North Carolina.

Emily stood to leave, feeling pressed by all the work that lay ahead.

"I'll let you know when Greg calls, and I'll keep you posted on the time frame," she said as she hugged her sister close and kissed her cheek. Emily hugged and said goodbye to her children, realizing that soon life would change for all of them.

Jennifer watched Emily leave, her eyes swollen from her tears. She sat with her nieces and nephew, and together they played until it was time to prepare dinner. The twins noticed her swollen face and asked why she was crying. Jennifer, unable to talk about what was about to occur, told them she cried because she loved them so much and didn't ever want them to forget her.

"We'll never forget you, Mama!" they both said, jumping into her arms. Jennifer's tears flowed again, and she held her little nieces close. She cherished the moment, and not wishing to make them sad, giggled with them before heading into the kitchen.

Chapter 5: The Move

> *"So, when you are doing your work of self discovery, self acceptance, and radical self awareness, remember that healing isn't a magic pill. It is permission to step back from whatever chaos is happening and see the soul of Who You Are."*
> ~ Christie Inge

It's been a long time since I allowed my emotions to get the best of me, Emily thought again, as she mindlessly rummaged through the refrigerator for leftovers. It was time to make up dinner, and she had to focus. *I must be losing my edge... I can't believe how I cried at Jennifer's house.* Dumping the remainder of last night's bean soup into a pan, she felt better prepared for Tom's arrival. *Still, I've got to admit it felt pretty good to get it all out in front of a real person, instead of all alone in my car.*

Although she had dreaded telling her sister the news of the move, she now felt relieved. And she had to admit to herself that she even felt a bit of excitement over the possibility of beginning a new life. *Starting over. What will it be like to start over with a clean slate?* "Of course," she thought aloud, "I'll miss Jennifer terribly." That's all it took to inch toward a slippery slope of negativity. Being without Jennifer brought up old, familiar worries, which flooded her thoughts. *How will we make ends meet? How will I find a babysitter who loves my kids as much as Jennifer does? How will I even afford a babysitter?!!*

The fears began mounting until they overwhelmed her. She was right back in the same old pattern that had always controlled her—and the abandonment issues of a small child who had been shipped out. Helpless. Alone. Afraid. *And now I'll be responsible for three children who will depend on me for everything.* In her mind, Emily still felt like a trapped, abandoned little girl in many ways.

Alone with her hopelessness, Emily gravitated to the one comforting spot in her house— the rocking chair that had been in the twins' room since they were born. Through fresh tears, she said a prayer: *Dear God ... please let Greg help us or make a way for us to stay here ... please, please God ... make some way for us ...*

Startled by the sound of the front door opening, Emily jumped up from the rocker. But Tom had already appeared in the doorway.

"Don't get up, honey," he said, crossing the room to where she was. Tom was in his sweet, caring mode, and Emily melted into his strong arms. "Everything will be fine, sweetheart. I promise. Greg will find us something—he's a successful guy. He won't fail us. Somehow I just know that everything is going to work out."

Tom knew that this change would be hard on Emily—not only taking the children from Jennifer, but also leaving behind her only sister. They had been so close through the years and had been through so much. He told her that Jennifer was always welcome to visit them once they were settled, and it could end up a great adventure for everyone.

A faint smile crossed Emily's face, and Tom felt a truer sense of himself—the kind-hearted, loving man he could be when he felt more connected to his family. He just knew this was going to work out.

***

Emily left for work early the following morning, wanting to get in as many hours as she possibly could. Bud, the owner of the restaurant, always appreciated her way with the customers, many of whom were loyal to his restaurant because of her ease with them. She was dedicated to serving them well and drew them in by treating them like family. Today, Emily gave extra attention to her customers with secret hopes of making more in tips.

An expert waitress, she would be greatly missed at the restaurant and its large following of regulars—repeat customers who had become friends. They knew she would be moving soon, and while they would miss seeing her, they wanted to help relieve the financial burden. Many left generous tips, and Emily felt grateful because it was true—

she needed every last dime to help relocate her family to North Carolina as soon as possible.

Emily and Tom both worked constantly. When they were not at their jobs, they were working at home in preparation for the move that was fast approaching. They had to be selective with what they packed, since they, along with their three children, took up most of the space in their station wagon. The space behind the back seat was only enough for the essentials.

With most of the packing behind her, Emily became lost in her thoughts, as she seemed to be quite often these days. She tried to concentrate on tying up some of the loose ends and sorting through items she would offer to Jennifer or to the neighbors. The phone rang and startled her. With a pounding heart, she knew that call must be Greg with some news.

"Hi Emily, this is Greg. How's everything going?"

Emily had been anticipating this call for days. She thought she'd be ready for it, but found herself trembling with a million potential "news flashes."

"Emily? Are you there?" Greg's voice brought her back to the moment.

"Oh yes. Hi Greg ..." In her nervousness, she began with small talk. "How are you and Claudia this evening?"

"We're doing great, Emily. It is so beautiful here in North Carolina, and autumn is just around the corner. It's our favorite time of year with all the beautiful fall colors! We just cannot wait for you and Tom to enjoy all this beauty with us!"

"Oh, it sounds lovely!" Emily replied, her heart filled with hope once again.

"I'm so excited to tell you and Tom that I've found a house for you!" Greg announced. "And you're going to love it!"

"I ... I ... I'm overwhelmed, Greg. You and Claudia are so kind," managed Emily.

"Now can you keep the secret for a couple minutes, Emily?" he teased. "I want to tell Tom the news myself. Is he at home?!"

Emily was overjoyed, "I'll go get him right now! He's outside, but it'll only take a minute. Hang on!"

She felt almost like a child at Christmas, and her eyes welled up with tears of joy and gratitude. She ran outside to find Tom, and she nearly knocked him over, he was headed back to the house. She hurried him inside and ushered him to the phone.

"It's your brother," she pointed, doing her best to hold back her excitement.

"Hello, Greg!" Tom boomed, beginning to catch the feeling of excitement that already permeated the room, "I hope you're calling with some good news!"

"Hey, Tom!" Greg called out just as loudly from the other end. "It's actually great news! I have a friend who is a real estate agent and spoke with him the other night. I let him know what you're looking for. He showed me a few houses that I wasn't all that impressed with, but now he's found what I think is the perfect house for you, Emily, and the kids!"

Greg barely took a breath and completely ignored any attempts by Tom to interrupt him.

"Tom, this is a great two story house with three bedrooms and one bath. There's a basement and a garage. The house is on two acres with a couple of old horse barns on the back side of the property. It's just a really great house, Tom, and it's only about twenty minutes from us!"

"Greg, this is great news …" began Tom, but was interrupted.

"And get this! The furniture comes with the house, so Emily doesn't have to worry. She can take her time decorating it."

Tom finally interjected, "Greg, I'm sure it's a great house. In fact, it sounds perfect, but it sounds like a lot more house than Emily and I can afford."

"Here's the best part, Tom," Greg said with even more excitement. "Claudia and I went over to take a look at this place. Get this— the owners wanted it sold quickly and took a really low price for it."

Tom's excitement evaporated as he tried to understand why Greg was even telling him about this great place. It sounded like it had already been sold.

Greg started laughing, reading Tom's thoughts. "I bought the house. I didn't want you to miss out and just couldn't pass it up, not to mention that it was a steal! Besides, when you're all settled in and get some work, you can start paying me back. We'll set up a payment you can work with. Does that sound okay to you and Emily?"

This time, it was Tom's eyes what welled with tears. "I don't even have words, Greg! This will make Emily's day!"

"It's a great deal for all of us," Greg agreed.

"It's the best news I could ever get. Emily's been wracking her brain trying to figure out how we were going to furnish even a small apartment on our budget, let alone a house for five people! She'll be over the moon to hear all of this!"

"Exactly. And best of all, we're only twenty minutes away. It will be great to have family around," said Greg.

"I wish I had words to thank you! I'll make it up to you someday, I promise I will," vowed Tom. He didn't know what else to say, considering his brother has just tossed him a lifeline. "I plan to find a job as soon as we get there. I can't wait to begin paying you back! Emily and I just cannot thank you enough, Greg! Please make sure you give our love to Claudia!"

"I will," Greg said. "And make sure you hug your beautiful wife for us too! We can't wait to see you all! By the way, if you've got a pen and paper, I want to give you the address. The place is just sitting there waiting for you and the family to move in!"

Tom wrote down the address and told Greg they would tie up their loose ends and let him know when they were on their way.

"Thank you again. And I won't say goodbye. Now I can say 'See you soon!'"

Greg laughed and said, "That's right. See you all soon!"

Emily could see the excitement in Tom as he hung up and hugged him even though she didn't know the details yet.

"Tell me all about it now! What did he say?!"

Tom went over the news, and she could barely believe what she was hearing!

"Is it true?" she asked. "Is it really true?"

"Yes, it really is true! We can finish packing and get ready to make this trip," Tom assured her.

It was becoming more real, and suddenly as Emily's thoughts shifted to Jennifer she said "Oh dear, Jennifer is really going to be upset."

"I know, sweetie. But this is going to be a better life, and we'll have our very own house and a brand new start. Jennifer will understand; that I know," he comforted.

For the first time in a long while, Emily felt real hope. They sat down to eat, and she decided to wait until tomorrow to tell Jennifer. She wanted to share these concrete details in person and hopefully lighten the pain.

***

Both Tom and Emily were so excited about the upcoming move that it was difficult to sleep that night. Emily envisioned that a new location, a new home, and an entirely new life could make all the difference for her and Tom, not to mention the kids.

This will be a great life, she told herself. It's everything I've always wanted! Everything seemed to be falling into place, which was a novel event. Rarely did anything run smoothly, and this was a positive situation for once. *The house sounds fabulous with outdoor space for the kids to play … I'm sure Claudia will know of someone who can babysit while I work … maybe Greg or Claudia know of a place that's hiring …*

She trailed off to sleep while Tom lay wide awake with thoughts of his own. *I know the boss will still keep a close watch on me, no matter where I end up … he'll never stop watching … I don't want to end up with death threats like Eddie did when he didn't follow orders … but I've never been a snitch, and I've always done as I was told … so, what do I have to worry about?*

He glanced over at Emily. She was so kind, so trusting. She had no clue he went to jail to cover for his boss. Fluffing his too-flat pillow, he turned on his side, not wanting her to wake and ask why he couldn't sleep. *I wish he would just trust me ... but people like him never trust anybody.* That fact was always heard loud and clear by all the guys. All of whom were dangerous. *Now I have to figure out a way to tell him I'm leaving the state.* Tom felt his chest tighten with the thought of some "accident" occurring with his family. Still, he knew that only the truth would work with his boss, no matter how risky.

I can't put it off. Tomorrow is the day, he decided. He almost said it aloud to convince himself. *He'll have to know when and where ... EXACTLY WHERE ...*

***

Emily's morning coffee was accompanied by mixed emotions, running the gamut from excitement over the new life ahead to near-depression over the conversation she needed to have with Jennifer.

Getting dressed for work was mechanical. Her thoughts were saturated with all the events scheduled for this day. The plan was to talk with Jennifer this morning before going to work. *I cannot afford to be dreading this conversation all day. I'll never make any tips*, she reasoned. Then she talked herself out of it. *I'd be a blubbering mess all day after leaving Jennifer with that news. What was I thinking?*

Driving straight to the restaurant was a relief, especially since all three kids were already at Jennifer's house. There was no reason to stop by until after her shift. She would face the conversation then and moved it to the back of her mind. Today she would focus her attention on her customers ... and their tips.

Telling her boss the news today would be easier. With her apron on and resolve intact, she asked for a moment alone.

"I hate that you're leaving in one short week," Bud said. "But I understand. And I hope I can find someone who is half as good with the customers as you."

His words bolstered her spirit. It was nice to be appreciated. No one ever knew her struggles, which were kept to herself. She always showed up with a smile on her face, lighting up the restaurant with genuine enthusiasm for customers and coworkers alike. It was telling that Tom often complained to her that she liked being at work more than she liked her days off.

Bud announced Emily's imminent departure to the breakfast customers. He did the same for the lunch crowd. The tips got larger, and comments sweeter. Well wishes were the talk of the day.

Emily played it up. "Hey, Bud! Add a few more fries to that hamburger for Ernie. He deserves it since he's been eating the same thing for lunch every day for five years!" She made every order special, remembering to comment on births, weddings, graduations and more. She knew these customers so well, and many of them rewarded her for the personal touch. The atmosphere at the restaurant was light and full of laughter, celebrating Emily who had spent the greater part of the past few years serving them all.

It hadn't really sunk in yet that she would not be there a week from now. She continued to push back the dread over the upcoming conversation with Jennifer. Yet the drive there was more peaceful than Emily had anticipated. More than likely it was due to the great day she had. Soon she was at the door, and Richard and the twins ran to meet her. She sat down and played with the children, who climbed on her and vied for her attention. For a fleeting moment, Emily felt that she was the luckiest woman in the world.

Jennifer walked into the room with two full cups—a coffee tradition that would soon no longer take place. She sensed that Emily was distracted and shooed the children from the room

"I can tell that you've got something you want to talk about," Jennifer opened. "I'm all ears."

Emily knew that stalling would only prolong the pain.

"Okay, Jennifer ..." Emily pointed to the seat beside her on the couch. "Have a seat here. I want to be close to my sister right now ..."

Jennifer sat next to her looking concerned. Emily took a deep breath.

"A week from now we won't have the luxury of our daily visits unless they're on the phone ..." she began.

Jennifer's body tensed.

"WHY OH WHY did I let down my guard and try to forget it?!" she yelled. "Why?"

Emily anticipated tears, not an explosion. "Jennifer, there is just no easy way. We both knew this was coming. I wish I could pack you up and bring you along with me."

Silence. Crickets.

"I cannot even comprehend how I'll get on without you, Jennifer! You've been my rock since I was a little kid!" Emily added.

"I wish with all my heart that it didn't have to be this way," said Jennifer, staring blankly at the wall.

"There is just no other way," Emily said, choking on her words between sobs. Composing herself as much as she was able, she told Emily about last night's conversation with Greg. "Jennifer, Greg has actually bought us a house. We'll be leaving one week from today, and once we're all moved in, I hope you'll come visit. Please promise me you will!"

Jennifer, still numb from the news, didn't respond.

"Jennifer, you're like a mother to my kids. We all love you more than words can express, and to hurt you is the last thing I ever want to do. It kills me to know that I have to leave without you. You know the story already—we can't stay, or Tom will be in danger—all of us would be in danger. I know you understand …" her voice trailed off, waiting for words that didn't come.

Finally, Jennifer sighed and stated in a near-monotone, "I know. I hear you. You're leaving one week from today. There is no other way."

She went silent again, and Emily knew her sister was still processing the news.

"Emily, those are my babies! Richard and the twins are no less than my own children! How? How can I ever say goodbye to them? I cannot imagine this house without them! I cannot imagine my life without my sweet baby girls … I'm their mama!" Jennifer sobbed, inconsolable, crumpling into Emily's arms.

The fact was, Emily truly wanted to mother her own children for a change. She pined for a normal family and children who called *her* Mama, not their aunt.

Suddenly, much like a robot, Jennifer stopped crying and stood up. "I'm sure it will all be okay," she managed, although her voice cracked. She walked Emily to the door and again assured her, "It will all be okay. I just need to take a bit of time to get used to it. Please leave all the children here until you leave, Emily. I want to spend every moment I can with them."

"Of course, Jennifer. Of course," Emily replied, grateful that the most difficult part was over ... for now, anyway.

Before she left, Emily turned and hugged her sister tightly. "I love you. So much. I'll see you tomorrow." Then she walked to the adjacent room and gathered her children in her arms, quietly relieved that soon she'd have them all under her own roof.

***

Tom's encounter was different from Emily's. If he had his way, she'd never need to know the tightrope of conflicting emotions that he walked. But this was the only kind of work Tom felt suited for, and though it seemed to rob him of his soul, he saw no way out of it.

As he approached his boss to let him know the news of their departure, his words had to be well thought out. He had to assure his boss there would be no trouble as a result of this move. Tom wrote down the new North Carolina address and phone number, and felt the glaring eyes of his boss—sort of a sixth sense that helped diffuse the personal threats some of his associates faced.

"You know the rules, Tom," his boss spoke with the kind of authority that transcended any state line. "You understand what happens if there is one utterance from your mouth." He lit a cigar and took a long draw.

Tom knew exactly what he meant. "I'm completely trustworthy and loyal," he said. "I swear it," he vowed, hoping his voice did not betray his nervousness.

"There will always be eyes, Tom… best not forget it," the boss warned, underscoring what he knew Tom already understood. A couple of his associates had gone missing after word got out that they had "loose lips."

"Yes, sir. I'll never, ever say a word," Tom assured again.

Walking back to his car, he breathed a visible sigh of relief and vowed to try to find honest work. He wanted to leave this chapter far behind him. His conversation with himself lasted until he arrived home, and then the doubts crept in. *Can I start over with a clean slate at forty-one years old? That's not too old. But with a criminal record and no real work history to speak of ... no references ... what am I thinking?*

He closed the car door and headed toward the house, trying to shake loose the worries.

Inside Emily was already hard at work packing. There were decisions to make about what to take along and what to leave behind. Still, when she heard Tom's car door close, she stopped her work and rushed to the kitchen to warm up last night's leftovers. It seemed their meals were a never-ending cycle of leftovers, although she rationalized that re-heated spaghetti was usually better the day after.

"How was your day?" she asked after serving him a plate.

Their conversation went as expected. Tom was relieved that he had told his boss. Emily was relieved for the same reason but was also less anxious now that Jennifer knew the plan. It had been an exhausting day for both of them, yet there was still much to accomplish.

"At least we made it through the roughest part," Tom told her. "It must have been hell for you giving Jennifer the move date."

"Yeah, and your day sounded like it wasn't a picnic either," Emily hugged him back with a sympathetic smile.

Tom offered to clear away the dishes while Emily resumed her sorting. The closet in Richard's bedroom took her memories back to when he was a small boy. He had been such a happy little boy. Now, at nine years old, he rarely smiled and often seemed dark and moody. *Maybe Richard can get some of his childhood back when we move,* Emily hoped wistfully, suspecting Richard's emotional issues stemmed from her brother-in-law's influences. From that perspective, she was grateful they were leaving and hoped it wasn't too late for Richard.

She chose the more positive thoughts. *He'll have plenty of space to run and play the way normal boys do, and maybe he'll make some good friends. I hope this move helps him—and all of us.*

Soon she had a couple of stacks of things she wanted to give to only Jennifer and Annie.

"Oh, Annie!" Emily groaned, "I'll have to face telling her tomorrow."

Annie worked at the restaurant with Emily, and it had been her day off. It would be difficult to say goodbye to her best friend. *I hope Annie will come visit me,* Emily thought, knowing the chances of that were slim to none at all, given that uncomfortable encounter when Tom was flirting with her. *What a prick!* she grumbled under her breath.

Suddenly feeling weary, she was aware she'd have to pace herself to get through the busy week ahead with work. She sunk down into that familiar old rocking chair in the twins' room and breathed a prayer for a better life for all of them. *God, I hope Jennifer is okay. I'm going to miss her. I know she is going to grieve losing the kids. Please, God, make a way for her to visit us in North Carolina ...*

With a new burst of energy, she returned to her tasks.

***

Reality hit again while seeing Annie at work the following day. Suddenly Emily was an emotional wreck and wiped away tears with the backs of her hand. Annie had already heard the news.

"I wanted to tell you myself, Annie, but it looks like someone beat me to it," Emily sighed.

"It makes no difference who said it. You're still leaving," Annie said, and reached out to touch Emily's arm. "We all knew, but now there's a date, and the reality is hitting me. I'm sorry, but I do not like it!"

Emily would miss Annie too, but she was so ready for this move. She hoped it meant some good changes were ahead.

The week flew by. She gave Jennifer some household items and a deep freezer filled with a few things. Annie teared up over the special things Emily gave her, mostly things from the recesses of her closets that wouldn't fit in the station wagon. It all began to feel lighter by Wednesday. On Thursday she had a yard sale—which was really a living room sale—and a few of the gals showed up and were tickled pink with all that Emily had set aside for them. Knowing Emily had a use for every penny, they paid her as much as they could and told Emily they'd always remember her.

With Friday came the final touches—organizing everything in one car, since Tom had sold the other one. Their last night in this little old house was peaceful, and Emily was grateful for the extra money of which Tom had no knowledge. She suspected he might have a few dollars up his sleeve as well.

Tom and Emily were ready for Saturday morning's arrival. Feeling more prepared to face Jennifer than she ever believed she could be, they first placed a quick call to Greg to let him know they were on the way. Then they took one last look around to be sure they hadn't missed anything and stepped out of their house for the last time. Backing out of the driveway, Tom took Emily's hand, "This place has been good to us, hasn't it, honey? I love you" he said.

Squeezing Tom's hand in acknowledgment, she said, "Yeah, it's been good to us."

The drive to Jennifer's was quiet, but there was no emotional distance between them. The aroma of coffee and bacon greeted them as they walked through the front door. Jennifer wanted to make this morning as normal as she could for all of them, including herself. With her sadness at bay, she could savor every last moment with the twins, who called her Mama. They all ate and chatted for a while. Tom was getting itchy feet to get on the road and gave that glance to Emily to let her know it was time. Emily stood up and went over to her sister for a prolonged hug felt good to them both.

"Thank you so much, Jennifer, for everything, including this wonderful breakfast! I always think of you when I think of breakfast done right," Emily giggled, doing her best to keep things light.

Jennifer joined in with the laughter. "It sure doesn't take much to please my sister, does it?"

With an exaggerated smack of his lips, Tom took his last bites and finished his coffee. "This will definitely hold us for quite a while Jennifer!" he complimented. "We won't have to stop until dinner time! You've outdone yourself!"

"That reminds me," Jennifer remembered, heading back into the kitchen, "I packed sandwiches and snacks for the trip. Let me grab them before I forget!"

Emily followed her sister into the kitchen and hugged her tightly. "I cannot thank you enough for all you have done, Jennifer! I hope you know how much I love you!" Walking with arm-in-arm, they brought the sandwich basket to the front door.

"I'm going to miss all of you, too. This house has been full for so long, and now it will be only me and Bill. I wish I could come with you!" Jennifer sobbed. For the first time in their lives, they would be separated by many miles. Tom helped the children gather their belongings and loaded them into the car. Emily and Jennifer walked outside for a bit of privacy, and Emily handed Jennifer an envelope that contained as much money as she could spare.

"It is nowhere close to the amount you deserve, Jennifer, but it comes from my heart, and I want you to use it in any way you wish."

Jennifer did not want to take the money, but Emily insisted. Jennifer finally gave in.

"Thank you, Emily. I'm truly grateful. I don't want to take this, but I know how stubborn you are," she grinned. With a more serious tone, Jennifer placed her hands on Emily's shoulders and looked into her face with strength and resolve. "Emily, I do know this move is the only way. I also know it's best for all three children to be together with their parents. Loving them as I do, I want what is best for them, even though it kills me to see them leave. We have telephones. We'll be in touch. I want you to be at peace as you leave. Make it an adventure for the kids. They deserve that."

Bill and Tom came through the front door carrying the remainder of the kids' toys and treasures. The children trailed behind them, ready to leave. Jennifer had done a great job preparing them for the separation.

Jennifer was the one who took command. "Come on kids … into the car! You're going to have a fun adventure now! Make sure you let me know how the trip goes and I want you to tell me all about your new house when you get there!" She kissed Richard and told him she loved him, and then she grabbed the twins and hugged them both very tightly. "I cannot believe how big you've gotten—overnight!" she said with a smile, squeezing them playfully. "Now you girls make me proud and mind your mom and dad!"

She had done her best to keep it light with them, but as the girls were climbing into the back seat, Jennifer grabbed them once again, hugging them and kissing their blond curls. Doing her best to keep her tears from flowing, she bent down and looked into their faces, studying them … memorizing them … and finally spoke. "Faith-y and Hope-y, Mama loves you so much! Don't you ever forget that!"

The girls hugged Jennifer back and kissed her face, telling her how much they loved her too. "Now get your little butts into the car and have a wonderful trip!" Jennifer managed.

Tom shook Bill's hand and kissed Jennifer's cheek, thanking them for everything. He took his place behind the steering wheel. Emily said goodbye to Bill, then took a private moment with her sister before she quickly stepped into the passenger seat to avoid more tears.

The kids were excited to go, and while she was overcome with emotion, Jennifer also felt contentment over a job well done over these past four and a half years—at least with the twins. She stood in the driveway until Tom and Emily's car was out of sight. With a tearful sigh she whispered to herself, "North Carolina is so far away …" as she abruptly turned and stepped into her house to busy herself by clearing away the breakfast dishes.

Chapter 6: Road Trip

"Although the world is full of suffering, it is also full of the overcoming of it."
~ Helen Keller

Emily turned toward the window to wipe away the tears, but it was too late. Richard had not missed it.

"Why are you crying, Mommy?"

"I was just thinking how much I'll miss Auntie Jennifer, that's all," Emily spoke honestly to her son.

"We'll see her soon, though," Richard responded with the innocence of a child.

Emily knew the children could not comprehend the time and distance between their old home with Aunt Jennifer and their new home in North Carolina. The twins kicked their feet, gigging softly together while Richard watched out the window. The familiar houses "disappeared" one by one. Soon they were on the highway, and everyone settled into the rhythm of the tires on the road.

Tom, alone with his thoughts, appeared to be focused on his driving and Emily, alone with her thoughts, continued to gaze out the window. Her mind wandered a bit and memories of the past tumbled over one another until she was brought back to the present. Her thoughts landed upon Jennifer. Tom glanced at Emily, knowing what she was thinking. He reached for her hand, "It will all be okay. I promise," he encouraged. Still, Emily privately wondered if he could truly ever change.

As always, Emily liked it when Tom displayed his caring, sensitive side. It consoled her that their trip had begun with such tender feelings between them, especially since he was so prone to outbursts of temper when he wasn't fully in control of a situation. Emily felt gratitude to Greg and Claudia for making it so much easier to leave the state. It felt to her as though Tom was encouraged by the help from his brother and glad to be leaving. Greg gave him a sense of brotherly love and some semblance of family warmth.

Maybe things will be better now, Emily thought, comforted again by Tom's sensitivity. *Maybe he's learning to control his temper ... I can hope.* Emily had often wondered what caused so much anger in her husband. That one time she had asked him about it taught her never to approach the subject again. His anger was off the charts over the mere suggestion that he might have an anger issue. She thought at the time, *He probably doesn't even know what it is ... poor Tom.* She felt it was her way of always protecting him, even at her own expense.

Between bathroom breaks and stops just to stretch their legs or grab a drink, the family had settled into the rhythm of the trip, sometimes chattering about what they saw along the way, or quietly lost in their own thoughts and imaginations of what their new life would be like in North Carolina.

Noticing some fields of corn through his window, Richard shouted out, "Look at the deer, Mom!"

The girls had never seen a deer before and squealed with excitement. A whole herd of deer was feeding in the field. Other sights came into view - horses, a few donkeys, and some cows. Of course, the children loved any type of animal. But soon the girls became restless after the novelty wore off.

"Are we there yet?" Hope wanted to know.

"No, honey. We have a long way to go. We won't arrive until very late tonight, and you'll probably be fast asleep!"

Tom did his best to help prepare his young children for the long distance they were traveling.

"We'll be on the road for a whole day," he explained. "That means you'll have to keep yourselves occupied. Maybe count all the colors you see. You know, on signs, on buildings, and the cars around us," he encouraged.

The drive, so far, went more smoothly than Tom or Emily anticipated. The children looked at their books and played car games, napping occasionally and waking up to watch the countryside pass by.

They snacked on the treats and the stops every few hours made the trip tolerable for children and adults alike.

With each stop, everyone was happy to get back on the road, anxious to see their new home. The closer they got, the more excited they all were. Tom talked about the property and told the kids all about the two old horse barns and how there was room on the property to run and play and explore. He painted a wonderful picture in their minds about how great life would be in their new home.

Nine-year-old Richard was beginning to comprehend that they were moving very far away from their old home. "Where is North Carolina, anyway?" he asked.

"Well," said Tom, "We'll be driving to the end of Ohio then through West Virginia and Virginia. Then when we hit North Carolina, we'll have a few more hours to drive before we get to our new house. It's a pretty long way, so I suggest you just relax and see what you can out the window before it gets dark outside."

"Wow, Dad!" Richard was amazed, "That's a lot of states! I can't wait to see what Virginia looks like!"

As the drive wore on, the kids wore on until they became fidgety. The girls were picking at each other and began raising their voices. Richard tried out his "big brother voice of authority" which, of course, only made matters worse.

Tom's frustration level began to escalate, "I don't count to three or even two! You kids have one chance to settle down right now! And none of you will like what happens if I stop this car, and I'm very close to stopping this car!"

The children immediately got quiet.

Tom felt Emily's eyes on him. "We have a long way to go, and I don't need all this fussing while I'm driving. The next time I'll pull this car over without even warning them!" he threatened.

Emily gave the kids a "look" over her shoulder and told them to make sure they keep it "on low." Three pairs of eyes looked at her miserably.

"Why don't you play the car counting game, Richard?" Emily suggested. Suddenly all three kids were excited to count all the cars that passed them. It kept them busy for a while, and Tom's frustration subsided. Emily's intuition told her they were growing bored with the game, so she asked if anyone was hungry. Everyone including Tom was ready for a stop.

"I need to fill up the gas tank, and I know we can all use a pit stop. When we're back on the road, let's dive into those great sandwiches Aunt Jennifer made for us," Tom volunteered, and Emily was relieved to see his pleasant mood reappear.

The stop at an old country store and gas station was a great choice with some interesting novelties. Although they were out of the car longer than Tom had planned, he knew it was good for all of them to stretch and walk around a bit, enjoying a few extra moments out of the prison on wheels.

"They really are doing pretty well for little kids," he whispered to Emily, who was happy to hear that Tom felt this way too.

Back on the road, everyone was ready for one of Jennifer's sandwiches. The conversation was light, and they recalled the interesting things they had seen in the country store. Richard had been very taken with the taxidermy rattlesnake. "You girls were funny to watch, making all your 'eeewww' sounds over a silly ol' dead snake!" he teased.

The girls in unison repeated, "Eeewww!!"

"Well, I liked it, didn't you Dad?!" Richard stated, proud to be a boy who appreciated such things.

"Yes, I thought it was great, Richard. Now finish your sandwich and settle down," Tom spoke loudly from his place at the wheel.

Sandwiches and drinks finished, Emily noticed that the children had heavy eyes as she gathered the trash from the back seat. Within minutes all three were asleep. Emily and Tom were both relieved and hoped the kids wouldn't waken until the end of the trip. After all, the hum of the engine and whirring sound of the tires should keep them lulled for a good long time!

The hours passed, and the sun had long set. The family made their final pit stop of the journey and the children climbing sleepily into the back seat, unaware of just how close they were to their new home. The children fell back to sleep, and it would have been the perfect time for a conversation between husband and wife over their hopes and dreams for a new beginning. But Tom and Emily kept their thoughts to themselves. Tom's mind was far ahead of him, working potential angles in his head for connections and deals as soon as he could get his bearings around town. Emily's thoughts were consumed with wondering if she even dared to dream this move could change her life for the better, especially since she now had responsibility for all three kids and no Jennifer around to lift that burden.

The only world that gave her any sense of self was her job at the restaurant, hundreds of miles behind her now. *Oh, God, I hope I can find a job right away,* her hopeless thoughts drifting toward heaven. *A job where I can work lots of hours, so I can keep my sanity!*

They pulled into town just before midnight. A light misty rain had just begun. The dim light from a phone booth shined through the misty darkness like a beacon. It was located at the first filling station they found. Tom was glad he still had a half tank left since the station was closed. He stepped out of the car to call Greg for directions. Greg was expecting the call and gave Tom easy directions to their new house, which was only a few minutes away.

"I'm glad to know you made it here safe and sound." Greg's voice sounded tired and happy. "You all get some rest tonight ... we can't wait to see you!"

"Thank you, Greg," Tom spoke with sincerity, "for everything. Please give Claudia a big hug. We can't wait to see you either!"

Tom hung up the phone with thoughts of how great it will be to spend time together with his brother and sister-in-law. Onward they drove, and the neighborhood looked perfect, even in the dark. They were both in awe of the house, and Emily felt like an excited child ready to explore the picture-perfect two-story abode, surrounded by a huge lawn. They were amazed at how much nicer this place was compared to their tiny house back in Ohio. Tom told Emily to wait with the kids while he went to find the house key and turn on some lights. Her heart pounded with anxious excitement.

"Please hurry," she said, not able to contain herself.

Tom, already at the back door before Emily finished speaking, reached under the mat for the key, opened the door, and turned on the lights inside and outside. Before he could call to her, Emily and the children, who had awakened the moment Tom closed his car door, were already beside him at the door. Together they walked through the kitchen, where Emily paused, surveying the appliances. Then into the dining room they went, where one of the two windows perfectly framed the moon. It had risen clear and full on this wonderful night, and Emily was in heaven in her new home.

The children, now wide awake, rushed past them to the wooden staircase leading upstairs, but Emily wanted to take it all in. So she walked toward the living room and discovered the fireplace she had always wanted. The door on the same wall as the fireplace opened to reveal a den.

"Greg was right about this house," said Tom, startling Emily out of her wonderment. "I'm so glad he got it before it was snatched up because this house definitely would not have waited long!"

They walked back to the large wooden staircase. Upstairs, the children had already discovered their rooms ... and not only had they found their rooms, but they also had already climbed into their beds and were sound asleep.

"Greg and Claudia are angels!" said Emily, prying shoes off her tired brood.

Relieved to be at his new home, Tom went back to the car to bring in what was needed for the night. Emily was amazed at the perfect furnishings in each room. Finally, she climbed into bed and pulled the covers up around her neck. Then she breathed a deep sigh of relief. *This bed is so comfortable ...*

Tom had told Emily that he would be up shortly, as he needed some time to unwind from all the driving before he could sleep. He went back to the car to bring in more of their things. In a sudden burst of energy, he brought all that was left in the car into the house. Securing all the locks, Tom once again walked through the downstairs of their new house, hoping against hope that he could make a new start and put behind him the troublesome old ways—things that had followed him for so many years. After checking on Richard and the girls to make certain they were sleeping soundly in their new beds, Tom quietly slipped into the new bed he shared with Emily, who was fast asleep. Drifting off, his last thoughts were already of the morning, when he knew the kids would be ready to play and explore the new property.

***

The first night in their new home was a short one, for the whole family was wide awake in the early morning as the sun was up. The kids dashed outdoors to explore while Emily threw together snacks that would have to double as breakfast. She was relieved that Tom volunteered to head over to the local market to pick up necessities for some simple meals. She immersed herself in unpacking and organizing, feeling energized in what she hoped would be a brand new, happy life.

Tom returned from the store with the supplies and news that he may have already found Emily a job.

"The manager wants you to come by tomorrow. I think it's the perfect job for you!" he said. The words were light and confident. While it would have seemed better to spend the first week at home, there was a part of Emily that was ready to dive into a job, not to mention that they could sure use the income!

Tom's voice on the phone with Greg signaled Emily that things were going well in Tom's mind, which was always a relief for her.

"It's perfect, Greg! Everything about it is perfect! Emily is so happy, and the children are excited. They were already out playing in the yard this morning. It'll be great to see you when you come by …" Tom's voice trailed as he ended his conversation and headed for the back door to do some outdoor exploring.

Clearing away some of the boxes, Emily noticed a door opposite the back door. Flipping on the light, the dim basement steps appeared. *I haven't looked down here yet,* she thought. Testing the creaky steps, she noticed the smell of musty dampness. That was quickly forgotten when she saw the washing machine and dryer across the room!

Oh, my! I've never had my own washer and dryer before! She was ecstatic as she pushed and pulled all the buttons to find that both machines were in working order. *Greg didn't tell us about this! I guess he wanted us to be surprised when we came down here!*

She walked over to the other side of the basement. The walls were old white brick that seemed hundreds of years old. It really did feel a bit scary. The light was dim and even darker in certain areas. Pushing on a heavy metal door, she wondered about the small space it opened up to. *It sure looks creepy in there.* Having enough "excitement" for one day, Emily quickly closed the door and returned to the steps, making her way back to the kitchen.

Outside in the garage, Tom was conducting some explorations of his own. Surveying the space, his calculating mind immediately began making plans for it. He was delighted to see a small enclosed area where he could set up a private office. Unconsciously grabbing the old broom that he found leaning against a corner, Tom began sweeping while his attention honed in on the "out of the way" hiding places that his criminal instincts were trained to notice. These were the nooks and crannies that most people would see no value in. But Tom was well aware of just how "valuable" such secret spaces were.

Yes, this old garage would do just fine. Yet the thought persisted, *I've been handed a new lease on life. It sure would be nice if I could do it right this time …"*

Tom's old life was ever present and overshadowed the future, always bigger than his wish to be free. He would always be dogged by the need to watch his back. The old boss had made that very clear, but showing fear was not his style, and Tom was too clever to ever be outsmarted by his own kind. *The trick is to keep my mouth shut and always be prepared. Never sit with my back to the door. Expect the unexpected and stay a step ahead of their game.* This was Tom's way, and it had kept him alive so far.

Regrets are for those who have the luxury to change, and while it seemed for just a fleeting moment that change could be within his grasp, the perpetual need to "watch his back" and the ever-present "dirty secrets" haunted him. He could share this secret life with no one, which kept him untrusting and filled with constant tension. It compounded a lifetime of anger stemming from the recesses of his childhood which could never be erased. Sometimes he was able to control it … and sometimes … well, he just could not.

It is what it is, Tom told himself, with not even a hint of self-pity. He set aside the broom and locked the door on his way out. *Ah, well, this old garage has held plenty of secrets so a few of my own won't hurt it any.* Satisfied with the garage, and leaving his thoughts and worries for the moment, Tom strode through the back door of the house whistling a made-up tune. The house was actually small, but somehow seemed perfect.

***

Emily had just finished the unpacking, and everything was now in its new place. She felt light on her feet with the feeling that this move was "just what the doctor ordered."

"Have you noticed that the "atmosphere" of this house is even better than our old house?" Emily spoke to Tom as he entered the kitchen. "Plus did you know, Tom, we've got a washer and dryer down in the basement! You've got to see it!"

Without waiting for an answer, she opened the basement door and directed Tom down the steps to show him her newest discovery.

"That little room is pretty creepy, so thank God it has a heavy door," Emily noted, pointing it out to Tom with only half-feigned fear.

Tom was happy for Emily, knowing that having a washing machine and dryer would mean a lot less work when it came to the laundry. He had a look at the "creepy little room" and the rest of the basement before they headed back up the steps. Greg and Claudia would be arriving soon.

"The place looks really great, honey. You've made a good start of things," he complimented as they wandered through the rooms of their new home discussing ideas for this room or that. They both noticed Greg and Claudia's car pulling into the driveway, and the kids noticed too because they all came running.

"Mom! Dad! Someone is here!" hollered Richard as he, with the twins at his heels, ran to his parents who were just coming out of the house into the driveway to meet them.

Greg and Claudia stepped out of their car, all teary-eyed and open-armed. Emily was surprised at her own exuberance, seeing Greg and Claudia for the first time.

"At last I can finally hug you!" she said, her gratitude overflowing as she embraced both Greg and Claudia tightly, with deep emotion.

Tom stepped over to hug his brother and sister-in-law, stated his own "thank you's" and then introduced them to the kids.

"This is your Uncle Greg and Aunt Claudia, who helped us get into our new house!" Tom announced.

The children were on good behavior and hugged their aunt and uncle. Greg whispered into Richard's ear, "There may be something in the back seat here that belongs to you kids. Why don't you go check it out?" Before the words were fully out of Greg's mouth, Richard had the car door open and was already bouncing one of the three large rubber balls he found.

"Thank you, Uncle Greg!" Richard said gleefully. The twins hugged Greg and Claudia with thanks and followed Richard to the backyard to play.

With a laugh, Tom and Greg instinctively headed toward the garage while Claudia and Emily made their way into the house for coffee. Emily was so happy to have another woman around who was a family member. Until now, she had not realized just how much she missed Jennifer and their coffee times together.

In the garage, the reunion between the two brothers was as though they had never been apart. Tom was happy to have a few moments alone to properly thank his brother for helping them with the house and furnishings.

"I want you to know that my top priority is to pay you back as soon as I'm able to," Tom assured his brother.

Pulling the newspaper from under his arm, Greg teased his brother. "Maybe there will be something in here to help you get started! Honestly, Tom, I'm just happy you're finally here. I didn't realize how much I've missed my kid brother!"

"Right back at you, old man," Tom kidded Greg. "And thanks for the newspaper. I'll start looking at the classifieds tonight. I can't wait to get back to work!"

Tom and Greg made their way back to the house just in time to take the grand tour with Emily and Claudia. Approaching the bottom of the stairs leading to the second floor, Emily took the lead.

"I just love this staircase with its railing all the way up ... " she pointed out as they made their way to the second floor. "... and how it wraps around at the top floor to overlook the staircase!"

Claudia chimed in to say how the staircase was one of her favorite features of the house as well. "You've done a great job so far Emily—and so quickly! I wouldn't have finished this much in a whole month, let alone a day! You're a regular whirlwind!" Claudia laughed, complimenting her sister-in-law.

The two couples spent the afternoon enjoying their family bond and making plans to spend more time together. While Greg and Tom talked about which trees on the property needed to be trimmed or cut down and how they would make great firewood, Claudia and Emily exchanged decorating ideas and planned their next get-together.

Evening approached, and it was time for goodbyes. "Good luck on the job interview tomorrow, Emily. They'd be foolish not to hire you," Claudia spoke sincerely, as Greg opened her car door.

"Thanks, Claudia. I'll just be glad when the interview is over, and I can get to work!" Emily chuckled.

Greg and Claudia waved as their car pulled away. Tom and Emily walked up the steps of their new home. Calling their children inside to clean up after a full day of fun and family interactions, a sense of "normalcy" began to settle in. All three of their children were now at home with their parents. They had a home they could be proud of, and the job market seemed promising. *Normal.* Emily liked the ring of that word.

With the children finally settled in their rooms and playing quietly, Emily said goodnight to Tom. Her mind was on tomorrow's interview, and she wanted to relax into a good night's rest before the big day. Tom sat alone in the living room with his newspaper, circling ads for jobs that he would contact tomorrow. He had high hopes of finding employment very quickly.

Suddenly distracted by the faint sound of the children playing upstairs, Tom's short fuse flew into over-drive. He yelled for them to quiet down and get into their beds, which they did immediately, Richard in his own room and the twins in theirs. In the stillness, little Faith put her hands together and recited the same prayer as always.

"Now I lay me down to sleep, I pray thee Lord my soul to keep. If I should die before I wake, I pray thee Lord my soul to take. Bless mom and dad, sister and brother, Aunt Jennifer, Jesus and the angels, and all the people in the whole wide world! Amen!" Then turning onto her side, little Faith yawned and soon fell fast asleep.

What seemed like only a few minutes became an hour. Finally, Tom was satisfied that he had done all he could for the night. After checking the doors and windows to be sure everything was secure, he turned off the lights and gazed into the street and his driveway for a moment, as was his practice, always making certain he wasn't being watched. He always had the feeling of being watched, though he was rarely bothered. Still, the kind of people in his past was not the type he wanted anywhere near him now.

Pausing at Richard's door to check on him, and then walking into the twins' room, Tom bent over each of their beds, kissing their heads and tucking the covers around them.

Ahhhh ... Tom breathed a deep sigh, realizing for the first time just how tired he was. Emily was already asleep, and his last thoughts were about the new jobs that awaited each of them. Finally, sleep overtook him.

Chapter 7: Daddy's Nap

"My past has not defined me, destroyed me, deterred me, or defeated me; it has only strengthened me."
~ Steve Maraboli

Tom awoke to the aroma of fresh coffee brewing. Making his way down the stairs, he followed the scent into the kitchen where he found Emily pouring a cup. She handed it to him and poured a cup for herself. Together, they sat at the table, appreciating the peaceful quiet while the kids were still sleeping. They talked about Emily's interview, and Tom told her that he felt hopeful about a few of the available positions he found in the newspaper last night.

"I'll make some calls today to line up some interviews," Tom spoke casually, confident that he would have no trouble finding a good fit. "Are you excited about your interview today?"

"Yes, I'm excited about it, although I must admit that I'm also a little bit nervous," Emily responded, "I'll just be glad to have it over with and get to work!"

"I know the feeling," Tom said agreeably. "You'll do fine, honey, and when they hire you, they'll see how great you are with the public. You won't have any problem getting this job."

"Fingers crossed," said Emily hopefully, blushing slightly from the compliment…his charm was intoxicating at times.

Tom stood and went to the living room in search of the newspaper. "And I can't wait to get a job too, so we can start paying off what we owe Greg," he added, heading back to the table.

"If I know you at all, I know you'll find a job quickly. And thanks for the encouragement. I hope they'll like me as much as you say they will," Emily replied with a quick laugh.

With one final sip of her coffee, Emily left Tom with the newspaper and busily prepared for her big interview. After brushing her teeth and putting the final touches on her hair and makeup, she returned to the kitchen.

"Wish me luck! I'm on my way," she called to Tom who had returned to the living room with his coffee and newspaper.

"You'll do great!" he called back, and Emily was out the door before the children were up. It felt good to get behind the wheel alone in the car. *This will be the perfect job being so close to home,* she thought as she positioned the car in the grocery store's parking lot. Checking her hair in the mirror and touching up her lipstick, Emily took a deep breath and headed into the store to meet the man she hoped would hire her.

***

With Emily off for her interview and the kids still quiet upstairs, Tom set out to tackle the employment ads that he had circled in the newspaper. "I'm sorry... we just hired someone a few minutes ago..." was the response from his first call.

Well ... I guess that's not the job for me ... he told himself and continued to the second ad. Just as the person on the other end answered, the children came racing down the steps laughing and making noise.

"Hello?" he heard the voice on the phone.

"I'm sorry, sir, please hold on for just a moment," Tom responded. Feeling the anger rise up, he glared at Richard, who was the first one he saw.

"Be quiet!! I'm on the phone!!" Tom hissed through gritted teeth. Frightened by their father's anger, all three children turned and ran back up the stairs. Tom's returned to the call with a more pleasant tone.

"I'm sorry, sir, my kids were making noise and I couldn't hear you ... I'm calling about the job you have in the newspaper ..."

The conversation ended on a hopeful note, and Tom felt good about the potential job opportunity. He only needed to go in and complete the application. Still, he seethed over the interruption. Stomping up the stairs, he yelled for the kids to come out of their rooms. His anger could never allow him to acknowledge their innocence, and when the three of them timidly appeared in the hallway, he exploded.

"When I'm on the phone, I expect complete quiet! Is that understood?" He glared at Richard. "Do YOU understand?"

Richard choked out a "yes," attempting to blink back the tears that had begun streaming down his face. The rage in Tom could not be controlled. It always took precedence over any compassion he may have felt later, and it had not yet been satisfied. It stared coldly through his eyes toward the two tiny girls standing before him, as though he were the great and powerful Oz.

"Do you two understand?" he boomed at them.

"Yes! Yes!" The twins reacted in unison, shrinking back in terror ...

"Good!" Tom shouted, shaking his finger at them, "Because if I'm ever on the phone again and I hear a peep out of any of you, I'll be taking off my belt and whipping all of you!"

The children glanced quickly at one another and ran back to their rooms. Tom's anger dwindled, and he headed back down the stairs just in time to see Emily pulling the car into the driveway.

He was happy when she strode through the back door, calling to him with great excitement, "I got the job! I got the job! I start tomorrow at ten o'clock!"

Tom hugged and congratulated her, and told her he felt hopeful about his own prospects. He had a few more calls to make.

"Would you mind keeping the kids occupied while I take a few minutes and finish up these calls?" he asked.

Emily agreed and left Tom to his calls. She gathered the children, asking them to be very quiet as they made their way down the stairs and outside. "Have fun exploring! But please keep the noise down so Dad can make his calls," Emily warned them.

As the children ran into the yard, Emily quietly returned to the kitchen where Tom was just hanging up the phone.

"Any luck, Tom?" she asked.

"I think so," he said. "I called about this traveling sales job; it was the one that makes the most money. They're out of New Jersey. The boss will be back in a few minutes, and I'm supposed to call back. So, cross your fingers!"

Emily beamed, stuck out both of her hands, and crossed her fingers. "I'm heading outside to explore with the children. Good luck!" she called over her shoulder, on her way out the back door. It was a lovely day, and Emily wanted to make the most of it since she started her new job the following day. She wandered through her new yard, taking her time looking at all the different trees and plants growing. She still could not believe this was her home.

***

While the children played ball in the side yard, Emily noticed a woman walking up her driveway. "Hello," Emily called out to the woman, "May I help you?"

"Hi!" The woman replied, "My name is Karen—I live across the street. I just wanted to introduce myself and welcome you all to the neighborhood."

"Hi, Karen, great to meet you! I'm Emily. My husband, Tom, is inside on the phone right now, and those are our children," Emily pointed in the direction where they were playing, "Richard is ten, and the twins are five."

"You're not going to believe this, but we have twin girls, too—and an older son! They are all the same ages as your children! My kids are with my husband, Sam, at the moment, but when they get home, I'll bring them over to meet your kids, if that's okay with you," Karen volunteered.

"That sounds great!" Emily was excited and called her children over to introduce them, "Miss Karen has twin girls the same age as you girls! And Richard! The twins have a brother your age!" They were all very excited to learn that there were children to play with—and just across the street!

"Can they come over and play?" Hope asked.

"As soon as they get home," Karen answered her. "They're with their dad right now, but when they get back, I'll bring them over to meet you all."

The children squealed with delight! The moms talked for a short while before Karen walked back across the street.

Strolling through her new backyard, Emily's thoughts were of how wonderfully things just seem to be falling into place. *A new house they all loved, a big yard for the children to play in, a new job that starts tomorrow and now children across the street that are the same ages as her own kids, and twin girls, no less!"* Emily smiled from the inside out.

I'll have to call Jennifer tonight, she reminded herself, and her thoughts drifted toward her sister.

Tom's excited voice calling her brought Emily back to the moment. "Yes! Yes! Yes!"

Stepping through the kitchen door, Emily laughed and commented, "You must have got the job!"

"I did! Emily, I did!" They hugged each other and Tom told her he would be starting next Monday. "And guess what, Emily? They'll be supplying me with a vehicle because I'll have to be out of town one to three days a week. Plus they pay for the gas and the hotels where I'll be staying."

Emily was happy that he got the job, but wasn't too excited by the idea that he would be out of town so much. "Are you sure you want to do all that traveling, Tom?"

Anticipating her feelings on the matter, Tom was prepared. "Emily, this job pays quite a bit and right now all I can think about is getting on our feet again and paying my brother back. With both of us working, we'll be out of debt in no time! Plus, I won't be going out of town for another month or so because they're sending someone here for training. He'll be coming with my company car, and when I finish the training, he'll fly back to New Jersey. Now, you can use our car for work, and I'll have my own. How can we pass that up, honey?"

Tom, changing the subject in his masterful way, indicated that the decision about this job had already been made.

"What about the children? We need to get Richard registered for school in the next couple of days, and we'll need to find a sitter," said Emily, worried.

"I'll take him to get registered tomorrow, and we can look for a sitter in the paper," Tom assured her.

"Okay! It sounds like you've got it all worked out," Emily sighed with relief. "That is a big load off me! Oh, and by the way, I have some good news for you too! I met our new neighbor across the street, Karen, while you were on the phone. You're not going to believe this, Tom, but they have twin girls and an older boy all the same ages as our kids! Karen said they'll come back over as soon as Sam, her husband, gets home with the kids. Maybe she'll know of a sitter."

Checking through the window for her kids, Emily noticed how much they loved playing in their new yard, and for the first time in a very long while, she felt genuinely happy. Her life had been filled with so much pain and loss. She finally felt some hope that Tom would change for the better, now that he was out of the business he had left behind in Ohio.

It's the start of a brand-new life ... all I've hoped for ... I can't believe this is happening! Yet Emily's thoughts drifted, and she couldn't help remembering Tom's con man tendencies. She wondered if her new found joy could truly last.

Outside, Tom checked the car over to be certain that Emily would have no problems with it after their long trip. As he reached for a rag to wipe his hands, he noticed the new neighbors crossing the street toward him.

"Hi, you must be Tom!" Karen called out as she and her family walked toward him.

"Nice having you in the neighborhood," Sam joined in.

"Thank you! It's great to be here—and to meet neighbors so quickly." Tom spoke in a warm neighborly voice. "We're still getting settled, and Emily starts a new job tomorrow up the street at the grocery store," he offered as Emily appeared from inside the house.

"Oh! Hi Emily! You're going to love working at that store!" Karen greeted her with a hug. "They are so nice over there. You'll fit right in!"

Emily returned the hug. "Well, that's great to know!"

The kids, not waiting for a formal introduction, disappeared into the backyard to play while the two couples chatted. Emily and Karen quickly agreed that Hope and Faith could play with Karen and Sam's twins one day a week and Karen had some good referrals for a sitter for the other days while Emily and Tom were at work. Sam and Karen said they needed to get back home, and they all agreed for Sandy and Sarah to stay for a while to play with Hope and Faith while Richard went across the street to play with John.

"It works out great for all of us," Tom remarked. He thanked Karen and Sam for coming by.

***

Over the following days, Tom took Richard to get registered for school. He and John would ride the same bus, which stopped right in front of the house. Richard was excited to have a new friend the same age who would ride the school bus with him.

Emily settled easily into her new job and really loved it. She was happy to secure the new sitter, Pearl, a kind and sweet woman with whom Emily fell in love very quickly. Just as importantly, so did the children. Relieved that everything was falling into place, Emily looked forward to putting in a full forty-hour week, with Sundays off.

Things were also going Tom's way with his new job. While Karen looked after the girls on Mondays, Pearl stayed at the house Tuesdays through Saturdays. It all fell together like clockwork, and life was looking very good for Tom and Emily.

The days were getting cooler and the twin's fifth birthday party was a great success. The twins across the street were now best friends with Hope and Faith, and they would often come over just to listen while Pearl read stories to all of them. Pearl soon became one of the family, and everyone loved her.

That Christmas was one to remember as the family of five were all under one roof together. It felt wonderful for Tom and Emily to surprise their children with lots of toys and loads of fun that the holidays bring. The girls loved their new baby dolls and a miniature metal kitchen set, which kept them busy for hours at a time. Richard loved putting together his new model cars and spent hours in his room gluing and painting and putting together all kinds of toy vehicles. It quickly became his favorite hobby! Emily bought him a tall metal stand to display his growing collection. When John or one of his school buddies came over, Richard proudly showed off his handiwork.

While it seemed like good times on the outside, dysfunction cast its shadow. There was that time when Hope and Faith were fussing at each other. It was late in the day, and Emily was still at work. Downstairs Tom could hear them and hollered. The twins didn't quiet down quickly enough for Tom, who stomped up the steps and burst angrily into their room. Reaching downward and grabbing ahold of Hope, he picked her up and shook her. Beyond anger, he spanked her, disregarding all thought that she was only a little girl.

Tearful and shaking, Faith knew she was next. He grabbed her and spun her around, then spanked her with the same force he had used on Hope. The girls, crying and screaming in terror, brought Richard into the room. Tom, still in a rage, ordered Richard to leave the room or he would be next. With a fright, Richard turned and ran down the hall to his room, hoping that his dad would not be coming for him. On his bed, frozen in fear, he could hear his sisters crying.

Soon Tom walked past his room and headed downstairs. Richard's terror gave way to a deep sigh of relief, as it was all too often that he was the object of Tom's wrath.

"I can't wait till Mom gets home," Richard muttered under his breath, still afraid that Tom could hear him.

The girls, through hiccupping sobs, had stopped their crying. Wiping the tears from their faces, they found comfort in clinging tightly to their baby dolls and rocking them, assuring their dolls that it would all be okay.

Emily's return from work was welcomed by everyone. Tom complained about the girls acting up while he had been busy with his paperwork. Emily, knowing that Tom would have been hard on the kids, did her best to soothe him, then headed upstairs to check on her children.

Peeking into Richard's room, she said, "Hi honey," she spoke quietly, "How was your day?"

"It was fine until dad got mad again and spanked the girls. They were screaming and crying really hard, Mom. I was sure he was going to get me too, but he didn't." Richard's voice was low and defeated.

"Oh honey, I'm so sorry," Emily said, hugging her son. "Let me go check on them."

She opened the door into the girl's room to find them sitting on their beds cuddling their dolls.

"Hi girls!" Emily saw that their little faces were still red from crying. She sat with them, quietly lost in her own thoughts as the twins continued rocking their dolls. She remembered the day, some time ago, when Tom had lost his temper with her. *He hasn't done that since we left Ohio,* she thought, wondering if he was going to begin taking it out on the children now instead of on her.

With the same defeated feeling she sensed in Richard, Emily went to the kitchen to pull herself together, sighing a wish that she didn't have to work so much. *But we really need the money, and sometimes it actually feels better when Tom is out of town,* she thought to herself. *At least it's peaceful around here when he's away ... I guess his new job is a good thing, after all.*

She kept busy clearing up the kitchen, although it was already clean. She could not allow herself much downtime and was driven to stay busy. It kept her from too much thinking.

***

Time passed, and Tom's frustrations seemed to subside as he fell into the flow of his new job. On a lazy Sunday afternoon, he announced that he was tired and was going upstairs for a nap. On his way toward the stairs, he turned to Faith.

"I'll give you a quarter if you rub my feet for me while I take my nap," he coaxed.

Faith was ecstatic. "You'll really give me a quarter just to rub your feet?" she called out, running up the stairs behind him. She left Hope and the coloring book behind to earn her quarter.

"Hope! Did you hear that Dad is giving me a quarter? Dad's giving me a quarter!"

Of course, Hope wanted a quarter as well and called out to Tom that she would rub his feet, too.

"Next time I take a nap, Hope, it'll be your turn to earn a quarter," he called back to her.

Hope was not happy that Faith was first to earn the quarter, but she knew better than to argue with her dad. "Okay, next time it's my turn!" she conceded.

Emily, always quick to diffuse tension, grabbed Hope's hand.

"Come on, Hope. Let's you and I hang the laundry out together." Emily made hanging the laundry on the clothesline into a fun game to help Hope forget feeling slighted over Faith getting the first chance at earning a quarter from Tom.

Upstairs in the bedroom, Tom removed his shirt and pants to lie down on the bed. Faith grasped her dad's foot in her little hands and began squeezing and rubbing it.

"How does this feel, Dad?" she asked.

"You're doing a great job!" Tom complimented and after she had rubbed both feet for a moment. He thanked her, saying, "That felt great, Faith! Take a rest now and come up here and lay beside Daddy for a while."

Faith scooted across the bed to lie next to her dad. Soon, the rhythm of Tom's soft snore sent her dozing off as well. Faith jolted awake at the touch of her dad's arm landing upon her stomach. Not wanting to wake him, she stayed very still. Faith froze as Tom's hand slowly moved down her tummy, stopping for a moment. Horrified, she felt her dad's fingers wiggling back and forth on her private parts. Faith's frantic thoughts kept her still as a statue.

If I wake him up, he'll get mad and whip me! she thought. There was no going back to sleep. Helplessly she did her best to stay very still as her father's fingers slowly moved on her. After what seemed an eternity to her, Tom "woke up."

He said nonchalantly, "Thank you, Faith, for the foot rub. You did a great job for Daddy. Let me get your quarter."

Running outside, Faith showed Hope the shiny new quarter their dad had given her.

"Next time, it will be my turn!" Hope stated emphatically. With that, for the remainder of the day, the sisters played together in the fresh Carolina air. Faith's thoughts did not return to that "finger incident" with her dad while he had been "napping." Instead, she turned to the excitement of having this shiny quarter and plans of how she would spend it.

Chapter 8: Candy Spree

"Who looks outside, dreams; who looks inside, awakes."
~ Carl Gustav Jung

With both Tom's and Emily's new jobs in full swing, they began to put away some savings and also had started to pay Greg back for the house. It worked very smoothly for the whole family. Tom worked away from home, the children were happy with their new friends, and Emily loved her job down the street at the grocery store. On the surface, life seemed idyllic for all of them.

The twins' new friends across the street were a perfect match. While Faith and Sarah made fast friends, Hope and Sandy gravitated together. All four were all very excited that the following year they would begin school together.

Winter that year was exceptionally cold, and Emily was certain that Tom was working very hard, as his naps became more and more frequent. *He must be exhausted,* she thought compassionately. As always, one or the other of their dutiful daughters "rubbed Daddy's feet" for that coveted quarter. It was also more and more frequently that Tom sent Pearl home early, offering to look after the girls while Emily worked and Richard was at school.

***

Once again, it was Faith's turn to rub Tom's feet while he napped.

Tom's voice was stern. "Hope, play in your room quietly while I take my nap. Today is Faith's turn."

Obediently, knowing she would be in big trouble if she made a sound, Hope went off to play very quietly while Faith followed her father to his bedroom. Closing the door, Tom removed his shirt and pants, then stretched out onto the bed. Pulling the sheet off his feet, he motioned for Faith to climb up and rub his feet. After a few moments, Tom praised Faith for the great job she did and patted the bed next to him.

In a voice that sounded very sleepy, he said, "Come up here and lie next to Daddy. You've earned a rest."

Faith crawled onto the bed next to her father, who pushed back the sheet and made room for her. She wasn't sleepy but knew she must lie very still, as Tom had already begun to softly snore. Faith faced the window watching the trees blowing in the wind. When she finally rolled over, she noticed that her dad's private part was exposed out of his underwear. Not wanting to wake him, she just turned back to look out the window.

Suddenly his large hand flopped on top of her hand. A moment later, he guided her hand around his penis. Faith's whole body froze, and the question raced through a five-year-old mind: *Why does Dad's hand do this while he sleeps?* She was too scared to move, but as Tom began squeezing her hand around his penis, she reflexively pulled away.

With a start, Tom woke.

"What's wrong, darling?" he asked in feigned surprise.

"Nothing," Faith quickly reacted. "It's just that I'm not sleepy. Can I go play with Hope?"

"Sure, I'm getting up anyway," Tom replied cheerfully, pulling on his trousers. "Here is your quarter, Faith, and that was a great foot rub!"

Relieved that her dad was happy, and excited as always to get her shiny new quarter, Faith ran to show her sister. Hope, momentarily glancing up from holding her baby doll, spoke softly, "Mom told me we should save our quarters and soon she'll take us to the store so we can buy some candy."

Faith's eyes lit up, and the girls went to the hiding places where they each stored the quarters. Faith ran to her side of the closet with its separate door and its own window. This was her private space where she loved to sit and just be quiet all alone. It was the perfect hiding place for her stash of coins. Pulling out the quarters she'd already saved from the little box beneath some toys, she counted her money and thought of the candy she would buy when Mom took them along with her to the store!

It was a happy afternoon spent playing in the backyard with Richard after he returned from school. Later that evening, the girls played with their dolls. Faith often wished that her mother would spend more time at home.

"Mom is always at work," she sighed to Hope upon Tom's announcement that Emily would be working late again. "How come Mom never plays with us?"

"I think she just works all the time," said Hope in her most grown-up voice, taking her sister by the hand. "I think Mom and Dad need money and that's why they work so much. Do you want to play Barbies, Faithy?"

The girls busied themselves with what they loved almost more than anything—playing with the Barbie Dolls they had gotten for Christmas. That always kept them busy for hours.

Bedtime came, and as always Faith recited her nightly prayer:

"Now I lay me down to sleep, I pray the Lord my soul to keep. If I should die before I wake, I pray the Lord my soul to take. Bless Mother and Father, Sister and Brother, Aunt Jennifer, Jesus and the angels and all the people in the whole wide world. Amen!"

***

The weekend finally arrived, and Emily surprised all three of her children.

"Come get your coats, we're all going to the store!" she called to Faith, Hope, and Richard. The twins scrambled upstairs to their hiding places to get their quarters. Squealing with glee all the way to the store, the girls talked about what they would buy.

"Why are you so excited?" Richard asked, annoyed at his pesky little sisters. The twins produced the quarters that their dad had given them for rubbing his feet during nap times. Emily noticed that Richard felt left out, which seemed to be common nowadays ... ever since they had moved to their new home.

As the girls directed themselves to the candy section, Emily leaned over and whispered into Richard's ear, "Don't worry, honey, I'll buy you some candy."

Richard was all smiles. "Thanks, Mom," he replied and turned to hug her.

It had not gone unnoticed that Tom treated Richard "differently" than he did the girls. *I wish he would give Richard as much attention as he gives the twins, and I really wish he was more patient with Richard,* Emily's thoughts flashed as she watched her children making their important candy decisions.

Back at home after the big candy spree, the twins ran to hide their newly purchased treats under their beds. Strolling into their room, Richard teased them, "When you go to sleep make sure you don't hang your arms down because those monsters under your beds will bite them off!"

Richard ran from the room laughing at the fright on Faith's face, which was much more telling than her loud words: "No there isn't, Richard!!"

Ever the champion, Hope comforted her sister. "He's just trying to scare us, Faith. Don't listen to him!"

The girls chased after him as Richard, very proud of himself, laughed all the way back to his room.

Later that night while lying in bed, Faith rolled over on her tummy to sleep. But the moment her arm hung down beside the bed, she remembered Richard's taunting and yanked her arm back up.

Although both girls told Richard they knew his monster taunt was not true, they were always careful to never hang their arms down again. Of course, they never let Richard know.

Chapter 9: Hot Stove

"Even in its darkest passages, the heart is unconquerable. It is important that the body survives, but it is more meaningful that the human spirit prevails."
~ Dave Pelzer

Spring was in the air and brought sunny days and warmer weather. Emily, happy that it was so much warmer here than back home, loved sitting outside, enjoying the sunshine and soaking up the rays. The children had friends, and both Tom and Emily were happily settled into their new jobs.

Still, Tom felt haunted by the memory of the boss's warning back in Ohio. He never stopped looking over his shoulder, no matter what—always scanning, always watching, just to be sure. In public places like restaurants, he made it a habit of situating himself where he could watch who was coming and going. One day a letter arrived in the mail with no return address, and it turned his palms sweaty. The walk to the office space he had constructed in the garage seemed a long trek, and with forced deliberation, he sat in the chair behind his desk. With a nervous sigh, he opened the envelope.

Although he had prepared himself as much as possible, he opened the envelope and jumped when a newspaper clipping fell on to the desk. The photo on the clipping told him all he needed to know, and it was now engraved in his mind. It was a photo of Tom's old associate, burned to death in a horrible car "accident." The chilling message was loud and clear. Tom sat with his head in his hands, gripped with the fear that comes with the territory, his thoughts racing. He knew without a doubt that his old boss had ordered the "hit" on his friend.

He has to know that I would never squeal! What if they come here to threaten me—and worse, Emily and the kids? What if the boss sends someone here and they do something awful? His nerves were completely shot. Peace of mind was a luxury that Tom had rarely known, and now he checked his gun, which was always within reach. Now his thoughts and actions became more deliberate. With purpose and determination, he secured every lock behind him and concluded that he should share the photo with Emily, reminding himself to ramp up his already intense watchfulness.

Emily knew a bit about how bad these people could be. *I was smart not to keep her in the dark,* Tom reminded himself as he stepped into the house to find her.

Emily's face clouded in fear as she glanced at the gruesome photo. "Are they coming here?" was her involuntary reaction as she glanced nervously through the window.

"No, Emily. I don't think so. I think the boss knows I would never say anything. This clipping is just a reminder to keep my mouth shut," Tom assured. He felt protective, even though he had his doubts. Throughout the day and into the evening, both Tom and Emily were quiet and lost in their own thoughts.

***

Tom felt agitated and nervous but did his best to conceal it. Over the next few days, he looked over his shoulder more often than usual. Although he would never give up his old boss or associates, he could not help but worry about whether his boss really knew that. Sleeplessness was a given these days, as Tom always had to be on guard and ready for someone to show up at the house or walk into his bedroom. Preparedness was his only security, and his gun was always within reach, even while he slept.

Regardless of Tom's reassurances, Emily could tell that he had that newspaper clipping on his mind. His sudden reactions to nothing gave him away. But she knew that any attempt to help would only create an argument, and she was glad to escape to her work down the street.

One day Richard had gone off to a friend's house, and Tom was at home alone with the twins. His tension hit an all-time high, and his daughters were there to take the brunt of it. They played in their room a bit too noisily for Tom's nerves, which created the catalyst his emotions required to explode. It began with yelling at them a few times. For a few moments, they quieted down. But as children at play often do, they forgot to be silent.

Tom needed an outlet for his agitation and now thundered for them to come downstairs. He pushed them into the kitchen and stood them side by side. Then Tom grabbed each of the girls by the wrist. Shoving his body against theirs, he turned the burner of the stove onto high heat. Ignoring their screams, he pulled their hands close to the redness of the burner. Traumatized and pulling away in horror, their screams grew louder and louder. Tom's rage would not permit him to release them.

"Daddy! No!! No!! Please!! Stop!!" They both screamed again and again. "Daddy!! You're burning our hands!!"

From Faith rose a scream that pierced the air: "DAA-DDY!!! STOP!!!!"

It was a scream so horrific that it reached Tom's senses. Suddenly his grip on their tiny wrists was released. Despite being stunned by his own behavior, he continued his yelling. Suddenly his voice became eerily quiet as he bent down into the faces of his two little girls and spoke.

"You must always do exactly what I tell you to do, and exactly when I tell you to do it."

The words and his tone were as frightening as his crazed behavior. Hope and Faith nodded their blonde heads, too afraid to speak.

"Go to your room and do not come out until your mother gets home," Tom barked his orders.

Doing their best to wipe the tears from their little red faces and swollen eyes, the girls turned and ran as quickly as they could to their room. After closing the door, they hugged each other for dear life, trying to control their sobs so that their father would not hear them. As they gained a bit more composure, their throats burned and their voices were hoarse from screaming. They inspected their hands for burns. Although very red and hot, their hands were not burned.

***

Time passed, and the incident with the hot stove became a memory. Tom could not afford to acknowledge it or even apologize to his girls for the horrific event. Nor did the twins ever mention the incident to their mother out of fear that their father might hurt them again as a punishment.

The following weekend, Greg and Claudia announced they were coming over. They all decided to have a picnic. It was beautiful that Sunday. Emily put the tablecloth on the picnic table and took out all the silverware and napkins. She made baked beans and a big pitcher of sweet tea. Claudia was bringing the potato salad. Tom planned to grill hamburgers and hot dogs on an old brick fire pit in the backyard.

Greg and Claudia mentioned they were bringing a "surprise," and Emily couldn't wait to see what it was. It wasn't long before the "surprise" arrived—Greg and Claudia brought a little girl with them that looked the same age as the twins. Everyone said hello, and Greg said, "I want you to meet our new daughter! Her name is Rachel."

"Well, hello Rachel!" Emily said, calling for her twins to come meet their new cousin. The girls came running, yelling, "Hi, Uncle Greg and Aunt Claudia!"

Greg held Rachel's hand and stooped down. "This is your new cousin," he told Faith and Hope. "Her name is Rachel, and I bet she sure would love to play with you two!"

"Yay!" screamed the girls. "Let's go inside and play dolls. Do you want to, Rachel?"

"I didn't bring my dolly over," said Rachel shyly.

"That's okay," said Hope. "I'll let you play with one of mine."

Rachel smiled, and they all ran inside. Emily called after them, "I'll let you know when the picnic is ready!"

After the girls went into the house to play, Greg explained that they just adopted little Rachel. Her biological mother did not want her. "We wanted to wait and bring her over to surprise you!" he said.

"Well, what a nice surprise!" said Tom.

"I'm so happy for you both!" said Emily.

Everyone got caught up on what was going on in each other's lives, laughing and cutting up. It was a fun time, but in the back of Emily's mind were questions. She was curious about how Rachel's adoption came about. Too polite to ask, she simply assumed that the details would be forthcoming sometime in the future.

It turned out that Rachel's unspoken backstory was quite sad and dramatic. What wasn't mentioned was that Rachel was Claudia's niece. Her sister was an alcoholic and got pregnant during a one-night stand. While pregnant, she tried several times to abort the baby but never succeeded. However, the various abortion attempts left the baby with slow motor skills, and limited eyesight. So Rachel, who was unwanted by her mother, was adopted by Claudia and Greg before she was old enough for school. And thus began her new life as a dear cousin of the twins.

***

Tom put the charcoal in the bottom of the pit and lit it. He then asked Greg to come into the office for a minute, and the two walked over to the garage. Tom pulled a key from his desk and opened a drawer. He reached for an envelope and handed it over.

"Here Greg. Here's the rest of the money we owe you!" exclaimed Tom. He reached over and gave his brother a hug. "Thank you again for all your help."

"Oh, thank you!" said Greg. "I'm happy that I could help, and it sure has been nice having family here. Well, let's go throw those hamburgers on the grill. I'm getting hungry!"

They walked back over to the picnic area as the ladies were bringing out the food. Emily handed Tom the plate of hamburgers and hotdogs, and he didn't waste any time putting them on the grill. Everything was out and ready on the picnic table.

"Richard, can you go tell the girls to come on outside?" she asked.

As the whole family gathered, they enjoyed fun and laughter. No one wanted to see the day end. Little Rachel and the twins got along well and bonded. But soon it was time for Uncle Greg and family to go, and they all hugged goodbye. With full stomachs, Tom and Emily cleaned up the picnic area, and before they knew it, the sun had set. It was time to get the children bathed and settled in for the night.

The girls were excited that they now had "picnic days" to look forward to and that any time Uncle Greg and Aunt Claudia came over, they would bring Rachel along. Throughout the years, the twins and Rachel would remain very close.

Chapter 10: The Slide

"The scars you can't see are the hardest to heal."
~ Astrid Alauda

Tom's work brought him back to the local area more often these days. The twins saw very little of their mother, whose stability was her work world. She put in as much time there as possible. The girls had begun school and life began a new rhythm.

Tom kept his nap time routine, paying a quarter for one of the twins to rub his feet. It was Faith's turn again—the usual thing—rubbing his feet and lying beside him. This time, as she lay down beside her father, his hand immediately landed on her stomach. Faith peeked to see if Tom's eyes were closed. Since he was sleeping, Faith knew that she should not disturb him. The hand slowly worked its way down on her skin from inside the top of Faith's skirt, past her abdomen, and rested on her private parts over her underwear. Suddenly, the fingers of the hand slipped inside her panties and stopped there. Frightened, Faith questioned silently, *Why does his hand do this? I can't wake him up to tell him where his hand is. He'll be mad that I woke him.*

The hand's finger jabbed her, which caused much pain for the poor girl. Startled from her thoughts, she jerked away and burst into tears. Then she slapped the hand and got out of bed quickly, heading for her own room.

Moments later Tom appeared at the door of her room, "Oh Faith, you forgot your quarter." Her father handed her the quarter and left the room.

When he was out of sight, Faith quickly went to the closet and put her quarter away in her secret place. Standing inside, she carefully put her hand inside her panties and checked to see if she was bleeding, because it hurt so very badly. Relieved that there was no blood, Faith reasoned, *He must not know what his hand does while he sleeps.* She decided that she would just not think of what had occurred.

That night Faith recited the same prayer as always: "Now I lay me down to sleep, I pray the Lord my soul to keep. If I should die before I wake, I pray the Lord my soul to take. Bless Mother and Father, Sister and Brother, Aunt Jennifer, Jesus and the angels and all the people in the whole wide world. Amen!"

Sleep came quickly to her, but she was suddenly awakened. Someone was at the side of her bed. Frightened, she forced her eyes open but quickly closed them again as tightly as she could. It was her dad. Tom put his hands under the covers and began touching Faith's private area. Petrified, she kept her eyes closed, hoping her dad didn't notice that she was awake. She didn't know what to do and laid as still as she could be, pretending to be asleep and hoping he would stop. He continued touching and playing, rubbing and rubbing, wandering all over her private parts. Finally, after what seemed like an eternity to little Faith, Tom straightened her panties and left her room.

Nap times ended abruptly. What replaced them was worse. Now he was coming to their room. Sometimes Faith would awaken in the night to see her dad kneeling at Hope's bed. The two little twins took on the burden of feigning sleep because they were terrified of him. Faith and Hope never discussed what occurred in the middle of the night. In fact, the girls never spoke of it to anyone, and now the frequency of his intrusions had escalated to a couple of times a week.

***

There was always an undercurrent of "smoldering on low" with Tom, and it seemed that Richard always provided a convenient outlet for Tom to take out his frustrations. One instance had to do with Richard's grades on his school report card. He knew that his dad was going to beat him for it. Any time he or the twins brought home anything below a C, Tom would take off his belt and beat them. Richard had a D and one F, and he was scared to show the report card to him. *Maybe since mom is here he might not beat me,* he thought.

Emily's presence was of no help. Richard handed his report card to his dad, who glanced at it and shot Richard a mean look. He slammed the report card down and started yelling. Richard started shaking, and Emily yelled out, "Tom!" Tom grabbed Richard by the arm and shoved him. He turned and looked at Emily in a way that always scared her, and told her to be quiet. He took off his belt. Richard was already crying. He swung Richard around and lifted his arm way in the air and came down hard on Richard's legs. The belt swung five times, and then Tom shoved him again and told him to go to his room.

Richard took off running up the steps and went into his room. Emily was horrified. She had her hands over her mouth and tears were streaming down her face.

"He knows better than to bring home bad grades," Tom said. "Maybe next time he'll have good grades."

Hope and Faith could hear the muffled sobs coming from Richard's room. Faith stood at the bottom of the steps as her father put on his belt and went out to the garage. She always felt deep pain whenever Tom beat her brother and sister, although she was never able to express those feelings. At times she would peek out her bedroom door to hear poor Richard crying on his bed. She could feel her heart sinking.

With Tom outside in the garage, Emily felt free to go to Richard and comfort him. But he was inconsolable. Through his tears, he choked out the words, "Why is Dad always so mean to me?"

Emily, still trembling, hugged him close. "I don't know, baby. I wish I knew," she said. How she dreaded these episodes when Tom lost his temper. But she knew if she tried to stop him, he'd hit her too.

As time went by, it became more and more obvious that Tom was deliberately kinder to the twins in front of Richard, and purposely and extraordinarily mean to the boy. Of course, the girls liked that their dad was nicer to them. They liked that he sided with them when they got into arguments with Richard. Without fail, Tom took up for the girls and Emily took up for Richard.

When Tom traveled, Richard got away with picking on the girls. If Faith complained that Richard was being mean, Emily's response was always to send her off to play without a correction for Richard. Faith and Hope felt slighted that Richard could get away with being mean while their dad was away. However, when Tom was at home, the opposite occurred. The twins would go to their dad to tell on Richard, and he was always in trouble, more than was warranted. They all learned to play against one another and pit parent against parent.

Over time Richard's resentment of the girls grew, and the girls resented him. The memories of Uncle Bill holding Richard down and telling the girls to hit him always came flooding back, and the siblings rarely got along. There was the time when Richard and one of his friends told Faith to lie on the ground. Richard held her hands, and his friend held her feet to swing her. Faith was excited to have some fun. It was a thrill for a moment until the swinging went out of control and they released her hands and feet, hurtling her into the air. In a free fall, Faith crash landed face first on the ground. Her lip was cut, and her arm bent under her rib. The boys laughed and laughed with no compassion.

When Faith ran to her mother crying over her bloody lip, Emily told her, "That's what you get," and sent her to her room. Of course, she was extremely upset and sat on her bed in disbelief that her mother would not even hug her or check to be certain she was okay. Tears streaked down Faith's cheeks as feelings of abandonment welled up. She was also in pain from what the boys had done to her. Faith felt unloved by her mother. She never heard words of love from Emily, who was always working. The abandonment took over her thoughts.

We barely even see our own mother ... she's here for dinner and a bath, and then it's time for bed. Faith recalled being sick with a fever. Her mom came into her room, touched her head and told her she had a fever. Emily made her some soup and crackers and told Faith she would be back to collect the dishes. There was not a hug or a sweet word from her mother. Only instructions. At times, both of the twins felt almost as angry with their mother as Richard felt at their father.

***

When the girls were not outside playing, they were in their room with their toys and dolls. At least they had each other. There was the time that one of Faith's friends invited the twins to a birthday pajama party. Of course, Faith knew her dad would agree, while she knew that her mother would not permit them to go. The girls always knew to ask their dad for whatever they wanted to receive the "right answer."

The day of the birthday sleep-over finally arrived. The girls were not a moment late getting to Janet's house. It was their first sleepover party and was great fun. The memories stayed with Faith long into adulthood. After all the fun and excitement was over, the group of chattering girls settled into their sleeping bags.

Lights were out, and all the girls quickly drifted off to sleep, except for Faith. She lay there half the night wondering when Janet's dad was going to come in and touch her like her dad did. She waited and waited. Still, Janet's dad hadn't come in. Faith began to think thoughts like, *I wonder if he fell asleep. Or maybe he'll be in later.* She laid there until the wee hours of the morning, but Janet's dad never came in the room. She finally fell asleep, and soon it was morning. Most of the girls were up, and the giggling woke Faith. She hadn't been to sleep very long and started rubbing her eyes. She could smell breakfast cooking. The girls got dressed and rolled up their sleeping bags and headed downstairs to eat. It would be soon time to leave. They all had a good time, and Hope and Faith always loved staying with their friends.

Soon Tom came to pick up the girls. They all hugged each other goodbye and Janet said thank you to each girl for coming and for the presents.

"We'll see you at school on Monday," shouted Faith.

Over the next few years, any time Faith spent the night with a friend, the same process occurred. She waited and waited for the arrival of her friend's father, but it never happened. No one's father ever touched her, and Faith wondered why. After all, her dad had been doing this since she was five years old, and she assumed it was a normal thing for dads to do.

***

When the girls got home, they took their sleeping bags upstairs and put them away. Richard was down the street with John. He was late coming home, and when he walked in the door, Tom was there to greet him. He shoved Richard and looked at his watch.

"What time did I tell you to be home?" he demanded.

Richard looked at him and said, "I'm just a little late."

Tom grabbed him and threw him against the steps. Richard tried to defend himself, which made Tom even angrier. He began hitting the boy as Richard tried to get away from him. Tom kept hitting him, and Richard finally got loose and ran up the steps. Tom was right on his heels and followed Richard towards his room. Richard tried to shut the door, but Tom busted through it.

"Oh, you're a tough guy now aren't you Richard?" Tom taunted and hit him some more.

Richard looked at his dad with fear and anger.

"No," he said.

"Oh, yes you are," said Tom. "I'll show you what a tough guy gets!" Tom walked over and grabbed Richard's shelf that had all of his model cars displayed on it.

"No, Dad!" Richard screamed. "No! I'm sorry!"

"It's too late for sorry," said Tom, who carried the shelf to the top of the steps and threw it down. The shelf tumbled, and Richards's beautiful model cars flew everywhere, breaking into pieces. Tom stomped down the steps, crushing what cars were in his way.

Richard was crying and screaming as Emily came into the house. She could hear the commotion when she pulled up, and her heart started beating faster and faster. She knew Tom had done something awful—again. She ran into the house and saw all of Richards model cars scattered everywhere. Tom stomped out, and Emily helped Richard pick up the mess.

Faith was watching out of the crack in her door and crying for her brother. Even though her dad always took up for them, she felt so sorry. She couldn't show any emotion, though, because she always thought her brother hated her. Plus, she was scared her dad would tear up something of hers or even spank her. Faith closed the door, and the girls sat in the room very quietly, feeling scared and helpless.

Emily got a big garbage bag and helped Richard clean up. There were a few cars that did not get broken, and there were a few that had just a couple of tiny pieces missing. Richard was distraught. He hated his dad. The anger grew in Richard and would continue to grow as he got older. To him, it seemed like his dad hated him and he didn't know why. Emily knew this and tried to overcompensate by taking up for him, unaware that Tom had other interests in the girls that they knew nothing about.

But Tom would lose his temper with the girls as well. There were a few report cards that were not to his liking, and he beat them with his belt across their legs, sometimes leaving bruises and blood marks. Faith remembered a time when she was about seven that her dad was angry and shoved her back against the wall, and then picked her up by her ears and banged her head against the wall until she cried. Then he dropped her and told her to go to her room. He then followed up after her, and picked her up and flung her across the room onto her bed. She hit the wall and fell on the bed. He then flung Hope into her bed and told them both to stay in their rooms. He walked out and slammed the door.

The girls just cried and cried. Faith always wondered where her mom was, not realizing that she was downstairs and too afraid to intervene. Sometimes Emily would be at work when things like this happened, and the girls would never tell what their dad did, simply because they were too scared. Faith remembered a time when she and Hope were watching TV in the living room. Faith could hear her mom crying and got up to investigate. She found her mom in the dining room leaning against the window, sobbing. Faith put her arms around her mom and told her she loved her.

She heard her mom say, "I can't take this anymore. You kids are driving me crazy!"

Faith didn't understand and went back into the living room. Her feelings were hurt deeply and she wondered what she had done to drive her mom crazy.

***

Months passed, and the children were slowly being separated by their dad, not ever realizing that he separated them so he could have control over each. It was deliberate and effective manipulation. As time went on, the children continued to experience a mix of many happy times, as well as the controlling, abusive acts of their father.

One night Richard wanted to go over to visit a friend who lived a couple of streets over. Her name was Mary. Over time, they became boyfriend and girlfriend. He asked his mom if he could go, and she said, "Yes." Tom chimed in and quickly said, "No."

"Why?" asked Richard.

"Because I said so," answered Tom.

"But I just told him he could go," said Emily.

"I don't care what you said. I said no, and no means no," insisted Tom.

Richard stomped up the steps and went into his room. Tom went out to the garage and Emily went into the kitchen to straighten it up. Richard peeked out his bedroom window and watched as his dad went inside. He snuck down the steps and out the front door. Then he got on his bike and went to Mary's house anyway.

About thirty minutes went by, and Tom went back inside. At the front door, he noticed Richard's bike was gone from the porch.

"Where's Richard's bike?" he asked Emily.

"It should be by the porch, like always," she answered.

Tom went up the steps and opened the door to an empty room. He came running down the steps and asked Emily where Richard was.

"He's not in his room?" she asked.

"No, he's not," said Tom.

Emily's heart started pounding, and she thought to herself, *Oh my God, I hope he didn't go to Mary's house.* Tom looked at Emily and said he'd be right back. *He knows exactly where Richard is,* thought Emily, and started to shake. She knew Tom was going to beat him again.

Tom peeled out of the driveway. A couple of minutes later, Mary's mom called Emily and was screaming.

"Your husband is here beating the hell out of Richard, and I'm calling the police," she said.

Emily was crying as Tom pulled up and threw Richard out of the car in the driveway. He began beating and hitting him with his fists. Richard had cuts and scrapes and was bleeding. Emily yelled at Tom to stop. He let Richard up and told him to go to his room and stay there until he said otherwise. Tom came into the house shaking from anger. A few minutes later, the doorbell rang, and he answered. It was the police.

Tom went outside, and the police said they got a call about him hitting his son. Tom looked at the police and blatantly told them, "This is my son, and you have no right telling me how to correct him."

The police officer said, "You're right, we don't have the right to tell you how to parent." Then they advised Tom to settle down and got in the car and left. When Tom came into the house, Emily held his arm and begged him to leave Richard alone.

"Please, Tom; he is hurt enough. He won't ever do that again."

Tom looked into Emily's eyes and could see the hurt. He walked off and went back out in the garage. *His anger has escalated so much over the years. Why does he have so much anger in him?* she wondered for the thousandth time.

***

The family dynamics did not improve. Tom continued to take his anger out on the children, especially Richard. One night, Tom was out of town. It was dark, and Richard was staying with a friend. Emily heard a car pull up in the driveway. She ran into the den and peeked out the window. The car had pulled up to the garage and had a man in it. He didn't get out of the car. Emily was frightened and quickly grabbed both the girls, told them to stay put, and made sure the front door was locked.

"Be very quiet and follow me into the basement," she told them.

As she passed the back kitchen door, she made sure it was locked as well. They hurried down the stairs.

"Don't make a sound," she whispered.

They huddled in front of the washer and dryer. Above the washer was a small window, about fifteen inches long and eight inches wide. It was just big enough that Emily could see out into the driveway and watch the parked car.

Hope said, "What's wrong, Mom?"

Emily quickly told her to be quiet. "Do not say a word!"

The man in the car was just sitting there. Emily remembered the threats that Tom's boss had made, and she thought someone was coming after Tom or her and the children. She was very scared.

About thirty minutes passed, and she heard the car start. The man drove off, but she waited a while and then took the girls upstairs. She told them to stay in their room and not come out. Emily picked up the phone and called Tom to report what happened. Tom said he would call his work and see if they had sent anybody there. After a while, he called back, and sure enough, they had sent a man down to train with Tom. He wasn't supposed to arrive until the following day. Emily was relieved, but she and Tom knew that fear would haunt them for the rest of their lives, especially Tom.

***

Tom continued to take his rage out on the children and continued to visit the girls in the middle of the night. Faith never told anyone what her dad did. She never even said anything to Hope. There were times when she just wanted to be alone. She loved the smell of the fresh cut grass and the pine needles all over the ground in the big side yard. Sometimes she sat in the pine needles against a pine tree all by herself. Through it all, she always seemed to find the things that made her heart happy. She found butterflies, crickets, or a praying mantis or two, and picked them up and loved them. She let them crawl in her hand and on her arm.

Hope enjoyed nature too. They found empty boxes and cut little squares out, making them look like windows. Then off they went to find crickets and Granddaddy long legs, and pretend it was their home. They played like that for hours and loved climbing the trees and picking honeysuckles. Most days, when they weren't confined to their room, they spent the majority of their time outside.

She and Faith often played in the woods beyond the back of the yard. They used to call the woods "the desert" because it had some hard orange soil with bare spots on the ground. It also had hills that they would slide down, getting their pants dirty. They had so much fun back there.

For Faith, it was a quiet place to get away. She felt safe, as if it were an extension of her very own home and yard. Sometimes she would sit in the trees and just be quiet. When she knew it was time to go back up to the house, she couldn't wait to visit the desert again. Faith and Hope had such good times and created fond memories in the desert.

***

One day Emily came home and asked the girls to join her in the kitchen.

"Guess what?" She said.

The girls knew their mom had something good to tell them by the smile on her face.

"Well, there's a lady who works with me. She was telling me about a lake that is just about thirty-five minutes from here. But, it's no ordinary lake. The owners built it to have two sides. A wooden boardwalk goes straight down the middle. One side is the deep end, and the other side is the shallow end for children to play!"

The girls were excited!

"When can we go, Mom?" they asked.

"Well, I'm off tomorrow and thought we could go out there and see what it's like."

The girls squealed, "Yay, yay, yay!" They were excited to spend some special time with their mom, as that didn't often occur—especially at a lake!

Emily told the girls to pack a bag with two beach towels and explained that in the morning they could put their bathing suits on underneath their clothes. The girls ran upstairs and found a big old bag with handles and packed their towels. Early the next morning they put on their bathing suits and got dressed. Then they ran downstairs as their mother was fixing breakfast. "Make sure you get the suntan lotion and put it in your bag, girls," she reminded.

They ate breakfast and Emily did one more check to make sure they had everything. They all hopped in the car and off they went. The girls couldn't wait to get to the lake. The drive felt like a fun adventure as they peppered their mom with questions.

"What's it like, Mom?" asked Faith.

"Is it going to be crowded?" asked Hope.

"I don't know," said Emily. "I haven't been there either, but we'll see when we get there, okay?"

The girls looked out the car window waiting to pull up. At last! There were quite a few cars in the parking lot, and they could hear loud music. They couldn't see the lake from the entrance, as a big wooden fence surrounded the whole area. They walked up the steps and entered a big open space. The ladies' restroom and showers were on one end, and the men's restrooms and showers on the other. There was a huge counter where food could be ordered, and the whole place had a very beachy feel to it. They walked down the steps and into the sand to find a place to sit.

The girls couldn't wait to get into the water. Emily found a spot and spread out her blanket, and told the girls to put their stuff down so they could get in the water.

"But you have to stay on this side, where all the sliding boards are," she instructed, pointing straight ahead. "Do not go on the other side because the water is over your head."

The girls looked wide-eyed at six diving boards, some really high.

"We promise," the twins said. "We'll stay away from the deep end."

The girls then ran off to the water. Oh, what fun they had! There were two metal sliding boards and other water toys. There were things they could climb on and jump off. This was the best place ever! Emily lay on the beach area and watched the girls have fun. She smiled as the girls laughed and had a good time. It was relaxing. She was always working and really enjoyed this time off.

She began taking the girls to the lake each day she had off, and Faith and Hope enjoyed this time with their mom. A couple of months passed, and one weekend they had a new experience.

Hope looked at Faith and said, "Let's go down the slide!"

"Okay!" said Faith. "Last one there's a rotten egg!"

The girls ran into the water to beat the others to the steps. Hope was always a little faster.

"I win!" screamed Hope. The girls got in line and made their way up the ladder. The tall metal sliding board rose about fifteen feet and was way, way over their heads. Hope finally reached the top and sat down to slide.

"Weee!" she hollered and landed in the water. It was Faith's turn, and she saw Hope in the water waiting for her. "Come on, Faith!"

"Okay, okay!" said Faith. She sat down and slid into the water. With a splash, she landed near Hope. "Wow! That was fun! And did you see how fast I went?"

"Yes," said Hope. "Let's do it again!"

They played for a long time on the slide. It was their favorite thing at the lake.

On a different weekend, the girls found a ball floating in the water. Hope told Faith to stay at the bottom of the slide and toss the ball so she could catch it before she landed in the water.

"That sounds like fun!" said Faith. "Then we'll take turns."

Hope went to the ladder, and Faith waited at the end. She finally saw Hope at the top, and when she slid down Faith threw the ball. Hope caught it. Hope was always good at catching the ball.

"My turn," said Faith. They each did this a few times, smiling all the way down. They decided to play until the person who caught the ball five times would win.

It was back to Hope. Faith waited at the end with the ball. She saw Hope get to the top, but then Hope held on the bars and turned to slide down backward. Faith watched in horror as Hope lost her balance and fell off the side. She watched her sister free fall, hitting the beams with her neck on the way down. As Hope fell into the water, Faith threw the ball down and got to her as fast as she could.

Hope hit bottom and then came out of the water holding her hand on her chin. Huge amounts of blood poured through her fingers and down her arm.

"Take your hand off your chin," Faith said urgently. When Hope pulled her hand away slowly, the underside her chin fell away, connected by some flesh.

"Put your hand back on your chin!" yelled Faith, even more urgently. She was so scared! Hope looked like she was in a trance and seemed confused, so Faith helped her sister towards the beach where their mom was laying in the sun.

"Mom! Mom!" screamed Faith. "Hope is hurt!"

By this time people were running towards the girls. Emily got up, saw all the blood, and started shaking.

"What happened?" She asked frantically.

"She fell off the slide," said Faith.

The lifeguard ran frantically down the boardwalk to get to Hope and wrapped a towel around her head. Someone had already called for an ambulance. People were gathering all around. The lifeguard picked up Hope and ran towards the front of the entrance, leaving a blood trail. Emily shook so badly she could hardly walk. Hope was in shock as the ambulance transported her to the hospital. Emily and Faith followed behind, and Faith prayed silently that her sister would be okay.

Tom met them at the hospital, and Hope had already been taken into surgery. They waited nervously in the waiting room, hoping to hear something soon. Emily was still shaking, and Tom comforted her as best he could. Emily held on to Faith to comfort her, knowing she was pretty shaken up.

Faith was in tears as she told her parents what happened. After a while, the doctor came through the door into the waiting room. Tom and Faith got up quickly and met him. The doctor looked at both of them and said that Hope was a very lucky young lady.

"If your daughter had hit her neck a quarter inch down, it would have snapped her neck," he explained. "She has suffered a broken jaw and a compound fracture, and we had to wire her jaw back together. She also has fifty stitches."

At least she was alive and will get better, thought Faith, although the doctor said that Hope would have a scar under her jawline. Tom and Emily were told that later if they wanted to make the scar look better, they could do plastic surgery. They headed to Hope's hospital room, and Emily was still shaken, believed that angels had watched over her daughter that day.

They entered the room and saw Hope's bandaged head, wrapped around her chin and concealing the stitches. She stayed in the hospital for several days, and every night when Faith went to bed, she prayed that God would take care of her sister and bring her home quickly. Emily never took the girls back to the lake again. The girls really missed going because it was always so much fun—a place where they could be children. The swimming, the laughter, the sand, the water, and all the water toys would be sorely missed. They also missed the music that played and the bar where they could get good snacks and food. They were special times, and those memories would last a lifetime, despite the trauma of the accident.

Chapter 11: Another Move

"You may trod me in the very dirt; But still, like dust, I'll rise."
~ Maya Angelou

The girls were almost eleven, and Richard was almost sixteen now. Having lived in their small house for almost six years, Tom and Emily felt it was time to move to a larger house. They loved the small house, but Tom and Emily simply wanted more square footage. So they sold the house and rented one on the other side of town for about a year, until they could find one they wanted to buy. The children hated leaving their good friends and their schools, but there was no choice but to pack up and settle in a new neighborhood.

Hope and Faith shared a big bedroom, and Tom and Emily were across the hall. Richard had his own room downstairs. It was a pretty nice house with lots of kids around Hope and Faith's age, and the new school was within walking distance. They soon made friends, including another set of twins that went to the same school and lived close by. Faith gravitated toward Bonnie, and Hope gravitated toward Brenda, which was perfect.

It took Emily about twenty extra minutes to drive to work. Tom was still doing great at his job and traveling a couple of days a week. He decided to start taking one twin at a time with him when they were out of school. His ways were getting worse. His anger was still the same.

He started a new game with the girls when Emily and Richard weren't home. He chased them and played hide and seek. When he found Faith, he grabbed her by the arm and threw her on the floor, laughing and giggling and making it out to be fun. He pinned her arms over her head and pulled her shirt up with his teeth. Once the shirt was up, he licked her belly and belly button.

Faith struggled to get away and became angry. She tried with all her might to get loose, but couldn't. Her father was too strong. He continued licking her and laughing for a few minutes, and then he let her up. Faith ran into the bathroom and locked the door, then took a rag and cleaned herself up. It was disgusting to her. He did the same to Hope, and this kind of play went on for quite a while. The girls hated it.

One day Faith was out with a friend, and Hope was home alone with her dad. He started playing his game and pinned her down in the living room. He had her hands above her head and started unbuttoning her jeans. Unbuttoned and unzipped, Hope was scared.

Tom started licking her belly again when he heard Richard pull up. Tom could see him approaching the door, and he looked at Hope. With a mean voice, he said, "You better pretend like you're playing. You better laugh and giggle and not let Richard know anything else."

Hope was petrified. As Richard came in the door, their father sat on Hope's hips, hiding the fact that her pants were unzipped. Tom tickled Hope, and she laughed, even though she didn't want to. Richard saw what was going on and felt jealous because his dad never gave him attention. All of Tom's focus was on the twins, and this made Richard angrier.

Tom looked at Richard and shouted, "What the hell do you want? Get the hell out of here!"

Richard gave them both a dirty look, slammed the door, and ran out to the car. He took off, feeling left out as always. This had been going on since Richard could remember, and his anger towards his dad and sisters deepened. Little did he realize that at the time Tom was in the middle of molesting Hope. Hope wanted Richard to catch her dad in the act, but Tom made sure Richard had no idea.

Tom got off of Hope, and she zipped her pants up quickly.

Richard's anger towards the girls grew and grew. Over the years, Tom had purposely pitted his daughters against his son, and vice versa, so that they didn't like each other. He knew what he was doing, and his plan of keeping them separated was working.

Tom's play time was escalating very quickly. Soon he was unzipping his pants and taking out his penis. Faith tried her best to get away when he rubbed it on her belly, but couldn't. He just laughed and laughed as hatred and disgust filled his daughter. Then he would tickle her and try to make her laugh. She finally did, just so he would quit. After she submitted as he wanted her to, he got up and let her go.

This kind of play went on for a couple of months, and he was still visiting the girls late at night in their bedroom. The crack of the door always woke Faith, and she froze and pretended to sleep while he took off her panties and played with her. Sometimes she wondered what he would do next, since it seemed he was getting bolder and bolder.

The girls turned eleven at their new house. They had a birthday party and invited their school friends and neighborhood friends who were a little younger. Faith was close to a girl who lived across the street named Cindy. Cindy liked hanging out with Faith because Faith didn't mind if she was a little younger, and was happy to be invited to the birthday party. Quite a few kids showed up, and the twins had a good time opening up gifts from their friends. The party didn't last long, but it was fun. After it was over, each of the girls took their gifts to their room and sat on their beds and showed each other what they had got. Emily cleaned up downstairs and started making dinner.

The next day as the girls were in school, Faith felt something warm in her panties. She went up to the teacher and asked if she could use the restroom. The teacher gave her a hall pass and let her go. When Faith sat down to use the toilet, she noticed a little blood in her panties. She knew what this was because her mom had talked to the girls about soon starting their period. Faith rolled up some toilet paper and stuck it in her panties. When she got home from school, she waited for her mom and then told her.

Emily went to the store and bought some pads for Faith and talked to her about it.

"You know this means you're a young lady now right?"

Faith was a little embarrassed and said, "Yes."

When Tom found out, he reminded Faith, when no one was around, that she was now a young lady ... but it just didn't sound right coming from his mouth. She hung her head in embarrassment because she didn't like the way he said it to her. She felt ashamed.

One day after school, Cindy came over. She and Faith played upstairs in her room. They were having a good time listening to music and laughing, when suddenly, the bedroom door opened and Tom peeked in.

"What are you girls doing?" he asked.

"Oh, just listening to music," said Faith. He walked over and started laughing and telling some jokes. The girls started laughing. Then he started playing around and tickled Faith. Cindy laughed because Faith's giggles made her laugh. Then Tom started tickling Cindy. Faith was alarmed. She knew what her father might do. Tom held Cindy's hands down and sat on top her. Faith knew now that he might pull her shirt up. She could tell Cindy was frightened by the look on her face.

Faith jumped on Tom's back and with all of her might started pulling her dad's arms off of Cindy, all the while acting like she was playing and having fun. She jumped up and down on his back, and finally, Tom got off of Cindy. Cindy quickly got up and ran out of the house back to her home. Faith could tell that she was scared to death, and she never came over again.

Faith was glad that she stopped her dad. She wasn't sure what he might have done, but she didn't want to take any chances. But her dad's face was really angry.

"So? You think you're tough, do you?" he said. Faith was scared but stood in front of Tom boldly.

"I didn't want you hurting my friend," she said.

"What makes you think I was going to hurt her?" Tom asked. He quickly grabbed her and threw her to the floor. He held her hands and pinned her body with his knee. He took the other hand and forcefully put it under her shorts and rammed his finger into her vagina.

Faith screamed in pain.

With a wicked look, her father said, "This is what you get for what you did to me!"

Faith cried. The pain was awful. Finally, Tom ripped his hand out, got off of Faith, and went downstairs. She felt like she was physically cut due to the pain in her private parts. Jumping up from off the floor, she was so angry at her dad and mumbled under her breath how much she hated him. She felt helpless and ashamed. *Why does he do this to me?*

For the next couple of hours, Faith thought of how much she hated her dad and the things he did to her and Hope. She felt so all alone knowing she could never tell anyone. Although she and Hope both knew he was doing things to each of them, they never discussed it. He had them that scared.

The rest of the day Tom never looked at Faith. He ignored her. She really did love her dad, but never understood why he would do the things he did. A few nights later after the girls went to sleep, Faith heard the usual sound of the bedroom door slowly opening. She knew it was her dad again. She peeked and pretended to be asleep. He walked over to her bed as her heart started racing. *Oh God,* she thought. *Please don't. Please.*

Tom knelt down by her bed and slowly pulled the covers down. He then took off her panties. Faith was scared. This time he climbed up in bed and straddled her. This time he took the abuse to the next level. This time, he raped her. She was eleven years old. *Mom, where are you?* The thought crossed her mind. She turned her head towards the wall and squeezed her mouth as tight as she could so he couldn't hear her scream. If he knew she was awake, he might take longer. The pain was excruciating. Tears leaked out of her shut eyes, and she hoped he would just hurry up and get off of her. He put his penis in far enough to take her virginity, and held it there for a few moments. Faith held her breath and wondered how long he was going to do this.

Finally, he climbed off, put her panties back on, and pulled the covers back up. She couldn't wait for him to leave. He finally turned, pulled his shorts up, and closed the bedroom door. Faith took a long breath and pulled the covers over her head. She held her hand over her mouth so no one could hear her gasp in pain. She was beyond frightened and would later call this her silent scream. No one knew. No one could hear it. No one could help her. *Is this what he is going to do from now on, she thought? Why does my dad want to hurt me like this?*

Faith felt so much humiliation and unworthiness. *"Why? Why? Why?"* tumbled through her head. *Why God? Why do you let him get away with this? Don't you love me? I don't understand why you let this happen!* As Faith was finally drifting off to sleep, she knew that the next day she would see him. She didn't want to run into her dad, but knew it was inevitable. *What is he going to do when he sees me?* she thought. *How is he going to act? Is he going to be angry at me? Is he going to glare at me?* She really didn't want to look at him at all and was terribly embarrassed.

When she finally did see her dad, he acted as if nothing had ever happened. He left her alone for a few days or so thereafter. This was confusing to her as well. She wondered if maybe he thought she slept through everything and didn't even know that it had happened. This was yet another secret that Faith could not share with anyone. Yet another incident that she buried within her being. She even wondered if he had done this to Hope yet, and she wondered if Hope saw anything that night that he raped her. The girls knew not to mention any of this to anyone, not even to each other. He had threatened them before, saying he would kill them.

***

One day Rachel was over, and Tom told the twins to go to the mall with their friends, which was within walking distance. Rachel stayed behind, and Tom told her that he wanted to make a movie. He asked her to take off either her top or bottoms. Rachel was nervous and told him she would take off her bottoms. Tom started fondling her, and she got scared and ran into the bathroom, grabbing her bottoms. She got dressed and came out, and Tom left her alone. Rachel was what they called a slow learner. She couldn't process things as quickly as others because of what her mom did while she was pregnant with her. Also, Rachel's way of thinking was naive.

Aunt Debbie (Greg and Tom's sister who was now raising her) came to pick her up later on. When they got home, Rachel, in her innocence, asked, "Mom, (that is what she called her), if you have a stomach ache, does that mean you're pregnant?"

Aunt Debbie asked her to explain what she was talking about. Rachel went on to tell her how Uncle Tom had fondled her. Aunt Debbie was furious. She called Tom and confronted him, saying that he was her brother and that she trusted her daughter with him. She was so angry that she didn't want anything to do with him ever again. The twins didn't see Rachel until many years later in 1978, and only after that did they see each other from time to time.

One weekend, Tom and Emily were home, and the girls were outside in the backyard playing. Tom wasn't in a very good mood. The girls argued and brought it indoors, just as Tom walked by the door. He immediately lost control and started yelling. The girls were already mad and started yelling back. Tom didn't like this one bit. He grabbed Hope and slung her across the room and then reached for Faith. He shoved her. Hope started standing up to Tom, and he shoved her again. Faith began yelling at Tom telling him to stop. She was always scared that he was going to hurt her sister, and she would rather him hit her than Hope. Faith jumped in the middle, and the three were yelling. Tom took his belt off and hit Hope, and she ran to her room. Then he went after Faith. At that time, Emily came in from outside after hearing all of the commotion. She raised her voice at Tom and told him to stop. Tom swung around and showed Emily the belt and told her to stay out of it or he was coming after her.

This was the first time that Faith had ever seen her dad act this way towards her mom. Tom swung the belt and hit Faith across the back and swung again hitting her across the legs. Faith took off running up the steps to her room as Tom was yelling at her to stay there. When Faith got in her room, Hope was standing there listening the whole time. They just both sat on their beds and started telling each other how much they hated him.

Tom was getting worse and worse, and the abuse was happening more often. Whenever Emily would come home after work, Faith looked at her and suspected her mother knew what was going on. She began to have hidden anger towards her mom. *Why won't she help me?* In Faith's mind, her mom never seemed to notice anything and always seemed to not care. Over time the anger grew—the hopelessness, the unworthiness, and the bitterness burrowed into her heart, deeper and deeper. But even in Faith's circumstance, even with all of those negative emotions buried, she always had a kind and loving heart. Faith seemed to actually feel everyone's pain and sadness. Her emotions were mixed, for she loved her mom, but still, the negative feelings always found its way into her mind.

At that time she didn't know what her mixed up feelings about her mom really meant, but she would find out much later. In the meantime, she learned to repress the horrors in her life.

***

Sometimes Faith wondered why Richard hated them so much. She felt he was the lucky one not to be at home, like they were. She never thought that if he knew what Tom was doing to her and Hope, it would make a difference. Over the course of the years, the anger and bitterness settled in all three of the kids. They all had bad tempers at times, and it got worse as they got older. There were so many mixed signals, confusion, and dysfunction in the home. But at the time, they just all thought that was the normal way of life… and it was for them.

Richard was in high school and had worked to buy the car he drove. Since he was gone most of the time, the girls were now getting the brunt of Tom's abuse.

One Saturday, Faith asked if she could go over Bonnie's for a while.

"Yes," said Tom, "but be home by three."

Faith started her walk up the street and through a little patch of woods to Bonnie's. Although she loved walking through the woods, at times, she felt scared. This was one of those times, and she couldn't wait to come out on the other end right at Bonnie's house. She ran up the steps and rang the doorbell, and Bonnie answered.

"Let's go to my room," Bonnie said. "I bought some new records, and we can listen to some music."

"Great idea!" said Faith.

The girls hung out in Bonnie's room for a while, and Faith had so much fun. She always liked it when she could get away. Still, she felt so different than everyone else. She laughed and told jokes to fit in, and she did. But she always had that feeling of not fitting in.

It was about two thirty in the afternoon, and Faith told Bonnie that she needed to go home. Bonnie walked Faith downstairs, and they said goodbye. Faith made her way back into the woods and was getting an eerie feeling. It wasn't a very long walk through the woods, but she couldn't wait to get to the road. Right before the road, she heard a rustle in the leaves and out jumped two boys who lived in the neighborhood.

"What are you doing, Faith?" They asked.

Faith told them that she just left Bonnie's and was on her way home.

"Oh, on your way home?" They laughed at her, and then suddenly both boys grabbed each of her arms and tried to pull her down. She was terrified and struggled and struggled to get the boys off of her. They fought tooth and nail to try and get her on the ground. One of the boys commented how strong she was. All she wanted to do was get away from them. She was scared what they were about to do. Thoughts of them raping her were in her mind. She fought with everything she had and eventually broke free and took off running as fast as she could. She ran all the way home, still terrified.

When she got to her house, she ran upstairs and closed the door to her room. She tried to calm herself down so her dad wouldn't know what happened. She thought if he found out, he would never let her go to Bonnie's again. She recalled that over the past few years, she and Hope helped their dad unload trucks with heavy boxes. It made them strong. She even thought of the times she fought, trying to get away from her dad. *This helped me get away from the boys,* she realized. Faith was just starting to calm down when she heard her dad coming up the steps. She jumped up quickly and pretended she was cleaning her room.

"Oh, you're home," he said.

Faith glanced at him. "Yes, Dad. I just got home a few minutes ago and decided to clean up my room. Sorry, I forgot to tell you I was home."

Tom just looked at her. "Okay," he said and closed the door. Faith felt relieved.

When she went to school that following Monday, she saw the boys. They pointed and laughed at her. She gave them a mean look and turned away. Faith didn't care too much for this neighborhood and the house that they lived in.

As the months went on, Tom continued to come into the girl's room. Faith never slept soundly. She never knew when he would rape her. Sometimes he would go a week or two and not come in, so Faith never got a good night's sleep. It didn't hurt as much, now that he had taken her virginity. Even so, she lay there pretending to be asleep. He would always do the same thing and then leave the room, and the next day act as if nothing ever happened.

Faith's grades were failing. She started losing interest in school even more. She didn't care if she ever did her homework or if the teacher would get mad at her for not doing the assignments. Worse, she sensed that the kids in the neighborhood were talking about them and their dad. She could feel it. Tom had played around with a few of her friends, never molesting them, but his behavior was odd. Her friends had never encountered anything like it before, and it was embarrassing.

Faith hated where she lived and couldn't wait until the day they would move. She found herself sitting in the backyard while her parents weren't home, and she decided to sneak one of their cigarettes. It took a few before Faith began to like them. She was now buying her own cigarettes and smoking quite a bit. She found that it calmed her nerves down at times. Faith knew if her dad found out, she would get in trouble. So she had to find a good hiding place for her smokes. One of her friends told her how they hid theirs, and Faith thought it was a great idea. She got one of her old hardcover books and hollowed out the middle a little bit bigger than a pack of cigarettes, and put them in there. She closed the book, and it was perfect! It looked like a regular book, and no one would be able to tell that anything was different about it. Now Faith had something her dad didn't know about and was proud of it.

After about ten months of living in that neighborhood, Faith overheard her parents talking about moving again. She ran downstairs and asked them about it, and they told her they were looking for another house. They were just renting this one, and the lease would be up soon. That gave them time to find one that they liked. Faith was happy, although she would miss Bonnie a lot. They had become good friends.

A few weeks before the lease was up, Tom and Emily found a house they really loved on the other side of town, near a beautiful lake. They were getting ready to pack up and move again, but a few days prior Tom and Emily took the girls over to see the new place. They would each would have their own room, and they were excited! Tom opened the door, and the girls ran upstairs. At first, they both wanted the same room because it was just a little bit bigger, but Faith had entered first and called dibs. Hope ran into the other room and was happy with it. After they got their rooms, they checked out the rest of the house. They all loved it.

Chapter 12: Pothead

"Though I can't change what happened, I can choose how to react. And I don't want to spend the rest of my life being bitter and locked up."
~ Tori Amos

The girls turned twelve in their new home, and the neighborhood was full of kids who thought it was cool to have twins for friends. This was the first time there were not any twins in the area. It was exciting to have their very own rooms this time, and it was fun to decorate the way they wanted. Tom was just as nice as he could be to all the kids in the neighborhood, and they loved him. He was the cool dad. He was the one they could talk about anything, and he always listened and gave advice. They grew to love him. Tom had always had that charm about him. Even the parents and adults in the neighborhood liked Tom and Emily.

It wasn't long after the girls turned twelve that they made specific girlfriends. They'd always come over and hang out, and sometimes spend the night. Tom was getting to know these girls.

One day during the school week, Faith had a headache. Tom told Faith she could stay home from school. She didn't like the new school much, so she was excited to stay home. She was in her bedroom listening to music when Tom opened the door. He had a little baggie of something in his hands.

"Here Faith, why don't you try this?" he said.

"What is it?" she asked.

Tom sat down on her bed and opened the baggie. He took out some papers and started rolling the brown stuff in the paper to make what looked like a cigarette. Faith had already started smoking cigarettes at the last house they lived in. It was something that she felt calmed her nerves, and she never told anyone. So this weird-looking cigarette seemed interesting, and she was very willing to try it.

Faith asked again, "What is it, Dad?"

He told her it was marijuana and would really make her feel good.

"You just smoke it like a cigarette, except you hold the smoke in for a while and then blow it out," Tom explained. "People call them joints or doobies."

He handed her the joint and gave her a lighter and an ashtray.

"Go ahead and smoke it," he said, and left the room, closing the door.

Faith was very curious and lit the joint and smoked about half of it. *Nothing seems to be any different*, she thought. She picked it up again, lit it, and took a few more drags of it before putting it out. After a couple of minutes, the effects of the marijuana kicked in.

Holy moly, she thought. *Wow, I really like the way this makes me feel.* Her head became a little heavy, and her eyes seemed to feel halfway closed, and she didn't seem to care about much of anything. Nothing bothered her, and she felt wonderful. She really liked this new stuff and wanted more.

***

The following weekend, one of Faith's friends came over. Emily was working, and Hope went to the mall with a friend and wouldn't be back for a while. Faith and Cassie were up in her room listening to music and talking and laughing. Tom knocked on the door.

"Come in," said Faith.

Tom came in and sat with the girls, laughing and telling jokes. Cassie loved Faith's dad. She thought he was the coolest dad ever—nothing like her dad at all. She enjoyed visiting Faith's house.

After a while, Tom looked at the girls and said, "Look what I have." He reached into his pocket and pulled out his bag of weed. He had already rolled a couple of joints and had them in the bag.

"Ah! I know what that is," said Cassie. "I've never smoked it before, but I know a couple of people that do, and my sister smokes it. I wanted to try it, but my sister said I was too young."

"No, you're not," said Tom. "Faith just smoked one last week, and she really liked it. Didn't you Faith?" He turned at looked at her, and in her mind, she wondered what Tom was going to do.

Sure enough, he gave the joint to Faith and told her to light it. She did and took a big inhale, and held it in as she passed it to Cassie. Cassie quickly took it and did the same thing.

"You girls have fun," Tom said and walked out of the room.

Faith and Cassie were as high as a kite and really loving this new feeling. The music seemed to get better, and everything was funny. They laughed and laughed and were having such a good time.

After about an hour, Tom came in again. "Cassie, come here a minute," he said.

Cassie stood up, and immediately Faith stood up.

"No! Not you, Faith," he said, giving her that look that was all too familiar.

Faith sat back down, and Cassie went with Tom. He took her into his bedroom and closed the door behind them. After a couple of minutes, Faith could hear Cassie laughing and laughing. She opened her door to see what was going on. Tom had Cassie laying on the bed and tickling her and making her laugh. Faith was scared to say anything and went back to her room.

After a few minutes, Cassie came back in. "Your dad is so funny! I just love being here," she said.

Faith sighed in relief that her dad didn't do anything to Cassie. She lit up another joint and she and Cassie smoked it all.

***

Tom began to supply Faith with her own weed. Faith hid it in her drawers so her mom would never find it. As a couple of months went by, Faith was now smoking one or two joints a day. She loved how it made her feel, like she was in her own little world. She was so relaxed.

There were times when Emily came home and asked, "What's that smell?"

Tom would always say, "What smell?"

But soon he introduced Hope to the drug, as well. After a while, Tom had all of the girl's friends smoking weed in the house. Once again, the kids thought he was the coolest ever. At times, Faith carried her weed down the end of the street where the kids hung out. She and Hope loved hanging out with this new group of friends in the cul-de-sac at the bottom of a hill, where they could always hear cars coming and put their joint out if need be. They sat in a circle and passed around the joint—about nine regular friends. The twins always had so much fun with them. Anything that kept them out of the house and away from their dad was just fine with them. Faith became very addicted to marijuana. After a while, all the kids called her pothead.

Two very good friends lived on the street. Gail lived down at the end of the street, and Lisa lived across the street. One time when Faith was hanging out with both girls, Gail held out her hand. Three pills were in her palm that she had taken from her mother's medicine cabinet, and she gave one to Faith and one to Lisa. It was some type of painkiller, and Faith quickly swallowed it. The other two did the same.

After a while, Lisa and Gail were feeling the effects of the drug. Faith didn't feel a thing. She kept telling Gail that the pill didn't work for her. Gail reached into her pocket and gave Faith another one. After a while, the other girls were acting silly, and Faith wondered why she couldn't feel anything. They all decided to go home and started walking up the street. Gail went into her home, saying goodbye to the girls. Lisa said goodbye and went into her house. As soon as Faith got into her front yard, the effects of the pills started to kick in. She could hardly make it up the front porch steps and was holding on to the railing. She opened the front door, and Emily told her to come eat.

Faith quickly said, "I'm not feeling good, I'm going to go lay down." It was all she could do to climb the four steps leading to her bedroom. She felt weightless, and soon her head began to spin out of control. She fell on the bed and was starting to get a little scared. Suddenly, the dizziness was more than she could bear. The whole room was spinning, and she felt nauseous. A couple of minutes later, she ran to the bathroom and threw up. Emily came up to her room to check on her and noticed how sick she was. She could hear Faith running to the bathroom and throwing up. The dizziness got so bad that Faith just put her trash can beside her bed, but by this time she was dry heaving.

The next day was the first day of school, and Faith knew she couldn't make it. The dizziness and the dry heaving lasted all night and halfway into the next day. Later the next day, she called Lisa and told her what had happened. The pills did not have the same effect on Lisa or Gail. Faith knew she would never do that again!

Faith made it to school the following day. She really didn't like this new school, although she and Hope loved the new friends in the neighborhood and had good times together. They spent every day after school with their friends, either over at their houses or the twins' house. Faith met a girl on the bus, Brandi, who didn't live too far away. They quickly became best friends and always sat together on the bus.

Tom continued to supply Faith with her weed, and she and Brandi smoked quite a bit in her room or outside. In some way, it helped Faith deal with all the monsters inside her that she kept hidden from everyone. All the pain and hurt seem to take a back seat, especially when she was smoking with a friend. Tom supplied weed and fun times to all their friends, anything that made the girls really like him. A lot of times weed and alcohol were present to loosen everyone up. When the girls were high, Tom would take one in the bedroom with him for a while, and they would come out laughing and carrying on. The door was always shut, and Faith knew not to ask. The girls never said anything.

***

As Faith lay in bed at night, and her heart hurt so badly at how her dad was treating her friends. He really liked her best friend, Brandi.

He started fondling whoever was with him and taking pictures of them, and then giving them money to do so. He made it fun. The girls, being young teenagers and high on weed or alcohol, loved the idea of getting money and spending it. This kept the circle going. This kept the girls coming over. Tom was the one that kept the marijuana and alcohol flowing, and everyone loved it. It always bothered Faith, but she could never say anything. She remembered well that her dad said he would kill her.

Tom had also started taking Hope and Faith out of town when he worked. There were many times he would let one or the other stay home from school and go out of town with him. They were usually gone one or two nights. Tom would continue to molest or rape them at night time after they fell asleep. The girls could never seem to get away from him. Sometimes he would take his camera out and tell Faith to take off all of her clothes, and then take pictures of her and give her money when he was done. He did this to Hope and some of their friends, as well. Everyone got paid.

The girls loved to take their money to the mall and buy lots of clothes and jewelry. Tom said he sold the pictures to people he knew and then he would give the money to the girls. Little did anyone know that he really kept the pictures for himself.

One late afternoon, Faith was in her room. Everything was getting to her. She was fourteen at the time. She got out her bag of weed and rolled a joint, lit it up and smoked it. She had her window open and would blow the smoke out the window. She knew her mom would be home soon and didn't want to fill the room up with smoke. She also lit a couple of candles to help with the smell. As she sat on her bed, she could feel all the ugly moments dashing through her mind—how her dad had been molesting her since she was five and then raping her since she was eleven.

Then one night as her dad entered her room and started feeling her private parts, she noticed a good feeling down there. She had no idea why she was feeling this new sensation, and at the same time, it made her sick to her stomach. She lay there with her eyes shut, pretending to sleep, but could not fight this feeling that was taking place in her body. After her dad was done and left the room, she covered her mouth and wept so no one could hear. *Why am I feeling this?* she wondered. *This is disgusting!*

She began to have feelings of guilt and shame and feeling so unworthy and dirty. She hated herself and felt so all alone. She dare not talk or share these feelings with anyone. She felt like her world was crashing down on her, and she couldn't take the sense of loneliness anymore. She just wanted to die. As she sat in her room thinking of ways to kill herself, she started crying. She fell to her knees and hung her head down. The cries were coming from deep within. Faith didn't want to live anymore. She didn't know if she could go on like this. The only thing she had was a full bottle of aspirin. She thought that would be the less painful way to die.

She unscrewed the cap, crying so hard she could hardly get the bottle open. She dumped some aspirin in her hand and was getting ready to take them. Then she began to think how Hope would feel if she killed herself. Hope would be all alone with their dad. Then something came over her... something strong. She didn't know it at the time, but it was a presence—something she never really felt before. Suddenly, she just couldn't do it. She didn't know what it was, but knew she couldn't kill herself.

As she was crying, she put the aspirin back in the bottle and walked over and fell on the bed. She lay there for a while in silence. She lit up a joint, and after a few minutes she got her notebook and pencil out and started writing a poem. It seemed to just come to her. The pencil seemed to move all by itself on the paper. Words just began to flow without effort as she sat in a trance-like state. She called her poem *The Rainbow*:

> I was dying while it was raining as the sun was shining bright,
> All I could remember was a beautiful rainbow,
> Each time the rainbow appears, I'll come back to life.
>
> The sun was shining bright, while the rain was falling down,
> There's a lot of things in sight, and there is a roaring sound.
>
> The rainbow in the sky made me wonder,
> The rainbow in the sky was bright,
> I could hear the crackling sounds of thunder,
> And feel the long sharp streaks of burning light.

> Night was coming overhead,
> Watching the rainbow getting dim,
> Now I know that I'm dead,
> But I'll come back again.
>
> The rainbow in the sky made me wonder,
> The rainbow in the sky was bright,
> I could hear the crackling sound of thunder,
> And feel the long sharp streaks of burning light.

Faith wrote that poem in about ten minutes. She read what she wrote and didn't understand quite what the words meant. She closed up her notebook and decided that would be her book of poetry. What she didn't know at the time, was that would be one poem that she would remember the rest of her life and understand the meaning of it years and years later. She crawled into bed and fell asleep.

At this point in her life, she didn't know that she'd be writing many poems over the course of several years, all about the sadness and helplessness she felt. Throughout this turbulent life, every night when she went to bed, she still prayed and asked God to take care of her and her family. She would say the same prayer but added a little more to it. *Now I lay me down to sleep, I pray thee Lord my soul to keep. If I should die before I wake, I pray thee Lord my soul to take. Bless mother and father, sister and brother, Aunt Jennifer, all of my friends, Jesus and the Angels and everyone in the whole wide world, and dear God, please keep my family safe, Thank you, God. Amen.*

Chapter 13: New Set of Wheels

I'm not the same soul I once was. A lot has changed. A lot had to change. So you shouldn't expect out of me what I embodied in the past. For that part of me no longer exists.
~ Author Unknown

At school, Faith quickly made friends with all the potheads, and there were a number of times she skipped classes and hung out with them. They always went across the street from the school, because there were a lot of hiding places where no one could see them. Faith made it a habit of cutting two or three classes each day and would go get high. The report cards didn't seem to matter much to her dad as much as it did when they were younger. She loved hanging out with everyone and couldn't wait to get on the bus to sit with her friend Brandi.

The weekend arrived, and Faith and Brandi had planned on going to the mall. They were excited at the thought of spending time with each other and going shopping. Faith looked forward to it because it got her out of the house. At the mall, Faith noticed a restaurant that was hiring. She thought to herself for a moment, *If I can get a job, I won't have to be at home so much.*

"Wait in the mall," she told Brandi. "I'm going to apply for the job."

Faith asked for the manager, and he brought her an application. She filled it out and handed it back, and the manager told her he would contact her soon. Faith felt a little excitement! When Faith's dad came to pick the girls up from the mall, she told him that she filled out an application for a job at the mall restaurant. She was a little apprehensive about what he might say, but she thought if he didn't like it, then she would just not work.

Much to her surprise, he was glad for her. "Why Faith, I think that is a wonderful idea!"

Faith was filled with joy by his support. Brandi and Faith giggled and told Tom what a good time they had shopping. When Faith got home, she ran into the house and told her mom that she filled out an application at the mall to be a waitress.

Emily looked at her and said, "I'm so happy for you. I hope you get the job!"

Faith opened Hope's bedroom door and told her she applied to be a waitress.

"Why do you want to get a job?" Hope asked.

"To have my own money, Hope," Faith answered.

She then went into her room and sat on her bed. She began to think ahead in time of what it would be like to work and not be at home so much. *If I'm not here, that would be less time that dad would be around me.* One thought after caused a sense of freedom to stir in her head. She felt so good, and a release came over her.

The next day, shortly after Faith got home from school, the manager called and told her she got the job as a waitress.

"You start the following Monday," he said.

Faith hung up the phone and squealed with delight! Emily was in the kitchen, putting the dishes up when Faith yelled, "Hey Mom, guess what? The manager just called and said I have the job!"

Emily's face lit up. "I'm so happy for you!" she exclaimed.

Tom was pulling up in the driveway from work and Faith ran outside and told him she got the job. He could see the excitement all over her.

"Well Faith, you know you're going to need a car, because we can't take you to work all the time."

"A car?" said Faith. Now she was really excited. She was almost fifteen and knew that she wasn't legally ready to drive, even though her dad had let her drive at times for almost a year, on and off.

"But Dad," she said, "We can't get our license until we're fifteen and a half and take Driver's Ed at school."

Tom looked at her and said, "Don't you worry about that. I know how to handle it."

Faith was confused, but the thought of her own car was exhilarating! She gave her dad a big hug and said, "Thank you!" and ran into the house to tell Hope.

Faith ran up the stairs and told Hope the good news.

"I want a car!" Hope said. She wasn't very happy that Faith got a car and not her.

"Well, I got a job, and I need a way to work. Mom and Dad can't take me all the time," explained Faith.

Hope didn't seem too happy that Faith would be getting a car so soon, but the car was all Faith could think about. She started work after school that following Monday, catching a ride with her dad. It took her a little while to get used to new people outside of home and school. Most of them were a lot older, but she managed. She decided she would put away a little money each paycheck. Faith knew saving money put her a step closer to escaping her parents' home and setting out on her own.

***

At this time, the twins were barely into the middle of ninth grade. Hope decided that she wanted to quit school. Emily was upset about it.

"You need to stay in school," she told her daughter.

When Tom got home, Emily told him that Hope said she wasn't going back to school.

Tom went outside and found Hope. "Why don't you want to go to school anymore?" he asked.

"I just hate it," She said. "I don't want to ever go back."

"If you quit school, then you'll have to work with me full time," Tom said. "After all, Faith is a waitress, and you need to work too."

Hope agreed. From that point on, she went to work with her dad. Tom's work carried him to the mountains twice a week, and he would have both girls go with him at times during these trips. The mountains were so beautiful. Faith went to work with him on one of these mountain trips during a break in her waitressing schedule.

Tom's job paid for the gas, food, and hotel. It never seemed to fail that every time they went out of town, Tom would molest or force sex on the girls. It was the same old thing of waiting until they fell asleep. He would get up out of his bed and make his way over. After he was done, he would pull the blankets back over and get back in his bed and go to sleep. The next morning he always acted like nothing ever happened.

Faith would wake up in shame, knowing that he knew what he was doing, but never said anything. He'd always have a good day after taking advantage of her and would buy her almost anything she wanted throughout the day. It became a ritual. This is how he treated the girls. The pain was always there with Faith. *Why does he do this to me? Why doesn't he stop?* She was a prisoner to feelings of guilt, shame, worthlessness, anger, bitterness, and feeling dirty. It flowed inside her—the hopelessness and wondering how long her dad would do these things.

When they left for work that morning, Tom turned to Faith and told her, "I know you want a car, and I'll get one for you."

Faith knew what he meant. *As long as I go to work with him and make him happy, I can get a car.* She was torn. Even though she knew what he was doing was wrong, and how it made her feel was wrong, he had been doing this since she was five years old. She didn't know any other way. In her mind, she reasoned, *Well, at least I'll get a car.*

The next morning at almost every stop, Tom would ask her if she wanted anything, whether it was food or a drink or something in the store. They would be going home that day after work, and Faith couldn't wait to get home. She had missed two days of school going to work with her dad, and couldn't wait to get back to her job at the mall.

***

One day after Faith got home from school, her dad approached her and Hope and told them to get in the car.

"I'm taking you to get your driver's licenses," he announced.

"How are you going to do that?" they asked.

"Don't you worry about a thing. You just need to tell them that you're eighteen and they'll give you a driver's test. And when you pass it, you'll both have your licenses. Now, remember, you need to change your birth year to 1957, and I'll take care of the rest."

The girls were excited! What teenager wouldn't want their driver's license, and especially getting it early! They never even thought of how illegal it was or what could happen if they got caught. They just knew that their dad was going to handle the details. So they hopped in the car, and off they went.

When they arrived at the building, Tom said, "Wait in the car until I come out."

He went inside, and after about five minutes, came out and told the girls to go in.

"Now remember, it's very important that you keep everything the same, except your birth year," he cautioned.

"We know, Dad," they said. The girls went in and took their test, and out they came with a driver's license that said they were eighteen. They didn't care how their dad did it, for they now had their I.D.'s, and that was all that mattered.

"Soon, Faith, I'll get you a car so you can have a way to work." Faith was excited about that. However, she knew within what it was going to take to get a car.

***

Tom took the girls driving a few times a week for more training. They were both very good drivers, and it wasn't long before Tom came home with a car for Faith. He had bought it from his brother Greg and got a really good deal.

When Faith arrived home from school that day, she saw the car and assumed someone was visiting their house. It wasn't until she went inside that Tom told her, "So what do you think about your new car in the driveway?"

"That's mine?" Faith asked. "Oh my God, I love it!"

She ran outside to the car and opened it up and sat in it. She grabbed the steering wheel and adjusted the seat to fit her. It was a 1965 Mustang convertible with bucket seats. When she turned to look at her dad, he threw the keys towards her.

"It's all yours Faith," he said.

With a huge smile, she put the keys in the ignition and started it up. She revved it up a little and asked if she could take it for a spin.

"Oh please, Dad, can I? Can I?" she pleaded.

"Okay," her dad said. "You can drive, and I'll ride with you. But just around the neighborhood."

"That's okay," said Faith. "Come on!"

Tom got in the passenger's side, and Faith put the car in gear. Off they went! She made sure she drove slowly and carefully as they headed up the street. About halfway, a bird flew in front of the car. Faith slammed on the breaks and Tom fell forward and had to put his hand out to stop himself from hitting the window.

Tom yelled at Faith, "Don't you ever stop for a bird or any animal. That's the way to get in a serious accident!"

"But I didn't want to hurt the little bird," she said.

Tom just looked at her, and they both started laughing. Tom told her again that she should never to stop for an animal because she or someone else could get seriously hurt or killed. She always had such a soft heart for little animals, though she knew he was right.

She drove all around the neighborhood about three times, and then Tom said, "It's time to go home." They pulled up at the house and got out of the car. "You did a great job driving, except for the little birdie incident!"

Faith laughed and went inside to call Brandi and tell her about her new car. Now that she was mobile, Faith always asked her mom if there was anything she needed from the store or any errands she could help with. She didn't care how big or small; she just wanted to drive her car. In spite of this willingness, Tom and Emily only let her drive it to work and back. She still had to take the bus to school, so the car sat quite a bit.

Chapter 14: Layers of Betrayal

Sometimes the strongest people are the ones who love beyond all faults, cry behind closed doors, and fight battles that nobody knows about.
~ Author Unknown

School was almost out for the summer, and Faith thought maybe she could practice more and improve her driving skills. Hope was upset that Faith had a car and she didn't.

At one point, Tom told Hope, "Don't worry, you'll get a car soon."

Hope knew, as well as Faith, what that meant. Tom had the girls trained that when he abused them, they were rewarded with material things.

Hope worked with her dad all the time now. Faith knew what he was doing to her, and because she wasn't going as much, Hope was getting most of his abuse. After a while, Faith was hardly going to work with her dad at all. She could tell he was treating her different. He was a little stand-offish and made sure that when Hope came home from a trip, she had all kinds of new things to show off. Hope would walk in with bags from all kinds of stores.

"Hey Faith," Hope would say. "Look what I got!" She'd take out all kinds of new clothes, earrings, necklaces, new socks, and shoes. Hope was accumulating quite the collection. But in the back of Faith's mind, she knew that Hope was paying for it.

Faith began to feel left out. Her sister had all this cool stuff and new clothes, and no one was bringing her anything at all. But she realized that all the things in the world weren't worth her dad's abuse. She felt more at peace, not going as much. Plus, she had her own job at the mall, but it was getting to her. Her coworkers weren't that friendly. After working there for about six months, she decided to quit.

***

Now that she was home again, Tom expected Faith to go to work with him more. Faith said she would, but would try and get out of it. She'd always come up with some excuse not to go, whether it was homework or a headache or feeling sick. Any excuse would do. She knew that Tom knew this, but wasn't saying anything. She could tell by the way he treated her. He had little patience with her and yelled more. But there were many times the excuses weren't good enough, and she had to go.

One weekend, Faith's friend Cassie asked her if she wanted to go to her parents' cottage with her on vacation. They'd be gone for a week. Faith was excited and asked her to come over and ask her dad because he'd most likely say yes if Cassie were there.

"Sure," said Cassie. She came over to Faith's house and approached Tom.

"Could Faith come with my family and me to our cottage for the week?" she asked. "My parents said I could bring a friend, so please say yes! Please!"

Tom looked at the girls and told Cassie, "It's fine. Faith can go with you. Just give me the details of where you all are going to be and the phone number."

The girls hugged him and said, "Thank you!"

Faith was excited to get away a whole week! That weekend, Cassie's parents came to pick her up. She was already packed and couldn't wait to go. Faith and Cassie had such a good time on the way to the cottage, which was about an hour and a half away. She felt so relieved that she didn't have to be at home. When they pulled up to the cottage, Faith fell in love with it. It was a huge log cabin on the river! The girls got all their stuff out of the car and Faith followed Cassie to their bedroom. When they entered the house, Faith stood in amazement. How beautiful and big it was!

"Wow," she said. "I've never been in a log cabin before!"

Cassie laughed and said, "Come on up the steps to our room!"

Faith had never felt so free in all her life! The girls put their stuff away, and then Cassie said, "Let's go out to the river and check it out."

"Sure!" said Faith.

They hurried down the steps and headed towards the river. A long pier went across the water, and Faith ran all the way down to the end and stood there looking over the water. *What a peaceful feeling,* she thought. *I love it here!* Faith was feeling emotions she had never felt before. She felt freedom—a sense of peace, safety, and most of all knowing that she would have a whole week without her dad being near her. It was the best feeling ever, and she didn't ever want to go home!

The girls had so much fun. They enjoyed many activities all week, including swimming, fishing, crabbing, boating and other fun things. The week went by much too quickly, and Faith was able to relax like she had never before. They were leaving the next day, and she could feel the heaviness starting to come back.

That night the girls stayed outside on the beach and watched the sunset for the last time. All of those peaceful feelings were all Faith could think about. As she thought about how good she felt, and being with a normal family, she knew she would be going back to dysfunction tomorrow… back to her real life. She didn't want to go.

The night seemed to fly by and morning came much too soon. The girls got up and packed their things and headed downstairs. Faith inhaled the wonderful smell of breakfast.

"Come on, girls," Cassie's mom said. "Breakfast is ready!"

"Our last breakfast here," said Faith. "Thank you for letting me come with Cassie!"

"Oh, you're so welcome, and I hope you had a good time!"

"I had the best time of my life," she told Cassie's mom, who didn't realize how much Faith meant what she said.

The trip back home was fun. However, as each mile passed by, Faith felt the awful dread of going home. They finally pulled up to her house and said goodbye. Faith thanked Cassie's mom and dad once again for the most wonderful time she ever had. Cassie and Faith hugged each other and said they'd talk tomorrow.

As Faith was going toward her porch, she noticed her car was not there. She walked inside, and her mom and dad were in the kitchen.

"I'm home," she hollered. As she walked into the kitchen, she asked, "Where's my car?"

Her dad looked at her and said, "Sorry, I had to sell it. I couldn't afford to keep it up."

Faith started crying and ran upstairs to her room and shut the door. She fell on her bed and cried her eyes out. She felt that the real reason her dad sold her car was because she didn't go to work with him. Her dad never mentioned the car again.

When would it ever end? She cried out to God in her mind and asked, *Why do I have to go through all of this? Why did you let him take my car? Where are you when my dad is raping me? Where are you, God? Where? Where are you when he is beating me up? Where are you when he is slamming me against walls or throwing me down on the floor and pinning me down? Where? Where?*

Faith grabbed her pillow and started sobbing uncontrollably. She felt so all alone. She had such a good time at the river, and then had to come home to this. She grabbed her weed that she had hidden in her drawer and rolled a joint and smoked the whole thing. She just didn't want to think. She just didn't want to feel anything at all. And most of all, she didn't want to be at home, and the weed helped her take her mind off of things a little. She stayed in her room until she fell asleep, and woke up the next morning still wearing the same clothes.

I need to get another job, was her first though. She really didn't want to go to work with her dad. It took Faith about three months to get another job, and in the meantime, she had to go to work with her dad. He'd take Hope one time and Faith the next. Every time he took Faith to the hotel, he molested and raped her in the middle of the night. Faith just laid there, hopeless, helpless, and starting not to care too much anymore. *What can I do anyway?* she thought.

The next day at work, her dad gave her money to buy whatever she wanted. Faith always bought clothes. Even though she knew the money given her was dirty money, she enjoyed shopping and getting whatever she wanted. It was her money, and she could spend it on anything she liked.

The following week, Hope went to work with her dad. When they got back from out of town, Hope came in so excited and was hollering.

"Faith, come here!"

"What Hope? What is it?"

"Come outside and look what I got!" Hope was running down the steps and Faith was right behind her. As they went outside, there sat a car in the driveway. "It's mine," said Hope! "I drove it all the way back here from out of town. How do you like it?"

"Why, that sure is a neat looking car," Faith said, but all the while knew what it really cost her sister.

All Hope could do was think about her car. "You want to go for a ride?"

"Sure," said Faith.

Hope yelled at her dad and said, "I'm taking Faith for a ride. Be back in a little while."

"Be back home within thirty minutes," Tom yelled back.

"Okay," they yelled.

The girls got in the car and drove off. Hope was always such a good driver, much better than Faith. Faith was always a little over cautious while Hope handled a car like a pro. She wasn't scared of anything. Faith always wished she could have more of that fearless attitude when it came to driving like Hope did.

They took the car down to the lake and drove around. Faith was very happy that her sister had a car, but the thoughts of her car being sold saddened her heart. They drove around for a while and then headed back home. Both girls knew what would happen if they were late. They pulled up along the side of the house and parked. Faith couldn't get over how excited her sister was. That car was her pride and joy! Faith was happy for her, but also knew she needed her own car to be able to get away whenever she could.

***

As time went on, Tom continued to abuse the twins. The late-night visits were about one to three times a week. Many times, when Emily wasn't around, the girls and Tom got into huge arguments. Hope was a lot feistier than Faith and much of the time stood up to Tom and yelled back at him. Tom never put up with Hope being so boisterous and came at her to put her back in her place. Whenever Faith saw this, she always stepped in the middle, because she knew Tom was going to hit her sister and she knew that Hope's temper was so bad that she didn't care what Tom did to her.

Faith's heart was always with her sister, and she never wanted to see her get hurt. This meant that Tom punished Faith for interfering, sometimes shoving her into a wall and then hitting her. He'd then go after Hope, and Faith would do the same thing all over again, leaving the three of them battling against each other.

One summer day, the same thing happened. Tom was getting ready to grab hold of Hope, and Faith jumped in. He knocked her down and flew into a rage. The look on his face was demonic, to say the least. He grabbed Hope and started ripping her clothes right off of her. Hope was screaming and trying to fight. Faith jumped in, and he started ripping her clothes off as well. Tom grabbed hold of Hope's shirt and completely tore it from her body, and then ripped her shorts and underwear off. Faith was screaming at Tom, and he did the same to her. He literally ripped off all Hope's clothes and underwear, and she was completely naked and ran up the steps into her room, screaming and crying.

He then grabbed Faith and tore the rest of her clothes off in a heated rage, and then shoved her up the steps. Faith was screaming and crying as well, and ran up the steps to her room naked, angry, and humiliated, slamming the door. Faith could hear Hope crying, and Hope could hear Faith crying. Faith locked her bedroom door and got dressed. To Faith, this was yet another one of the most demeaning acts her dad had perpetrated – both of us this time! It stoked the burning hatred towards her father.

They stayed in their rooms for quite a while until Tom hollered at both of them to come downstairs. They both opened their doors and looked at each other and went downstairs. Tom, still angry, told the girls to never defy him again. Faith never forgot that day. Anytime she would ever think of it, all of those negative feelings would surround and fill her being. She hated how it made her feel.

When Emily got home from work, she never learned what happened that day. She just knew everyone was upset, and no one ever gave her an answer. Faith felt such a disconnection with her mom. She had always hoped that her mom would stop what he was doing to them, and this impacted Faith's feelings for her mother. Home life was usually chaos and good times, all tumbled together. The girls were young teenagers, and by now all of those emotions that came from abuse were embedded in both of them, and in Richard as well.

***

Richard hated being at home and moved into his own apartment at the first chance. Faith was glad he was free from the abusive reins of Tom. He soon was dating a girl named Vicky, who he eventually wed and had two little girls. This made Emily very happy. She loved those little girls and loved being a grandmother. It was a treat when Richard, Vicky, Donna, and Diana came over.

Tom had eased up on Richard by then and enjoyed the girls at the house. Faith always watched her dad around the girls. She didn't trust him one bit and made sure he never was alone with either one of them. Faith loved Donna and Diana so much, and they never knew how Faith protected them whenever Richard or Vicky wasn't there.

Hope and Faith continued to work with Tom, and sometimes both girls brought a friend or two along. Faith and Brandi would go together at times, and sometimes Hope and Brandi would go together. One day when Faith and Brandi went out of town with Tom, they got back to the hotel early. Tom always had plenty of weed to give the girls, and both of them would always smoke it. The girls rolled a few joints and began smoking, laughing and carrying on, and having a good time.

Tom looked at the girls and said, "Hey, I have an idea. How about I set up a movie camera and take movies of each of you separately. It will be fun!"

The girls looked at him with a puzzled look.

"This is what we'll do, and after the movie camera goes off, I'll give you each a hundred dollars!" The girl's eyes got real big.

"One hundred dollars?" They asked with excitement.

"That's right," said Tom, "One hundred dollars."

"What do we have to do?" asked Brandi.

"Well," said Tom, "I'll set up the camera, and you and I will lay on the bed, and I'll play around with you." Tom got out the camera and set it up. He told Faith to stay in the bathroom and close the door, and he'd tell her when to come out.

"How come?" Asked Faith.

"Just do as I tell you," said Tom. "It will make Brandi more comfortable if you're not looking."

Faith saw that look on his face and went into the bathroom and closed the door. She could hear Brandi giggling, and even though she couldn't see what was happening, she figured it out. As she sat in the bathroom, she began thinking of how embarrassing this was. She wondered how Brandi felt. This was her best friend, and she couldn't stand what her dad was doing to her. More and more anger was building up inside of Faith.

After it was all over with, Tom hollered at Faith to come on out. When she opened the door, Brandi was laughing as Tom handed her a hundred-dollar bill.

"Okay," Tom said. He looked at Faith and said, "Your turn." He told Brandi to go into the bathroom and close the door. Brandi got up and went into the bathroom. Faith studied Brandi's face, and she didn't seem to mind what was going on. In fact, she seemed okay, which was a relief for Faith. But at that time, Faith didn't realize that Brandi harbored strong negative feelings about the experience, similar to hers.

Brandi closed the door, and Tom turned on the camera and told Faith to lie down on the bed. He quickly put his arm under her neck and told her to lift her hands up above her head. As soon as she did, Tom quickly grabbed her wrists and held her hands. He then used the other hand to lift up her shirt and expose her breasts. He started playing with them and running his fingers down her stomach. Faith was not laughing at all. She hated this. Faith started squirming to get away but Tom had his leg over hers, and she couldn't move. He laughed and carried on like he was having such a good time. Faith couldn't wait until the camera stopped. After he was done, he let Faith up, and she pulled her shirt back down.

Full of disgust and anger and humiliation, she got up and grabbed another joint and lit it.

"Come on out, Brandi," Tom yelled.

Brandi opened the door as Tom pulled out yet another hundred-dollar bill and handed it to Faith. Faith took it and put it in her pocket, not even making eye contact with him. Tom laughed and made it all seem like it was just so much fun.

Faith turned to Tom and asked, "What are you going to do with the movie?"

"I have someone who buys them from me, and he pays me a hundred dollars per movie," Tom said.

Faith wondered who else was going to see this. She felt so ashamed and humiliated once again, but also felt trapped and couldn't gather the courage to do anything about it.

When Hope took a friend, the same thing happened. This was now one of Tom's favorite things to do when they were out of town. He always paid the girls a hundred dollars, and the girls loved having the money to go shopping. They could hardly wait to spend their money. *What teenage girl doesn't like to go shopping at the mall?* they thought. Plus, a hundred dollars was a lot of money back in the seventies, especially for a teenager.

Chapter 15: More Dysfunction

"Don't allow your wounds to transform you into someone you're not."
~ Paola Coelho

At this point in their lives, Tom and Emily were relieved that the "bad guys" and Tom's former boss had pretty much left them alone. However, Tom was aware that they sent someone from time to time, without being obvious, to make sure he was still keeping quiet. This is why Tom always slept with a gun and had one in his truck. He never sat in a restaurant with his back to the door and was ALWAYS looking over his shoulder. So even though there was no physical contact, a sense of knowing they might be there haunted him. He never knew who they might send. It could be total strangers.

At the same time, his pedophilia only got worse. Every time Faith went alone with her dad, the same familiar ritual occurred. The TV was turned off, she fell asleep, and Tom got up and pulled her covers off. She would become wide awake but always pretended to be asleep, even though her heart was pounding. It helped her think that if her dad knew she was asleep, then she could play it off the next day and pretend nothing had happened. But even that thought never relieved any of the negative emotions.

One time on a trip, Faith was watching TV and had just finished smoking a joint. She was pretty high. It was long before bedtime and Tom got in front of her and told her to lay down.

"I want to show you something," he said.

Faith was scared and just looked at him.

"I said lay down!" Tom spoke in a stern voice.

Faith did as she was ordered. She laid on the bed, and Tom started removing her jeans. She was shaking. *Oh no,* she thought. *He's going to do something to me when he knows I'm awake.*

"Now hold still," said Tom. "I'm going to show you what an orgasm feels like. So you just lay there."

He removed her underwear and dragged her to the edge of the bed. Faith was so nervous and so embarrassed. She kept thinking, *Why does he do this to me?* She wanted to throw up.

Tom started performing oral sex on her. Faith didn't know what he was doing, but after a minute it stimulated sensations in her genitals. *Oh, my God,* she thought! *Why is this feeling good? This is my dad!* But she couldn't help the feelings that were running through her body. They were just there.

Suddenly, she had an orgasm, and Tom knew it. Even though she felt humiliated, disgusted, and angry, the orgasm was the best thing she had ever felt.

He knew she was done and got up with a big smile on his face, and said, "See? I told you it would feel good!"

Faith grabbed her underwear and put them on quickly, and then put her jeans back on. Tom walked away again as nothing had happened. He did not seem to care what he had just done to his daughter. She didn't even want to make eye contact with him. She got up and went into the bathroom and took a shower, all the while feeling so dirty. She stayed in the bathroom for a long time until Tom yelled at her to come out. She came out and sat in bed and started watching TV so she wouldn't have to look at him. Tom never said anything to her.

As it was time to go to sleep, Faith kept thinking about what happened and feeling so guilty about it. There was such a mix of emotions. She hated what her dad done to her. Still she couldn't get over the new feeling she had experienced. Her emotions were running rampant inside her head. *What the hell just happened?* she wondered. She laid there with tears running down her face, trying to muffle the sounds, and just silently cried herself to sleep.

***

Over the summer, Brandi got an after-school job. She wanted Faith to work there too. It was a little candy store, just around the corner, and they were hiring.

"Come put in your application," encouraged Brandi.

That evening after dinner, Faith asked her dad, "Can I get a job and work up the street at the candy store where Brandi is working?"

"Okay, I'll take you there to fill out the application," he agreed.

That week, Faith was hired, and both of the girls worked together. They always had so much fun. Tom took Faith to work and dropped her off. When he was out of town, Emily dropped her off. Faith loved going to work, for it meant more time away from her dad.

Hope, however, didn't get a job and worked with her dad more often. The only time Hope stayed at home was when he took Faith. One day Faith was off of work and Hope had stayed home as well, since Tom was working in town that day. A neighborhood boy drove down and parked in front of the girls' house. Faith and Hope went outside and stood around talking with Dave, who was a very nice, shy boy.

The girls and Dave talked and laughed for about an hour, and Tom came home. As soon as Tom pulled into the driveway, he glared at both the girls and yelled at them to come inside.

"Just wait here," Faith told Dave. "We'll see what Dad wants and be right back."

"Okay," said Dave as the girls ran inside.

It was a nice day, and all the windows in the house were open. Dave could hear Tom yell at both the girls, and then he heard Hope crying and yelling. He knew that the twins' father was mad at them and felt bad as he waited outside, witnessing the anger in Tom's voice.

Tom had taken off his belt and was beating Hope. Faith was in her room, knowing she'd be next. Tom walked in as Faith sat on the bed. He raised the belt up and yelled, "How many times have I told you girls, no company when we're not home?" He swung the belt across Faith's back. She glared at Tom and was determined not to cry. He swung hard again, and again and again. Faith stood her ground.

"Oh yeah?" said Tom. "You think I can't make you cry?"

Faith just looked at him as he swung the belt even harder across her back until she couldn't take it anymore and started crying. She knew he would stop as soon as she started crying.

Tom made his point and left the room. Faith saw Dave outside hang his head. He got in his car and left, and they never saw him again.

Over the next several days, Faith's back was sore. She wanted to show an adult or the police or someone what her dad had done to her, but was too scared. She figured that no one would do anything about it, and then she'd have to face the wrath of her dad again. It was best just not to say anything at all.

***

One time while working with her dad, Faith asked him about a car to get back and forth from work, and that way she could drive herself. Tom told her when they got back home they would look for a car for her. Faith was excited! She couldn't wait to go back home and look around.

As they chatted, Tom suddenly said, "There's something I want to tell you."

Faith felt a lump in her throat because she had no idea what was going to come out of his mouth. Was it going to be something that was going to totally embarrass her? She looked at Tom and said, "Okay, what?"

"Well, your mom and I had a baby girl before your brother was born. We couldn't afford to take care of her, so we gave her up for adoption."

Faith was stunned and speechless. "What?" she said. "We have a sister out there somewhere? Do you know where she is? Do you know what she looks like? Are you able to contact her?"

"Whoa!" said Tom. "First of all, all the answers to your questions are no. We've tried a few times to see if we can see who adopted her or any information at all. They said it was a closed adoption, and there is no way to ever find out. But your mom has always faithfully sent a Christmas card to the attorney every year, just in case we might be able to find her someday."

"Wow," said Faith. This was such a surprise, and she hoped one day they would be able to find her. In her mind, she wondered what her sister looked like, and also felt she was lucky to be adopted, which saved her from the abusive hands of Tom. She smiled and wondered what her life was like, and hoped it was much better than hers. In fact, in the years to come, Faith would think of her sister and wondered what she was doing.

After the road trip and when they got back into town, Tom told Faith he would look around and see what he could find. He left that next day and took Hope with him. They came back with a car for Faith.

When they pulled up, Hope ran into the house and hollered, "Faith, come here and see your new car!"

Faith was doing the dishes and ran out of the house. She saw a beautiful car just for her, and loved it! "Thank you, Dad!" she screamed. "Thank you!"

Hope handed her the keys and Faith got inside.

"Hop in, Hope," she invited. "Let's drive down to the lake."

Tom saw how excited the girls were and told them to go ahead. The girls took off and drove for about an hour, and then came home. When Faith saw her dad, she hugged him and told him, "Thank you," once again.

Tom gave her a big hug. "You're welcome," he said.

Faith ran upstairs and called Brandi. "Guess what? Dad just bought me a car!" she announced.

Brandi was excited and said, "From now on, you can pick me up when we both work the same shift."

"I sure will!" said Faith. "In fact, I'm going to drive over and show you my new car!"

"Okay!" said Brandi, who couldn't wait to see it.

When Faith drove up, she rang the doorbell, and Brandi's mom answered. Everyone called her Granny.

"Hey, Granny! I just got a new car and came over to show Brandi!"

At that moment, Brandi came out the front door.

Granny smiled and said, "I'm so happy for you!"

The girls ran down the steps to check out Faith's new car. Brandi loved it!

***

Brandi and Faith worked at the candy store for a little over a year. They had so much fun, and the owners liked them. One night the girls worked till closing, and after work, the owners sat down at one of the tables. One got up and locked the doors, and pulled out a bag of weed.

"Do you girls want to come smoke?" they invited.

"Sure!" said Faith and Brandi.

They all sat down and passed the joint around. Faith enjoyed the sense of freedom when she worked and, honestly, anytime she was away from home. She wasn't working with her dad much anymore, but he still came to visit her at night when he was home. But these encounters were getting less and less frequent, which was fine with Faith.

However, whenever they went out of town, Tom always gave Brandi and Faith one-hundred-dollar bills for each movie they did. This went on for a couple of years. It just seemed to be a lifestyle, one that Faith didn't want. Her wheels were always turning on how to change it, and soon. She still kept away as much as she could, now that she was working at the candy shop. In the back of her mind, she felt bad that Hope was still with Tom most of the time.

Chapter 16: Out of Town Escape

"Not until we're lost do we begin to find ourselves."
~ Henry David Thoreau

One morning before leaving to go out of town, Tom and the twins got into a pretty big argument. Tom was so mad at the girls that he told them neither was going with him this time. He grabbed his coffee, and out the door he went.

The girls really didn't care that they weren't going. In fact, they had the house to themselves that day and could do whatever they pleased. Faith went back into her room and turned on the music and lit a joint, and Hope went back to her room and turned on her music. They went back and forth to each other's rooms, looking at the different albums they each had and playing records. It was fun being there alone.

Later that night, right before the girls were going to bed, Tom called. Faith answered the phone and could hardly make out what her dad was saying … something about being at the hotel and not feeling good. The way he sounded made Faith really upset, and she thought he might be having a heart attack. Faith was scared.

"Do you want me to call an ambulance," she asked.

"No," he shouted, "don't call one."

Faith could hear that his voice was weak, and then he wasn't on the phone at all. She ran into Hope's room and told her what was happening.

"We need to drive out there and make sure he's okay," she said.

The twins grabbed their bags and climbed into Faith's car, and drove just over an hour to Tom's location. Both were terrified. They thought of their argument that morning, and Faith started feeling guilty. She drove fast all the way there.

They arrived at the hotel and dashed inside, asking what room her dad was in.

"Room 117," said the guy at the desk.

The girls ran to the room and started knocking on the door. There was no answer. Hope began to bang on the door, and still no answer. They were afraid that their dad was laying inside, dead.

Faith ran to the front desk and asked for a key. "Call an ambulance! I think my dad might have had a heart attack!" she told the clerk. She ran back with the key and opened the door.

Their dad was sitting up in bed, slumping over.

"Dad!" the girls screamed! "Are you okay?"

"I'm fine," said Tom, and then got mad at them for coming down. Faith was puzzled at why he was yelling at them for checking up on him. He still didn't look good.

"Well, I told the guy at the desk to call an ambulance, and they should be here soon."

Tom was furious. "Why the hell did you do that?"

"Because I thought you might be having a heart attack, Dad, that's why!" said Faith.

At that moment, there was a knock on the door, and the EMT crew came in. They started asking questions, and Tom told them he was fine.

"The girls are overreacting," he said. They took his vitals, and he seemed to be okay.

"Do you need to go to the hospital?" they asked. Tom said, "No."

"Call us if you have any more problems," they instructed. After they saw the siuation was under control, the EMT crew packed and left.

It was already late, and the girls were tired.

"Let's take turns staying awake and watching Dad to make sure he's okay," said Faith. Somehow their love and concern transcended his abuse.

Hope got in the other bed, and Faith sat in the chair, carefully watching out for her dad. Two hours went by, and she could hardly hold her eyes open. Hope was already sleeping. Faith tried to wake her, but she wouldn't get up, and Faith didn't want to wake their dad by persisting. So Faith sat back in the chair and stayed awake most of the night. Finally, in the wee hours of the morning, she fell fast asleep in the chair.

Four o'clock came early, and Tom was up like nothing had ever happened. He was his same usual self, and it was confusing to Faith. He ran up to the front desk and brought back coffee and sat and drank it with the girls. Faith's mind was boggled.

He got ready for work. "Get ready to come with me," he said.

"I'm staying here and going to sleep," said Faith. "I'm tired from being up all night."

Hope joined in. "I'm still tired and don't feel like going, either," she said.

Tom got mad. "You girls are lazy, and you don't care about anyone but yourselves," he yelled. Faith could hardly believe what she was hearing after they drove down there and she stayed awake most of the night to make sure he was okay. The twins just looked at him. He grabbed his coffee, and right before he left said, "I'll be back at noon, and you better be ready to go home." He slammed the door and was gone.

The girls got back in bed and slept for a few more hours. They got dressed before Tom arrived back at the hotel. He started an argument again. All three of them were yelling at each other, and Tom started getting that usual look of rage on his face. His eyes always looked demonic when he was like this.

"Both of you pack your shit and get the hell out of here!" he screamed. "I don't care where you go, but don't either one of you come home. Get out!"

The girls grabbed their stuff and got into Faith's car. Faith started it up and looked at Hope. "Where do you want to go? I only have a few dollars, and I'm going to need gas, and we have to eat and find a place to stay."

Hope grinned a huge grin and said, "Let's go to the mountains in that tourist town and get a hotel."

Faith looked at Hope and said, "Didn't you hear what I just said? I don't have enough money to do that!"

"That's okay," said Hope. "Dad gave me his credit card the other day, and I haven't given it back to him yet."

They both started laughing and said, "Let's go!"

They drove about thirty minutes outside looking for a hotel for the night. Hope didn't pick out a cheap one, either. They parked the car, got their bags, went to the front desk, and paid for one night, figuring they would just do one night at a time until they could go home.

They took their stuff up to the room and got settled in. "What do you want to eat?" asked Hope.

"I think we should take it easy on the credit card," said Faith. "Let's just go to the grocery store and buy a loaf of bread, some bologna, and some drinks." After all, their room had a small kitchen with a microwave and refrigerator.

"That sounds good," said Hope. "We can have bologna sandwiches for dinner and fried bologna sandwiches for breakfast!"

"Sounds good to me," said Faith, and off to the store they went. It was still early. They got only what they needed and went back to the hotel. They hung out at the hotel, and later that afternoon decided to go in town where all the kids hung out. They took showers, fixed their hair and put on makeup.

Hope looked at Faith and said, "Why don't we dress alike tonight?"

"That sounds like fun," said Faith, "but I don't think we have exactly the same clothes."

"Well, let's try and match as close as we can," said Hope.

So they both put on jean shorts and tube tops and flip-flops. The tube tops were close in color, and with the girls' long blonde hair and pretty faces, the majority of people would know they were twins. After they got all dolled up, they hopped in the car and followed the road into the touristy part of town.

Faith found a parking place, and they strolled along the sidewalks, enjoying the souvenir shops. Guys blew their horns and screamed out of the car windows, whistling at them. "Look, they're twins!" Faith heard someone shout.

All of the compliments swelled their heads, and they grinned from ear to ear. Faith really enjoyed this time with her sister. It wasn't often that they were able to be alone together, just to have fun. Faith would hold this memory in her heart and smile every time she thought about it.

It started to get late, and they decided it was time to go back to the hotel. On the way to the car, they giggled and chatted about the fun time they had, without a care in the world! Back at the hotel, they got ready for bed. Faith was getting sleepy, although Hope was still wound up a little. Finally, both fell asleep.

When morning came, the girls got up.

"Want a fried bologna sandwich?" Faith asked Hope

"Of course," said Hope! "Yummy!"

Faith fried up some bologna and put bread in the toaster. They ate their breakfast and had a soda. They talked about the night before and how much fun they had together. It felt a lot like a "get out of jail" pass. To Faith, it was an inspiring feeling of what could be. Both girls always felt so trapped under the controlling reins of her dad. He always had one eye on them, and they found every way possible to get away with things. But most of the time their dad knew almost everything they did.

Faith pondered these thoughts and said to Hope, "I wonder if Dad is still mad at us and wondering where we are?"

"Who gives a shit!" Hope shouted. "He's the one who told us to leave!"

"Yes, I know," said Faith, adding "But you know how he is." Even though she was having the time of her life, she could sense that something wasn't quite right. But being with Hope made Faith feel a lot better about herself. Hope was the stronger one. Faith just wanted to keep things as happy as possible so there would be no fussing or fighting. She played it safe and was a born peacemaker.

After the girls got dressed, they returned to town and did some sightseeing. They decided to spend one more night at the hotel, and later on that evening, Faith told Hope that she felt like she needed to call home. Hope finally agreed and told Faith to call in the morning.

***

It was great staying at the hotel, knowing that they could actually sleep and get up when they wanted to. It was a refreshing feeling. Checkout time was at ten a.m., and shortly after Faith awoke, she picked up the phone and called home. The phone rang, and Tom picked up.

"Hi Dad, just calling to check in," she said.

"Where are you?" he asked.

"We're not too far away from the hotel you were staying in," she said.

"Well, you girls need to come on home," he said.

"Okay," said Faith. "We're going to a store here, and then we'll head home this afternoon."

Tom said, "That's fine," and they hung up the phone.

Even though the girls knew they couldn't stay, they sure wanted to. Faith felt relieved that her dad didn't seem mad. The girls checked out and went into town for a little while before they headed home. It was almost a two-hour drive.

As the girls got on the road, they started talking about the fun they had. It felt invigorating to not have a care in the world!

"Well, we better enjoy these last two hours," said Hope, "because we know what it is going to be like when we get home." They both agreed, and as they got within a mile of home, they both felt that all too familiar feeling of helplessness and constraint.

They pulled into the driveway and could see that Tom was in his office. The girls were a little nervous and quietly got their bags out of the car and went in the house. They both went to their rooms to put their stuff away and could hear their dad coming up the steps.

Hope ran out of her room and said, "Hi Dad!" with a big smile, and then Faith came out and gave him a hug and said, "Hi Dad, we're home safe and sound!"

"I see that," said Tom. "I Just wanted to check on you two." He went back downstairs and out to his office. Faith waited to see him outside her window and ran into Hope's room.

"Whew!" she said. "I really thought he was going to yell at us or punish us or something!"

"I thought so too," said Hope. "He must have cooled off while we were gone!"

They both smiled at each other and went back to cleaning up their rooms. They were still thinking about how much fun they had the last couple of days! Faith couldn't help but think of all the mixed signals that she had received over the last few days. At first, she thought her dad was having a heart attack and was so scared that her heart pounded. Then she decided to drive two hours to rescue him at a hotel, being scared the whole time and praying that he was okay. And when they get there, he seemed to be okay but got extremely angry at her for calling an ambulance. Then she stayed up almost all night watching him breathe to make sure he was okay. Worn out and extremely tired, both physically and mentally, she fell asleep, only to wake up to an angry Dad yelling at them, and then finally kicking them out and telling them to leave.

Those thoughts swirled in her head, and she couldn't make heads or tails out of them. It only left her in a daze until the next round of turmoil, when it would start all over. Faith felt sorry for Hope because it seemed she didn't care about most things. Hope just wanted to have fun and buy things that made her feel good. Faith, on the other hand, couldn't wait until she was eighteen to get her own apartment. She enjoyed buying things with her own money.

Night time came, and right before Faith went to bed, she stepped into Hope's room and told her what a good time she had. "I have to go to work tomorrow afternoon. Are you working with Dad tomorrow?" she asked Hope.

"Yes, he's going back out of town, and I'll be going."

"Okay, then," said Faith, "I guess I'll see you in a couple of days."

"Nighty night," said Hope as she hopped in bed and turned off the light.

"Good night," said Faith, and gently closed Hope's bedroom door.

Faith went into her room, closed her door, and lit her candle on her nightstand. Once again, she looked out the window and prayed: "Now I lay me down to sleep, I pray the Lord my soul to keep, If I should die before I wake, I pray the Lord my soul to take. Bless mother and father, sister and brother, Aunt Jennifer, Brandi and all the people in the whole wide world. God, please don't ever let anything happen to Dad and Hope. God, please, when Hope and I get married, please let us live close together so we can raise our kids together. I always want our family to be together. Thank you, God. I love you. Amen."

Faith lifted her head off her pillow, blew out her candle and drifted off to sleep.

Chapter 17: Never Again

You have been assigned this mountain to show others it can be moved.
~ Anonymous

Morning came, and Hope had already left with Tom to go to work. Faith went downstairs and got a little coffee, and then went into the bathroom to take a shower. When she came out, her mom met her in the hallway.

"Good morning," said Emily to Faith.

"Hi, Mom. I have to work this afternoon, but should be home by seven tonight."

"Okay," said Emily. "I have to work too and will be home at five." Emily went downstairs and grabbed her keys and went out the door.

Even though her mom seemed to almost always be in a good mood and would try and talk to Faith, the negative emotions Faith felt were always simmering under the surface. Once again, that thought slipped through her mind: *Why doesn't Mom ever say anything to Dad about what he does to me, Hope, and our friends?* In Faith's mind, her mother just always seemed to smile and not care. *Why doesn't she yell at Dad or take up for me?* These thoughts would invade her mind quite a bit. Faith was too embarrassed and humiliated to bring the topic up, so she just left it up to her mom to do the right thing. But she never did. Faith would be nice to her, but a lot of times show disrespect whenever her mom would correct her for something. Her mom was an easy target and would hardly ever argue with Faith when she was disrespectful. Faith kept the majority of negative emotions for her mom inside.

Faith was now working and going to high school. After going into the second year of high school, she couldn't stand it anymore. She hated the school she attended, and by the time she was in the middle of tenth grade, she quit. She started working more, and her dad didn't say much when she told him she dropped out of high school. It was an easy way out.

Hope had already quit the year before and now was working with Tom full time. As for Faith, she just wasn't interested in school whatsoever. Studying was not her thing, and she never could really focus much on school or homework. She had spent a lot of time cutting classes and going across the street to get high with some friends. Her grades fell terribly. *What's the point?* she reasoned to herself.

When Faith wasn't working, she stayed high on marijuana. She never really liked the taste of alcohol, but she sure loved her weed. It helped her to cope with things—things no sixteen-year-old girl should have to endure.

***

One night when Emily got home from work and was fixing dinner, she told Tom that a customer had a real nice above ground pool that she wanted to see.

"Since it's so hot here in the summer, I thought it would be a good idea to go look at it and see what you think," she said.

Tom looked at Emily. "That sounds like a great idea. Ask your customer when would be a good time to come and see it," he said.

Emily set it all up with the lady, and a few days later Tom and Emily went over to look at the pool. It was a very nice pool with an aluminum fence all around it. At the other end, it had step going up to the pool and a deck surrounding the whole area. Tom and Emily fell in love with it and told the lady that they would buy it. The lady had it all disassembled and ready for them to take it the following week. Tom worked hard at putting it all together, and when it was done everyone enjoyed it!

Hope and Faith loved their new pool and would swim almost every day! The world inside the home was a hive of confusion, to say the least. Tom could be the nicest father and have a lot of fun with the family, and then could morph into the opposite. With it being that way all of Faith's life, it left her and her siblings with so many mixed, deep-rooted emotions.

One morning as Faith was getting ready for work, the phone rang, and she ran downstairs to answer it. It was Brandi.

"Hey, girl! What's up?" greeted Faith.

"Hey Faith, I just wanted to tell you that while you were gone, I quit the candy store and got a job at the Country Store Market! I love it there, and I just couldn't take that other little store anymore."

"Oh my God," said Faith. "It's not going to be the same without you there. It makes me not want to go to work today." She didn't like that she and Brandi would not be working together anymore. They had become inseparable.

"Well," said Brandi, "I have to go for now. I'm leaving for work, and I'll talk to you tomorrow."

"Okay," said Faith. "Don't forget to call me!"

"I won't," said Brandi, and they hung up.

Faith went back upstairs to get ready. She turned on her favorite music and started singing the lyrics to put herself in a better mood. At work that day, it was not the same. However, she continued to work there a couple more months.

***

One weekend Brandi called Faith and told her they were hiring again at the Country store Market, and to come down and put in an application.

"I'll tell the manager about you as well," promised Brandi.

"I'll be there Monday morning," said Faith.

She drove down to the country store, talked to the manager, and put in her application. He looked it over and told Faith she had the job and could start in a few days. Brandi was working that day, and after Faith left the manager and went over to her friend.

"I got the job!" she announced. "We'll be working together again!"

Faith couldn't wait to start her new position. The next day at the candy store, she told the manager that she'd be quitting and had another job. The owners were both sad to see Faith leave. In the next few days, she started her new job, and the girls had so much fun working together once again. Faith really liked the Country Store Market and began thinking: *I'm going to save some money out of each paycheck and start buying little things for an apartment.* She thought it was prudent to plan ahead. When she turned eighteen, she wanted to move out of her parents' house.

Faith would usually pick Brandi up if their shift hours were close together or the same. The girls had many laughs at the store, and the customers just loved them both. Many said the only reason they shopped there was because of Faith and Brandi. After working there for a year, Faith had everything she needed for a kitchen. She also started putting money into her own little savings account.

There was a time that Brandi and Faith were both off of work and went with Tom out of town. Tom had always liked Brandi a lot. She was so funny, and her sense of humor made people laugh. Tom connected well with that. Brandi was also a very pretty girl and Faith's best friend.

When they finished work and went back to the hotel, Tom started flirting with Brandi and threw her on the bed as if to play fun games. Faith felt that sickening lump in her stomach because she knew what Tom was doing. As usual, Tom told Faith to go into the bathroom and lock the door until he told her to come back out. Faith grabbed a joint and went into the bathroom. She sat in there for about thirty minutes smoking her joint while she could hear laughter and giggles in the room. Faith wondered how much longer this was going to keep happening. All she could think about was moving out.

After a while, Tom yelled at Faith to come out. Faith opened the door, and the smoke rolled out of the bathroom.

"Holy crap!" said Brandi, "How much did you smoke in there?"

Faith just cracked a slight grin. "The whole thing," she said and sat down in the chair.

"Are you girls hungry?" Tom asked. "I'll run and get everyone something to eat."

"Yes!" The girls yelled.

"Okay, I'll be right back." Tom left, and the girls sat and chatted for a while. Brandi pulled out some money and said, "Look what your dad gave me."

"Okay," said Faith as she smiled a smile that was totally fake, although Brandi seemed happy to have money in her pocket. Faith hated what her dad was doing to her friend.

Soon Tom came back with some food. They all sat at the table and ate and talked and laughed. As nighttime came, everyone went to sleep because they were headed back home in the morning. As Faith lay there, she said her prayer that she would say every single night and then asked God to please help her get out. She didn't know how much more of this she could take. As tears filled her eyes, she fell asleep.

Morning came, and the girls got ready to leave. They packed up and got dressed and took their things out to the car.

"I'll stop by a breakfast place and get something to eat before we head home," Tom said. "Is that okay with you girls?"

"Yes!" they said. "We're hungry!"

After a couple of miles, Tom spotted a little restaurant up the road and pulled in. They all sat down to a really nice breakfast.

"This is so good," said Faith as she chomped down on her biscuits and gravy. Both girls ate like they hadn't eaten in a week!

After breakfast, they hopped in the car to head home. About fifteen minutes into the trip, Faith pulled out a joint. She nudged Brandi and then lit it up. Brandi cracked the window to let the smoke out. She did not want to go home smelling like marijuana. The girls passed the joint to each other and were quiet. They were enjoying the ride.

After a while, Tom broke the silence and said, "Hey Brandi, I found a good deal on a car. Would you like to go see it? I'll buy it for you."

Brandi's eyes got real big. "Why yes! I'd love to."

"Okay then, come on over this weekend, and we'll go look at the car and see if you want it."

Brandi looked at Faith, and they both screamed with joy. "I can't wait to see it Will you come with me?" She asked Faith.

"Well, of course, I will. I wouldn't miss that for anything."

They finally got back into town, dropped Brandi off at her house, and then went home. Faith got her bags out of the car and went inside. She had to work the next day and went to her room to straighten it up and get her laundry done. As night fell, she was tired. She got on her PJ's and crawled into bed. As always, she would say her prayer before she fell asleep: *Now I lay me down to sleep, I pray the Lord my soul to keep. If I should die before I wake, I pray thee Lord my soul to take. Bless mother and father, sister and brother, Aunt Jennifer, all of my friends and all the people in the whole wide world. God, please always take care of my sister and when we get married, please let us live close by and raise our children together and please don't let anything bad happen to dad. Thank you, God. I love you with all my heart. Amen.*

Sometimes she would imagine her and Hope living just down the street from each other, each of them having children and doing fun things together. All kinds of wonderful thoughts would dance in her head until she fell fast asleep.

It seemed like she had just gone to sleep when she heard the familiar sound of her door opening. Faith had been high all day and was really groggy. However, the strangest thing happened. She began feeling an excitement in her genitals again. *Oh God, why is this happening?* she thought. Tom was right at her bedside, pulling her blankets off. She pretended to be asleep, figuring that her father knew she was pretty well out of it after all the pot she had smoked. He began molesting her again. She just laid there and noticed that she was enjoying the feelings that were running through her body. After Tom was done, he pulled her panties back up and put the blankets back on her. When he shut the door, it was all Faith could do to keep quiet and not let anyone know she was crying.

All those filthy, nasty, humiliating feelings were filling her mind up. *Why?* she asked God for the thousandth time. *Why am I feeling these feelings? It is not right! I hate myself! I hate myself.* It took her a while to get back to sleep because she was so angry at her dad and even angrier at herself. *How is this even possible?* She could not bear the added humiliation of telling anyone. She put her hands over her face and silently screamed. She lay there for a couple of hours feeling ashamed, and then she finally fell asleep.

The next day was always the same. Tom acted like he didn't know a thing and the disgusting emotions were still inside her, trapped and not going anywhere. Faith just went about her day as usual. She would still always laugh and tell jokes as if nothing ever happened. She always put on a big front, while deep inside she was torn apart.

The weekend came, and Brandi had come over early Saturday morning. Tom took Brandi and Faith to look at a car he had spotted a week earlier. Brandi was so excited! She loved the car. Tom checked it all out, and it was in good running condition, so Tom talked the owner down a bit on the price.

"Do you like it," he asked Brandi.

"Yes!" she answered.

Tom worked out all the details, and after about thirty minutes the man handed Tom the keys. Brandi and Faith got in and followed Tom back to the house. Brandi knew that her mom would be upset about Tom buying a car for her, so she said she bought the car with the money she saved up from working with him. It took a while before Brandi's mom was okay with it. Between Faith and Brandi, they convinced her that they worked really hard with Tom. Brandi's mom finally gave in, and Brandi finally had a car of her own.

Brandi had gone many times with Tom out of town. There were times that Faith didn't go with her, but Hope did. It was always the same each time. Tom would molest the girls and pay them. They would go out shopping buying all kinds of clothes and jewelry. Faith worked more at the country store and did all she could to keep her dad away from her. It seemed to work. The times were getting few and far between, but still, when it did happen, she felt progressively more ashamed. She knew that Hope was getting abused by Tom more than anyone because she was practically his full-time worker on out-of-town trips. There were many times that Hope went by herself because Brandi was working or other friends couldn't go.

For some reason, Tom treated Hope worse than everyone else. Not just the sexual abuse, but also he talked down to her and at times and degraded her terribly. This had a profound effect on her. She became more and more withdrawn. It seemed like all she wanted to do was buy things and go out and have fun. That seemed to make her happy. But Faith knew her sister was just burying her emotions deeper and deeper until they seemed to disappear. She was also getting braver with her anger towards her dad. Hope didn't care if he beat her, and she gave it right back to him no matter what. This bothered Faith.

Faith, who was not almost seventeen, was home alone with her dad one day. He called her into his room and told her to lay on the bed, and then he raped her. He told her that he was going to show her how to treat her husband when she got married. As Faith lay there numb, she finally said in her mind: *This is the last time he'll ever do this.* After Tom was finished, she got up and took a shower, thinking: *Whatever it takes, this will be the last time.* She had enough. She got out of the shower and went to her room. Over and over in her mind, she kept telling herself, *No more! I don't care what he does to me! I don't care if he beats me! No more! Never again.*

She finally put her foot down. From then on, she locked her door at night. She didn't care if her dad got mad. She figured that if he knocked on the door late at night or tried to pick the lock that it would wake up her mom. Faith knew she had to do this no matter what. The first couple of weeks it was hard for her to fall asleep. She wanted to listen and see if her dad came to her door. She heard the handle jiggle a little one night, and then nothing. Faith's heart pounded. She didn't know what he would do. He never came in that night.

The next day he asked, "Why was your door locked?"

Faith just said, "Because I locked it."

The next night Faith lay awake, listening for any sound near her door. This went on for a few days, and again one night she heard him at his door. Once again, she froze. She could hear the handle jiggle a little as she was frozen in fear. Finally heard him walk away.

This continued over the next few weeks, until one day Tom asked her again why she was locking her door. Faith just looked at him and stood her ground and said, "You know why." Tom walked away without saying anything. That was the last time that he ever touched her. Faith continued to lock her door every night. But Tom continued abusing Hope.

After a year of working at the country store, a friend of Brandi's asked her to come work at the local food chain store. Brandi used to go to this store on a regular basis to grocery shop for her mom. After a while, she decided to give it a try and told Faith about it. Then she quit the country store and started working at the local food chain store.

"I'll put in a good word for you," she told Faith. Brandi had already told her friend, the assistant manager, about her best friend. Brandi brought Faith an application to fill out, and sure enough, Faith was hired. This was a big store compared to the little country store they worked, and it wasn't long before Faith and Brandi were a big hit with the customers. Faith was eighteen by now and really enjoying this job. She had a big collection of apartment furnishings and would be ready to move into her own place when the time came.

It had been two weeks at her new job, and Faith really loved it. She enjoyed going to work and made friends quickly. Everyone who worked at the food chain store was very nice, and most of them were around Faith and Brandi's age. There were times at the end of a night shift that they and a few other employees hung out in the parking lot, sharing a bottle of wine and just laughing and telling jokes. Then it was time to go home after a long day at work. Faith would hug Brandi goodbye and tell her she'd see her over the weekend.

Once, during a late night parking lot get together, Brandi said, "Oh, I forgot to tell you, Faith, I'm going out of town to visit my cousin for the weekend." She had met a man there several weeks before, and they started seeing each other every time she came into town.

"That's great," said Faith. "I'm happy for you two!"

"Well, I'll see you at work next week," said Brandi. "Okie dokie," smiled Faith.

The weekend was pretty quiet for Faith since Brandi was not around. She was perfectly happy to work on Saturday, but it was never the same without Brandi there.

Chapter 18: Independence Day

"When you change the way you look at things, the things you look at will change."
~ Wayne Dyer

Faith usually worked the night shift, since she had been on the job for just a couple of weeks. However, she didn't mind and had told the manager that she liked the night shift. One night she got off of work early and headed home. When she came into the house, Hope and their dad were arguing. Faith jumped in and sided with Hope. Tom didn't like it at all that the two girls were standing up to him. He got very angry and shoved both of them out the front door.

"Get out and don't come back," he hollered at them.

They both got into Faith's car and drove over to Brandi's house. They went to the front door and knocked. Brandi answered and let the girls in.

"What are you all doing here so late?" she asked.

"We were arguing with Dad, and he kicked us out. Is it okay if we spend the night here?" asked Faith.

"Why sure it is," replied Brandi. "Just let me go tell Mama that you all are here." She instructed the girls to go back to her room and said she'd be there in a minute.

The girls walked quietly to Brandi's bedroom and sat on the bed, waiting. She finally came in, shut the door, and asked what happened. Brandi listened while fetching two sleeping bags out of her closet and handing them to the girls. The three chatted for about an hour, and then were ready to go to sleep.

As Faith lay there thinking of everything that had happened, she said, "Hey Brandi, what do you think about you and I getting an apartment together?" Brandi sat straight up in bed and grinned from ear to ear.

"Wow! That would be fun! But I don't know if Mama will let me or not."

"Well," said Faith, "we both work, and I have everything we need for an apartment except for a couch and kitchen table. You know I've been saving up for this day."

Brandi said, "I'll talk it over with Mama and see what she says."

Faith was excited! "Hey Hope, if you want to move in with us, you can get a job, and we'll all three split the bills."

"I'm not quite ready to move out," Hope said.

"If we get an apartment, you stay with us anytime you want to," said Faith.

"That sounds good," said Hope.

The next morning Faith had to go to work, and Hope stayed at Brandi's for the day. Faith worked an early shift that day and could hardly wait to get back to Brandi's to see what her mom said about them going out on their own. She couldn't help but think of how exciting it would be to get her own apartment and be away from her dad. Her mind raced and it was all she could think about!

Meanwhile, Brandi discussed getting an apartment with her mom. Her mom wasn't that thrilled about it at first but knew that Brandi had been working hard. This was her time to start being a little more independent. She had a long talk with Brandi about responsibilities and having important bills to pay. As they sat down to discuss these things, Brandi's mom was reassured that Brandi had it all figured out and was doing a great job. Between the two girls, and as much as they worked, she eventually said yes.

By the time Faith got back to Brandi's house, she could sense the good news the minute she saw Brandi. Both girls were off the rest of the day and the next day. They decided to start looking right away! As the girls sat in the kitchen, Hope could see how completely her sister and Brandi were fired up.

"This was a good idea," she said. "But I wonder what Dad is going to think about it all."

Faith looked at Hope and reminded her, "You're eighteen and can move in with us if you want."

***

Faith and Brandi knew the area well and had an apartment in mind. They both had seen these apartments before and thought they were nice. Brandi looked up the number and Faith called, asking about the details. The apartment manager said they could come over anytime between nine and five to look at the model apartment. The girls squealed with joy!

"Since we're both off work tomorrow, let's go over and check it out," said Brandi.

Faith quickly said, "Yes! I do have to go home and at least let my mom and dad know what we're planning, though."

"Okay," said Brandi. "Why don't you and Hope go and we'll talk later."

"Sounds good," said Faith. The girls got into the car and went back home, figuring their dad would be expecting them anyway. He always did. It didn't matter if he told them to leave a couple of days earlier. He just acted like nothing had ever happened and knew they would be back. When they pulled up, neither parent was there. The girls went in the house to their rooms.

Faith told Hope, "I'll take a shower first, just in case Mom and Dad get home." She wanted to talk with them about the apartment.

"Sure," said Hope. "I'm going to clean up my room until you're done."

Faith hopped in the shower and then went into her room to gather her thoughts. About two hours later, their mom came home, and about an hour after that, their dad came home. Tom went straight to the garage to do his paperwork for the day. Faith was a little nervous about talking to them. However, she had actually dreamed of this day and was going to be straightforward with them.

Emily was in the kitchen trying to find something for dinner. Faith came in and said, "Hi mom."

"Hi honey," she said. "When did you get home?"

"We got home a couple of hours ago. We stayed over at Brandi's house."

"I figured that!" she said with a smile.

"Mom, when Dad comes in, I really need to discuss something with both of you, okay?"

"Why yes, Faith. Are you alright?"

"Yes, mom," said Faith. "I just want to wait until Dad gets in. I hope he's in a good mood," she said with a slight smile. "What are we having for dinner?"

"Well, I'm fixing pinto beans, fried potatoes, and cornbread. What do you think?"

"Oh Mom," said Faith, "that's my favorite!"

Emily smiled because she knew it was the twin's favorite meal.

Faith ran upstairs and went into Hope's room. The girls sat on the bed as music played.

"So Faith, when are you going to tell Mom and Dad about your plans?"

"Well," said Faith, "I'm waiting for Dad to come in, and will give him a little bit of time with Mom. Then I'll go downstairs. I just might wait until we're having dinner."

"Good idea,' said Hope. "I've got your back!"

"Thanks," said Faith.

The girls flipped through albums trying to find the next one to put on. "Hey Hope, can we listen to one of my albums?" asked Faith.

"Which one," asked Hope?

"Well, I was thinking about my Bad Company album. They always remind me of our times at the lake. I remember a lot of their songs played during that time."

"Okay," said Hope, "go get it, and I'll put it on."

The girls sat in Hope's room, listening to the album as Faith recalled how much fun they used to have. It was like a movie playing in her head. She sat there, back against the wall, grinning ever so slightly as if in a trance and remembering the water and the sand. Her mind took her back to moments that she would remember the rest of her life. Then the thought came of when Hope fell off the sliding board. The movie kept playing in her mind of how awful she felt that day to see her sister fall and hit the water. She stopped thinking of that and looked over at Hope, who was going through all of her albums and trying to figure out which one to play next. Hope's scar was still visible, which was a minor thing, mostly because Faith felt so blessed that her sister survived that horrible accident and was there with her.

The moment was interrupted by the opening of Hope's bedroom door.

"I see you girls are home now." It was Tom standing at the door and waiting for a response.

"Yes, we got back a few hours ago," said Faith. "We stayed over at Brandi's house."

"Okay," said Tom. "Your mom said dinner will be ready in about a half hour." He closed the door, and the girls just looked at each other. Without saying one word, they both thought the same thought—their dad walked away without saying anything to them about kicking them out. A sigh of relief came over them.

"Well, I guess we should wash up and go downstairs," said Faith. "I need to have that talk with them. You come with me, Hope."

Faith went down first, and Hope followed shortly after. They sat at the table, and Faith said, "Mom, dinner smells so good. I can't wait to chow down."

Emily laughed out loud. "Eat as much as you want girls!" She chatted with the girls as she set the table. "What have you girls been up to the last couple of days?"

Faith was in the middle of talking when they heard the front door open. Hope changed the subject quickly and said, "Dinner smells wonderful, Mom."

Tom came in and washed his hands in the sink. Emily began putting the food on the table. The mood in the air was positive, and Faith felt it would be a good time to talk to her parents. Tom had sat down beside Hope and looked at a crossword puzzle she was working on. He reached over and said, "Five down is apparel."

Hope said, "That was on the tip of my tongue. Thanks!" She quickly filled in the answer.

Once the family began to eat, Faith said, "I have something I'd like to discuss."

"Tom and Emily looked at her and said, "Okay, let's hear it."

Faith started out slowly. "Well, the past couple of days we were staying over at Brandi's house. Anyway, Brandi and I were talking and thought it would be a good idea to get our first apartment together. We've both have been working for a while and have saved up money. So, what do you all think?"

Tom and Emily looked at each other. Emily said, "Have you considered all the bills that you'll have when you move out?"

"Yes," said Faith. "I've been thinking about it for a while, and have some money in my savings account. I've bought all kinds of stuff for when I move out."

Tom didn't say anything.

"Brandi talked to her mom, and her mom said yes," added Faith. "We've already found an apartment and are going to go over there tomorrow to look at it."

Both Tom and Emily could see the excitement and determination in Faith. They knew she was pretty responsible.

"Dad, what do you think?" Faith waited impatiently for his answer. He was in the thinking mode, and no one knew what to expect.

"I think this could be a good idea," said Tom.

Faith stood up and ran over and hugged her mom and dad. "Thank you! Thank you!" she screamed.

"Okay Faith, while we're eating, we need to discuss some things," said Tom. "I want to take you and Brandi over to the apartment because there might be some things that you all don't know about and I can help. I should be home from work at two. We'll go then. Tell Brandi we'll swing by and pick her up about two thirty."

"That's fine, Dad! Can I take my bedroom furniture with me?"

Both Tom and Emily said, "Yes, of course," at the same time.

Faith could hardly believe her ears! "I'll be right back," she said, and ran upstairs, and then brought down a piece of paper. "I have all of the bills figured out," she said. "The lady told me how much the apartment is a month, and Brandi and I are splitting everything."

Tom and Emily saw how Faith had written all the bills written down and how much she'd put back each week from each paycheck.

Emily glanced over and said, "Faith, I'm proud of you for doing all this in advance." She could tell that Faith had been working and thinking about this for a while, and also knew she wanted to escape Tom's anger and all the arguing. Looking at Faith's face all lit up, Emily was happy for her.

"I'm going to call Brandi and tell her the good news. Thanks for dinner, Mom, it was really good!"

"You're welcome," said Emily said as she gathered up the dishes. Faith ran upstairs and could hardly push the buttons on the phone from all of the excitement.

"Brandi, Dad said yes, and he's taking us to see the apartment tomorrow!"

The girls were so pumped, they could barely stand it. After Faith hung up the phone, she lay across her bed and just couldn't believe that tomorrow would be the day that she had long awaited. She knew in her heart that the apartment manager was going to say yes. She closed her eyes and said, "Thank you, God!" She could feel the tears leaking out of her eyes as she had so much thankfulness in her heart. It seemed as if all of the violations and horrific events she had gone through with her dad were coming to a final close. No more would she be under his control, and she hoped that her sister would join in the "getaway." She opened her eyes, wiped her tears, and sat up in bed, then lit the candle on her nightstand. She could hear Hope in her room playing music and walked over to say goodnight.

Faith opened her door. "I'm going to bed now. Tomorrow is a big day for me. Are you coming with us to check out that apartment?"

"Of course," said Hope. "I think it will be fun!"

"I'm glad," said Faith and closed the door. She crawled into bed, but couldn't get to sleep for hours just thinking about her future. She then leaned over and blew out the candle and closed her eyes to pray. *Now I lay me down to sleep, I pray thee Lord my soul to keep. If I should die before I wake, I pray the Lord my soul to take. Bless mother and father, sister and brother, Aunt Jennifer, Jesus and the Angels, all of my friends and everyone in the whole wide world. Amen. Please God, always take care of my family. Please take care of Hope, and I pray that when we each get married and have children, we can live close by and raise our children together. Thank you for letting dad say yes to me moving out. I love you with all my heart. Amen.*

***

Faith rolled over and closed her eyes and soon fell asleep. The next morning, she woke to bright sunshine and the sound of birds singing. She always loved hearing the birds, and it sounded like there were hundreds outside her window and in the trees that surrounded her house, nesting in the neighborhood. She tried to figure out which sound went with which bird, and could always guess the Blue Jay, the Crow, the Cardinal, and a few others. She launched out of bed, went downstairs, grabbed a cup of coffee, and called Brandi.

Brandi had just woken up too. "I was just about to call you. What time are we going?"

"Oh, I was so excited that I forgot to tell you. Dad will be home about two, and then we'll come get you shortly."

"That sounds great," said Brandi. "I'm going to get dressed and grab something to eat."

They both hung up the phone, and Faith sat and drank her coffee. Soon Hope came downstairs with bed head and grabbed a cup of coffee.

"Hey Hope," said Faith. "We're picking Brandi up around two-thirty to check out the apartment. Do you still want to go?"

"Yes, I'll go," said Hope. "I'm going to take a shower and get dressed in a few minutes."

"Good," said Faith. "I'll go ahead and jump in the shower now."

Hope went back to her room and turned on her music until Faith was done. Faith got out of the shower and headed to her room to get dressed. As she closed the door, the excitement escalated. *How much fun it will be to decorate!* she thought. Her mind was going a thousand miles a minute, and then she thought, *what if they turn her and Brandi down?* She never really thought of that until now. She quickly got dressed and ran outside to the garage.

"Hey, Dad! What if they turn us down at the apartment?" Faith said, somehow always knowing which side of her Dad would answer.

Tom turned around. "They'll do a credit check. Don't worry; I know how to handle these things. This is why I want to go with you and Brandi. You all are new at this, and I'm an old pro."

"Thanks, Dad!" Faith felt a whole lot better and went back inside to make her bed and clean her room. She looked at all of the things she had bought in preparation for this day. There were many packed boxes in her closet and the attic, and she wanted to open each one to see what she had accumulated over the last couple of years. *I'll just wait,* she thought. *I'm getting myself all worked up and don't even know if I'm going to get this apartment or not.*

Faith finished cleaning up her room and then went into Hope's room to chat with her. Hope was fiddling through her closet, trying to find something to wear. Faith started jumping up and down, telling Hope how excited she was.

"Calm down," said Hope. "You look like you're going to have a nervous breakdown!"

Faith started laughing. "I feel like it! I just can't wait to get over there and see what it looks like and what the manager has to say!"

"I know," said Hope, "but seriously, you need to calm down!"

The girls laughed at each other and Faith went downstairs to wait for her dad to get home. She was fidgety all morning and afternoon pacing the floors. She cleaned up the kitchen and then went upstairs to get some boxes ready. Time was flying by. She happened to glance at the clock, and it was already one thirty. Finally, she saw her dad pull into the driveway, home a bit earlier than expected.

"I'm taking a quick shower and then we'll leave shortly," he said.

"Okay," said Faith. She quickly called Brandi and told her that they'd be picking her up soon. Faith didn't know who was more excited—her or Brandi! She could hear Hope playing her music and went in her room.

"We'll be leaving soon," Faith announced and went back downstairs to wait anxiously in the kitchen.

Tom came downstairs. Faith spun around and asked, "Are we going now?"

"Yes, Faith, just give me five minutes, okay?"

Faith yelled for Hope to come down and the girls ran outside to wait by the car. Tom came out, and they headed over to Brandi's, who was already waiting on the front porch swing. She yelled to her mom, "Faith's here! I'll be home in a little while," and went running down the steps to the car.

Tom noticed how pumped up the girls were and was genuinely happy to take them over to the apartment. He knew which one they wanted to get and headed that way.

"I get to pick the first bedroom," said Faith.

"How come?" asked Brandi.

"Well, because it was my idea!" said Faith.

"That's works for me!" said Brandi, smiling warmly at her best friend.

The ride over to the apartment took about twenty minutes, and during that time Tom told the girls that they'd have to fill out an application and the manager would have some questions for them. As they pulled into the complex, Tom drove around until he saw the office sign and found a parking place right up front. They all got out of the car and went into the office.

At the desk, an older lady with a big smile said, "Good afternoon, my name is Sarah, can I help you?"

"Yes please, my name is Faith, and this is my friend Brandi. We'd like to look at your two-bedroom apartments."

"Will it be the two of you?" Sarah asked. "Yes ma'am," replied Faith. "By the way, this is my sister Hope and our dad Tom."

"Nice to meet you all," said Sarah. "Now if you'll follow me, the model apartment is just a couple of doors down."

Faith and Brandi were giggly and couldn't wait to get inside. Sarah got her keys and headed out the door with everyone following. They arrived at the model apartment, and the girls were like coiled springs until Sarah opened the door.

"Go in and look around," invited Sarah. "When you're done, please meet me back at the office."

"Yes ma'am," the girls nearly shouted in unison.

When the door opened, Faith already knew this was going to be her new home. She entered with Brandi on her heels, both scurrying through the apartment.

"The downstairs is perfect," Brandi said.

"I agree," said Faith. The bottom floor was fixed up nicely and had a kitchen, separate dining room, a living room and a half bath. The girls loved it.

"Time to go upstairs," said Faith as she ran up the steps to two bedrooms and a full bath. Faith quickly glanced in each bedroom and said, "I want this one!" pointing to the bedroom at the top of the steps.

"Okay," said Brandi, "I guess this one is mine!" Both were happy with their rooms, though they would have been happy with anything.

Hope said, "Hey, where am I going to sleep when I come over?"

"We'll figure out something," said Faith. "There's plenty of room!"

They all went back downstairs, and Faith asked Tom, "So, what do you think, Dad?"

"Well, I think it's a very nice apartment," he responded.

"It is," said Faith. "The only thing we don't have is a couch or kitchen table, but I'm sure we'll get them soon."

Tom looked at the girls and said, "You remember the couch and leather loveseat that I have in the garage, don't you?"

"Yes," said Faith.

"If you all would like to have them, they're yours." Faith and Brandi looked at each other and yelled YES at the same time.

"Now all you need is a kitchen table," Hope said.

"Oh, I'm sure we'll find one somewhere," Faith responded.

"Time to go to the office to talk to Sarah," said Tom.

Hope, Faith, and Brandi grinned from ear to ear as they rejoined Sarah.

"What are your thoughts?" she asked.

"We love it!" The girls said at the same time.

"Well then, let's sit down and get some paperwork started."

They all sat down, and Sarah went over the paperwork with the girls. After she took all the information, she noted that the girls were first-time renters without established credit.

"What does that mean?" asked Faith as she felt her heart slowly sink.

"It just means that I'll need someone to co-sign the rental agreement," explained Sarah.

Faith turned to her dad, and he saw the concern in her eyes.

"These are two responsible young ladies," he told Sarah. "If you need a co-signer, I'll be happy to do so."

Faith reached over and gave him a big hug. "Thank you, Dad."

Brandi got up, hugged him and thanked him as well.

"Okay then," said Sarah, "I'll need the girls to sign here and here." She pointed to the x marks on the papers. "When the girls are finished signing, I'll need you to sign at the bottom on the co-signer line," she told Tom. "Then I'll call you tomorrow afternoon and let you know if everything checks out."

Everyone stood. Tom told Sarah, "I'll be waiting for your call." After shaking hands, they loaded back into the car.

BEHIND CLOSED DOORS

Faith asked Tom, "What exactly is a co-signer?"

He explained, "If you don't pay the rent, I'm responsible for it. You girls will be paying the rent every month, now won't you?"

"Yes Dad," said Faith.

"Of course," said Brandi.

"Good! That's all I wanted to hear," said Tom.

"Hey Hope," Brandi yelled from the back seat, "Are you going to come over and help us move?"

"Yes," she answered. "I think it'll be a lot of fun!"

"That's great, and yes, it will be fun!" agreed Brandi.

They soon arrived at Brandi's house and dropped her off. Both she and Faith had to work the next day and had the same shift.

"I'll pick you up tomorrow," Faith told Brandi.

"Okay," said Brandi. "I'm going in to tell Mama everything. See you tomorrow!"

Tom backed out of the driveway and headed home.

"I can't wait to tell Mom," Faith said with a huge grin.

"Remember, we have to wait on Sarah to call and make sure everything went through," he commented.

"I know," replied Faith. "I'm just going to tell Mom all about the apartment."

Tom pulled into the driveway, and Faith ran into the house and up to her room. She started pulling boxes out of her closet to see what all was in them. The first box held dinner plates, and she noted that with a felt marker.

Hope came in and said, "Don't you think you're rushing things a bit?"

"Not at all," said Faith. "I really feel like I'm going to get the apartment!" She continued to pull boxes out and go through them.

Hope closed the door and went downstairs. Faith wondered if Hope was unhappy with her for leaving, so she hollered down the steps for her to come back up for a minute.

"Hey, anytime you want to come over, you can," said Faith. "You can even move in with us. You know that, right?"

"Thanks," said Hope. "I'm sure I'll be over from time to time." She sat on Faith's bed and watched her go through her things. Faith was starting to feel bad that Hope would not be moving in with her and Brandi. She knew Hope was getting the brunt of Tom's abuse, especially when they went out of town.

"You know Dad would get mad at me if I moved out with you," said Hope.

"So what?" said Faith. "You're eighteen and can do what you want!"

"I know, but I don't have a job, and I'm still working with him. I'll just see how it goes."

"Okay," said Faith, "but remember, anytime, okay?"

"Okay," said Hope as she leaned over to look at the contents of some boxes.

"There are a few more in the attic," Faith said as she heard their mom arrive home. She quickly ran downstairs yelling, "Mom! Mom! We just got back about an hour ago from seeing the apartment! It's so nice!"

Emily could see that her daughter was all worked up. "Well, that's absolutely wonderful. Tell me what it looked like."

Faith described every detail. "We both love it, Mom!"

Emily was all smiles. She could feel the joy coming from Faith. "I can't wait to go see it."

"I can't wait either," said Faith. "The lady is supposed to call tomorrow and let us know if we're approved, and if we are, we can move in this weekend!"

"Well, I'm sure you all will get it," said Emily. "You and Brandi have been working for a while now and are pretty responsible."

Faith smiled and ran back upstairs and retrieved the rest of the boxes from the attic. After stacking them in her room, she flopped on the bed and called Brandi. The girls gabbed away for about two hours and hung up. Pretty soon Faith noticed the aroma of dinner filling her bedroom. Dinner was ready! She ran downstairs, and all she could talk about during dinner was how she couldn't wait until tomorrow to hear from Sarah.

"What time do you work tomorrow?" asked Emily.

Faith replied, "I have an early shift. Brandi and I both work nine to five. I'm picking her up in the morning, so I guess I won't find out until I get home. I'm going to be curious all day!"

Hope said, "If Sarah calls early enough, I'll drive up to your work and let you know."

"Oh wow! I didn't even think of that! That's a great idea," said Faith. "Thank you for thinking of that! Oh, Hope, I'm just so excited I can't think straight!"

When it was time to go to bed, Faith laid there with her eyes wide open. She put her hands together to pray and said, *Oh God, please let Brandi and me get that apartment! Please!* Then she went on to her usual prayer. She never left Hope out, always wanting to be together and someday raising their children together. Sometimes she'd lay there and actually see her and her sister living a few houses from each other and babysitting each other's children, and doing things together. Before she fell asleep, she locked her door. Then she pulled the blankets back and crawled into bed and was soon slumbering, exhausted from a long and exhilarating day.

It seemed like only a couple of hours had gone by when she heard the alarm go off. Startled, she reached over and slammed the button on the clock radio. *Ugh,* she thought, *it feels like I just went to sleep.* She laid there for a few minutes gathering her thoughts, and then flung the blankets off and went to take a shower and get ready for work. As the sleepy-eyed Faith walked to the bathroom, she remembered this was the day that Sarah would be calling. Suddenly, she was wide awake, and the excitement began all over again. She showered, dressed, and ran downstairs to brew coffee, almost spilling it coming back up the stairs due to the eagerness she was feeling. It didn't take her long to dry her hair, put on makeup and dress for work. In fact, this was accomplished in record time. She could hardly wait until five o'clock!

***

Hope had already started her day with Tom. Today they would work in town, and it was not going to be a long day. Faith headed out the door to pick up Brandi. As soon as Brandi got in the car, the girls screamed with joy! They did a high five and were so full of energy!

"I can't wait," said Brandi.

"I can't either," screamed Faith. "Hope told me that if Sarah calls and leaves a message by the time she and Dad get home, she'll to drive up to our work and let us know!"

"That's awesome," said Brandi!

The two girls were at the cash registers, chatting so much to each other that the manager came out and moved Faith down three registers so they could concentrate on their work.

"Both of you are talking too much, and it doesn't look professional," said the manager.

"We know," said the girls together. Faith explained, "We're waiting to hear from the apartment manager to let us know if we'll be getting our new apartment."

"Well, neither of you get off work until five, so let's try and focus more on your work, okay?"

"Yes, ma'am," said the girls as they grinned at each other. "I hope today is a busy day," said Faith, "so the time will go by faster!

It did turn out to be a busy day, and the girls were glad! Every customer commented on Faith's attitude that morning. They could tell she was beaming and full of energy! Quite a few customers asked her what was going on, and she must have told fifty people the exciting news. Everyone wished her luck, and that made her happy. Lunchtime rolled around, and the manager closed off Brandi's line so she could go to lunch first. During the quiet times when there were no customers, Faith silently prayed and asked God to please let the apartment go through.

During a slow period, the manager told Faith to go in the back room and start working on a variety of stock. Faith closed off her line and walked into the back room, as the manager told the other two checkers to call for Faith if they needed her. Faith could feel the silence in the stock room. It felt good to her. She got the cart ready, grabbed the label gun and headed back out to the aisle to start on the stock. Faith liked this quiet time away from the registers. She focused on getting everything labeled and put in its right place. It wasn't long before the manager told her to go to lunch. "I'm sending Brandi to work on the cart," she announced.

Faith put down the label gun and went to the deli while Brandi started on the rest of the stock. Faith ordered a sandwich and drink, and went into the break room. A couple of other employees were at lunch, as well, and they started chatting with each other. It was already a little after one in the afternoon, and Faith kept watching the clock as each minute passed.

Meanwhile, Brandi was reaching the top of the shelves putting up stock when someone came behind her and yelled "Boo!" She spun around to see who it was and heard Hopes' all-too-familiar laugh!

"You scared the crap out of me," said Brandi.

"Yes, that was a good one," said Hope, laughing. "I just got home from work and ran in the house to check the recorder, and Sarah left a message." Hope looked a little sad.

Brandi said, "Oh no, we didn't get the apartment, did we?"

"Well …" said Hope, "Sarah said …" She paused for a dramatic effect as Brandi stared at her. Then Hope lifted her head up and said with a shrill voice, "You all got the apartment!"

Brandi playfully slapped Hope on the arm. "You had me worried!" she said, jumping up and down with excitement and keeping her hand over her mouth so no one could hear her. She glanced down the aisle to make sure the manager wasn't around.

"I was looking for Faith, but didn't see her," said Hope.

"She's upstairs on lunch," said Brandi. "You need to go up there and tell her!" She could hardly contain herself and thanked God for the good news!

Hope walked quickly up to the break room and decided to fool her sister just like she fooled Brandi. Hope loved playing tricks on people. It made her laugh and laugh! As she got to the top of the steps, she put on a serious face and approached Faith, who looked up and knew Hope was there with the news.

"Oh my gosh!" said Faith. "What did Sarah say?"

Hope glanced at the floor and said, "Well Faith, I just don't know what to say." She continued to stare at the floor and knew Faith was probably getting ready to cry, so she looked up and continued, "I don't know what to say, Faith, except ..." she paused for a moment.

"Yes Hope? What?" Faith was getting nervous. "What Hope?"

Hope busted out, "You got the apartment!"

Faith squealed with joy! "I'm going to kick your butt for making me think that we didn't!"

Hope laughed and told Faith she did the same thing to Brandi. The girls laughed quite a bit, and Hope sat down with her sister until she finished lunch.

Facing Hope, Faith said "See, I told you that we were going to get it! I knew it!" Faith could not wait until she was off work to make plans.

Hope said, "Sarah says you can move in this weekend since Monday is the first of the month."

Faith crammed the rest of the sandwich in her mouth. "I have to get back to work. Thank you, Hope, for coming up here and telling me the good news!" She looked at her watch and noticed she had three more hours left of work, and could hardly wait to punch the clock to go home. As she came down the steps, she saw Brandi in the check stand. They both knew what the other was thinking and grinned from ear to ear. Faith got back to her check stand and could feel herself shaking. It was a good shake!

***

Five o'clock rolled around, and both girls quickly punched out and got in the car. They hugged each other and were raring to go!

"By the way, Brandi, Hope told me that Sarah said we can move in this weekend. I'm going to start packing up as soon as I get home," said Faith. It was Thursday, and the girls had planned on getting everything ready and move in on Saturday. "Get your stuff ready, and I'll let you know what time we can head over there. We'll both pack our cars with as much stuff as possible, and Dad has the van to load the furniture in."

"Sounds like a plan," said Brandi.

"I'll call you with all of the details," said Faith.

"Well, I have to work on Saturday, but I'll ask the manager if I can have off," said Brandi. "I have no idea how you got to have the weekend off!"

Faith reminded Brandi that she had to work the last weekend, so they gave her this one off. *Perfect timing,* thought Faith.

"I'll call you later," Brandi shouted as she got out of the car.

"Okay," said Faith.

When she pulled up to her house, she ran inside and straight to her room to rip off her smock and kick off her shoes. She started pulling boxes out of her closet and stacking them in the hallway. Hope was in the backyard and came inside to see her.

"Holy Moly, Faith, slow down a little!" She could see that her sister was in high gear.

"I'm just beside myself," she told Hope. "I'm so excited; I can hardly stand it!"

"I can see that," said Hope. "Do you want me to help you?"

"That's okay," Faith said. "Everything is already in boxes, and I won't start loading my car until Friday after work. You can help me then if you like."

"I will!" said Hope. She went downstairs and looked for something to fix for dinner. Emily wouldn't be home till around seven thirty, and Hope thought she would find something for everyone. Hope was a natural cook. Everything she made tasted so yummy!

Faith couldn't wait until her mom got home so she could tell her the good news. Faith was so busy getting things in order, that she didn't realize how fast the time went by. Emily came into her room and saw boxes everywhere!

"Well, hi Faith! By the look of things, I'm assuming you got the apartment?"

Faith stood up and shouted, "Yes, Mom, we did!"

Emily could see her eyes beaming and was so happy for her. It was going to be different now that Faith was moving out. While she worried about adjusting to her not being at home, she smiled at her daughter and said, "Congratulations!"

"Thanks, Mom, I can't wait!"

"Oh my, something smells good," said Emily. "I wonder what Hope is cooking up?"

"I don't know," Faith said, "but it sure smells good! I'm just too excited to eat right now."

Emily went back downstairs and saw Hope fixing her plate. "What did you make?" she asked.

"I made some baked spaghetti and garlic bread. It's ready, Mom. Come on and fix your plate."

"Where's your dad?" Emily asked.

"I think …"

Before she could finish, Tom entered the house.

"Dinner is ready," Emily told him.

"I thought so. I could smell it out in the garage," he said.

The three sat down to eat while Faith stayed upstairs getting things ready for her big day.

***

After dinner, Tom went upstairs to Faith's room to see what she was doing.

"Will you help me get my bed and dresser out of my room on Saturday?" she asked.

"Of course," said Tom.

"Thanks, Dad. I'll get all the boxes together."

"We'll load as much as we can in your car first thing Saturday morning," he said, "So be ready."

"I will," said Faith. "Don't you worry about that!"

Tom left her room, and Faith picked up the phone to call Brandi before she went to bed. Both girls were working the next day, and Faith thought she'd better get some sleep because she knew she was going to have a busy weekend. She went downstairs and told everyone goodnight, and then went back to her room. As soon as she closed her door, she locked it and then put on her pajamas and crawled into bed. Eyes closed and hands folded, she said her usual prayer and included a big thank you to God for her new apartment.

Chapter 19: A Home of Her Own

"Every day is a journey, and the journey itself is home."
~ Matsuo Basho

Saturday morning came, and Faith awoke early to the beautiful sound of chirping birds. They were telling her that today was moving day! It was 5:15 and still dark outside. She tossed the covers off and got out of bed, turned her nightstand light on and began dressing. She could hear her parents downstairs talking.

Tom and Emily always got up early, usually around four a.m. every morning. As five-thirty approached they could hear that Faith was now awake. As they were drinking coffee and talking about the busy day ahead, Emily said, "Faith is pretty responsible." At that moment, Faith came running down the stairs. "Good morning! I need coffee!" She grabbed a cup and told Tom, "I'm going to start loading my car with the boxes from my room." She took a long sip of coffee and added, "Mom, the coffee tastes really good this morning."

Emily smiled and said, "Yes, and I'm on my second cup already!" She was proud of her work ethic and loved the early morning hours.

"Do you have to work today, Mom?" asked Faith.

"Yes, honey, I do. I'll be leaving here at eight fifteen this morning. You have fun moving today."

"I sure will," said Faith as she sat down for a bit to finish her coffee. It was starting to get light outside. She sipped the last bit in her cup and put it in the sink, and then dashed back upstairs to grab one or two boxes at a time and out to her car. The twins were pretty strong due to working with Tom and lifting a lot of boxes since they were six years old. It didn't take her long to fill her car up. It was loaded back and front and even in the trunk.

Hope finally got up and asked, "Need any help?"

"Well, there's a few more boxes left. Can you put them in your car?"

"Sure," said Hope.

They loaded the rest of the boxes, and both cars were full. The only things left were the bedroom furniture. Faith rested a few minutes and then asked Tom, "When will you be ready to load the furniture?"

"I need to get my screwdrivers and take the bed apart. Why don't you girls get all the dresser drawers out and stack them outside, and then we can take the dressers out," answered Tom.

It didn't take Faith long to go back upstairs to get started. One by one, the girls removed the drawers and stacked them near the van. Tom took the bed apart and taped the bed frame together. They all loaded the van and still had a small stockpile to move.

"It looks like we're going to have to make another trip," said Tom. "When we come back, we'll load that up and then head over to Brandi's and get her things."

They went inside to get some water and Faith called Brandi.

"We're moving stuff to the apartment," she announced. "Are you ready?"

"Of course I'm ready!" said Brandi. "I've been up since four this morning! My car is packed, so I'll meet you over there."

"Okay," said Faith. "We'll be leaving in twenty minutes. See you there!"

Brandi hung up the phone and sat with her mom for a few minutes before leaving.

After a while, Tom came in and said to the girls, "Let's go!"

Both girls grabbed their car keys and purses and ran to their cars.

Tom said, "Drive behind me."

"Okay," they yelled as they both started their cars.

Tom pulled out of the driveway, and the girls quickly fell in behind him. Faith had never been happier! This was a dream come true, and all she could think about was moving into her apartment. *This will be my first night in my own place,* she thought with a huge smile on her face!

Thank you, God! Thank you! It wasn't long before they pulled up, and Brandi was already outside to greet them.

"I beat you!" she said, smirking at Faith.

"You're so funny, Brandi," Faith said. "I'm just too excited to even care! I'm just glad we're here!"

"Me too," Brandi smiled.

Tom told the girls to help with unloading the van first. They all worked together, and before they knew it, all of Faith's bedroom furniture was upstairs in place. The girls started unloading the cars. Faith told Hope to put all of the kitchen boxes in the dining room up against the wall so she could unload them later.

"I can't wait to get my bedroom furniture, and guess what? Mama gave us a kitchen table!" said Brandi.

Faith yelled out, "Thank you! Now we have everything we need! After we're done here, we'll head over to your house."

Soon everything was unloaded, and Brandi told Tom, "Everything is in my garage just waiting to be loaded."

"We'll head to your house now and get all of your things," he said.

Once again everything was loaded up. Tom gave Hope some money and told her to stop off and get them something to eat. Hope wrote down everyone's order and told them she'd see them back at the apartment. Tom and the girls made it to the apartment and started unloading again. After a while, Hope drove up, and they all took a lunch break. The girls wolfed their meals down quickly because they wanted to finish up and start organizing.

***

Faith got the kitchen boxes and put the contents away. She wanted to cook breakfast in the morning and wanted everything she needed out of the boxes.

"Bye, girls," said Tom.

Faith and Brandi hugged him and thanked him for helping with the move. *He was so normal in so many ways…* Faith thought to herself.

Faith looked at Hope and asked, "Are you going to stay?"

Hope said, "No, not tonight. I have a date."

"Okay, Hope. I'll see you soon. Have fun on your date!"

As Tom and Hope walked out the door, Faith and Brandi collapsed on the couch, just looking at each other with twinkles in their eyes!

"I cannot believe I'm finally out of the house," Faith said. "It feels so strange but so wonderful, all at the same time."

The girls sat and talked for a while.

"I'm going to call Danny to let him know we're moved in," said Brandi.

"I'm going to take a shower and get into bed," Faith told Brandi. The feeling of getting her own towels and getting in her own shower was something she never experienced before. It was peaceful. It was freeing. It was relaxing. Those feelings made way to a memory that crept its way into her mind. Once, a while back at home, she noticed a hole in the tile around the shower handle. She turned off the water, opened the bathroom door, and then opened the linen closet. Squatting down, she could see the bathtub through the hole—a hole made by her dad so he could peek at whoever got in the shower. After that discovery, Faith covered up the hole with a wet washcloth, sealing it so he couldn't see. *I don't have to worry about that anymore,* she thought with a sigh of relief. Still, her mind was trained to look for holes in shower and bathroom walls, which was something she'd do for the rest of her life. She had actually encountered a few over the years, especially in gas station bathrooms and sometimes hotel rooms. Anytime this happened the memories came flooding back, and she always found a way to seal the hole.

Her mind quickly shifted to her own shower in her own apartment, and the peaceful feelings came flooding back as the water sprayed all over her. *This is the longest shower I've ever taken,* she realized. She got dressed and went into her bedroom, then scooted around a few things and admired her surroundings. She could hear Brandi downstairs still talking to Danny.

Faith yelled down the steps, "Good night." Then she crawled into bed and was relieved she didn't have to worry about her dad coming in her room late at night. Even at her new apartment, she kept her door closed. It made her feel safe. She stared at her bedroom door with a peace that she had never felt before. *It's finally done. It's finally over,* she thought and closed her eyes. She said her usual prayer: *Now I lay me down to sleep, I pray the Lord my soul to keep. If I should die before I wake, I pray thee Lord my soul to take. Bless mother and father, sister and brother, Aunt Jennifer, Jesus and the angels, bless Brandi, all my friends and everybody in the whole wide world. And God, please watch out for Hope and remember that when we get older and have kids, to let us live close by so we can raise our kids together. Thank you, God, for my beautiful apartment! I love it! Amen.*

As she drifted off to sleep, she had no clue that it really wasn't over. Although her dad wouldn't be coming in her room, the years of being violated remained within her mind and heart. From here on, day after day, all the wounds bottled up inside her would poke through from time to time, rearing ugly heads. Faith didn't realize how much she had buried—all the hurt and pain—keeping them locked away in a safe place. Her feelings had never seemed to matter. There were many trigger words that her friends, boyfriends, and people, in general, would say or do that struck a chord or haunted her full force, stirring up anguished memories. However, when the memories stirred she never told anyone, and they kept getting suppressed deeper and deeper. Later they manifested in all sorts of ways, like yelling, slamming things and losing her cool very quickly. Faith just always assumed that her lashing out was because she had a bad temper. But in truth it all came from a psyche scarred from abuse, rather than a bad temper or some flaw in her character.

For the first time, she slept soundly. She wasn't awakened and didn't sleep restlessly as she did at home. She didn't have to worry anymore. Before she knew it, she was opening her eyes to a brand new morning, well-rested. She lay in bed for a few moments, enjoying the peace and quiet. It was a wonderful feeling to be on her own—and safe. *This is what it's like. I love it!* She couldn't help but think of her sister back home. *I really want Hope to come over,* she thought as she got out of bed and stretched.

Faith opened her door and quickly went into Brandi's bedroom. "Wake up!" she screamed. Brandi rolled over and glared. "I was sleeping so good," she said.

"Well, not anymore! Let's go downstairs and fix our first cup of coffee and our first breakfast," she yelled.

"All we have is cereal," said Brandi.

"That's okay," said Faith. "It's still our first breakfast in our own place!" She reached over and grabbed the blankets off Brandi. "Now get up!"

The girls laughed, and Brandi told Faith, "Payback is hell, and I'm going to get you for waking me up!" The girls giggled and ran downstairs like little children on Christmas morning. Faith fixed a pot of coffee and Brandi got the bowls, milk, and cereal out and set them on the table. They both sat at the kitchen table and couldn't believe how fast everything had flown by.

"Just think," said Faith, "yesterday we were both still living at home, and now today we have our very own apartment!"

Brandi smiled and nodded as she shoved cereal into her mouth. The coffee was finally ready, and Faith poured herself a cup and sat back down. "We have a lot of unpacking to do today, and cleaning up."

"I know," said Faith. "After breakfast, I'll start unpacking, and if you want, you can go to the store to pick up some things that we need."

"Sounds like a plan," said Brandi. The girls enjoyed their simple breakfast and Brandi went back upstairs to get dressed. Faith cleaned up and started going through boxes and putting all the dishes in the dishwasher. She was having the time of her life! It was fun and relaxing just going through box after box.

Pretty soon, Brandi came downstairs with pen and paper in her hand. "Hey Faith, come over here and let's make a list of what we need."

The girls sat down and made a shopping list. Faith reached into her purse and handed Brandi some money. "We'll just split everything down the middle," she said.

"That's fine with me," Brandi agreed. She finished up her coffee and went out the door.

Both Faith and Brandi had to work the next day. Brandi had the earlier shift and Faith had the late shift. The next few days went by quickly, and the girls worked very hard at getting their home in order. It wasn't long before Faith was at the stove learning to whip up new meals. She enjoyed cooking and exploring new recipes. She already knew how to make quite a few culinary dishes by now.

***

One night while Faith was working, a customer named Parker came in as he usually did. He was a regular customer and seemed to have taken an interest in Faith. He always picked on Faith and Brandi, and they always gave it back. He had a great sense of humor, and the girls didn't cut him any slack. He liked that. Faith enjoyed seeing him, and they laughed while he was there. If Faith wasn't busy, she'd chat with him.

As they were standing there, Parker asked, "Would you like to go get dinner one night?"

"Why yes!" Faith said with a big smile. "That sounds awesome!"

Parker wrote his number on a piece of paper and handed it to her and told her to call him. She felt all tingly inside and couldn't wait to go out on a date. She had gone out with a few guys before, but was single now.

After Faith and Parker went out on a number of occasions, their relationship became serious. Faith went over to his house most of the time because he was raising his five-year-old son. Whenever his son went to his mom's house and Parker wasn't busy, he stayed the night with Faith. Every time they were intimate, there was always something that reminded Faith of her dad. This bothered her terribly. Individual memories of her dad came back to haunt her, and she could not get it out of her mind. She just held it all in and continued the intimacy with Parker, never letting him know the secrets she was hiding. In fact, she didn't let anyone know. In her mind, she knew that this was the way it was going to be the rest of her life and she would just have to deal with it the best she could. She didn't realize that it was eating at her. Faith became accustomed to shifting her thinking to something else in order to cope with the feelings.

By now, Faith and Brandi had lived in their apartment for a few months and were really enjoying their new life! There were so many fun times they would never forget, even well into their future years. But there were lessons, too. Once Brandi went to visit Danny after hearing that her favorite band was playing in concert at the coliseum. Brandi called Faith and told her she was buying the tickets and would wait for Faith to drive up the next day. Faith always loved driving. She turned the radio up full blast and sang her little heart out. She finally got to Danny's house, and she and Brandi primped a while before leaving for the concert.

They left early to beat the crowd. As they walked around the bottom of the coliseum, the crew for the band waved them over and started talking to them, asking where they were from and other small talk.

"Do you want backstage passes?" the lighting director for the band asked them.

They yelled, "Of course we do!"

The guy leaned over and gave them both the passes. "Follow me," he said.

The girls were excited! They had never had backstage passes before. He took them behind the stage and then outside.

"Where are we going," Faith asked?

"I'm taking you out to the band's bus, and you can meet them," he responded.

Faith and Brandi looked at each other in amazement. They could hardly wait!

The lighting director took them on the bus. The band was there along with some of the road crew. A few were drinking and smoking weed. The girls sat down and introduced themselves as one of the guys passed a joint to them. They smoked just a little and had a drink and laughed and partied with them until the band had to go on stage. They were having a grand time and thinking *this is living!*

When the band was ready to go on stage, the lighting director took the girls up there and told them where to stand so they would be out of the way. They were on the stage the whole time until the concert had ended. The girls tapped their feet and sang some songs while the band was playing. They had the time of their lives! After the concert was over, they were invited out to dinner and accepted. Everyone was so very nice, and they had such a great time. They left the concert and went back to Danny's, and Faith stayed with them for a couple of days.

Little did they know that work was trying to call both of them to come in because they were short of help. There wasn't anyone back home who knew where they were because they just packed up and left on the spur of the moment. They didn't think of telling anyone. After all, they had their own apartment and didn't even think to say anything to anybody.

When the girls were ready to come home, Faith said, "We should follow each other on the road." It was a two-hour drive, and as they were pulling into the parking lot, Faith saw her dad standing by his car. He walked towards her with an angry look on his face, which frightened her. She never knew what he was going to do when he was angry. As she got out of the car, Brandi had already parked and was getting out of her car too.

Tom screamed, "Where have you two girls been?"

"I went to stay with Brandi at Danny's apartment, so we could go to a concert," Faith explained.

Brandi could see that Faith was scared and stood beside her, piping up to say, "We didn't do anything wrong. Our favorite band was playing, and we wanted to see them."

Tom began to scold them. "I don't care where you go, what I care about is that you let me know where you are so I don't worry. Your work has been calling both of you, and they were worried just like the rest of us. The next time you all decide to go out of town, you have to let someone know!"

Faith just wanted to agree with him so he'd stop yelling. "Okay Dad," she said. "We didn't even think about telling anyone, but yes, if we ever go out of town again, we'll let you know."

Tom turned around and got in his car and left. Faith and Brandi went into the apartment and understood what he was saying, but on the other hand, they felt that they were out on their own and didn't have to answer to anyone. But they both agreed that it was the safest thing to do. Faith knew that Tom was right, and this was "normal-dad stuff" but still couldn't help but resent his control. The girls went into the apartment, and chilled out for a while. They talked about how much fun they had and laughed and reminisced all evening.

Both girls worked the same shift the next day, so they rode together. When they came into the store, the manager and a couple of other employees all shouted, "Where have y'all been?"

"Wow, we go off for two days, and everyone is having a hissy fit," said Brandi.

The manager looked at both of the girls and said, "It isn't like you to leave for a couple of days and not say anything to anyone. We were all just concerned and glad that you two are back safe and sound."

The girls both realized that everyone was right. They apologized and said it would never happen again. Then they clocked in and went to work. It felt good to have work friends who cared and were happy they were back.

While living on her own for the very first time, Faith made the huge decision to no longer smoke pot. It was a crutch she no longer needed, and she made this promise to herself while she was still just seventeen.

***

Faith noticed that Parker wasn't coming in the store as much and seemed to have excuses for not going out. She could tell that something was up. One night he came over to Faith's place and seemed to be acting somewhat distant. She never did say anything to him about it. He didn't stay the night and left after a few hours. They said goodbye, and she felt like it would be goodbye forever.

After work one late afternoon, Faith decided to go over to Parker's house without calling him first. As she got closer to his house, she noticed a woman getting into her car and leaving. As the woman left, Parker looked up and saw Faith heading his way. She saw the surprised look on his face as she pulled up in the driveway and knew something was wrong. In fact, she knew in her gut that he was seeing this woman—she could feel it all over.

"Who was that?" she asked as she got out of her car.

"Who?" said Parker.

"The woman who just left."

"Oh," said Parker, stuttering. "That's a friend of mine at school. I let her borrow a book she needed for a class."

Faith could tell he was lying. She could feel it. He started walking into his house as she followed close behind. "So, Parker, do you want to tell me who that really is?"

Parker turned around and said, "I just told you who she is."

Faith told him straight up that she didn't believe a word he said. He got angry and told her that she could just leave, which surprised her. He had never behaved like that before, and she decided right then and there that the relationship was over.

How could he do this to me? she thought. *How could he just not care about my feelings and do this behind my back?*

She looked at Parker and said, "I'm not going to see you anymore."

"Fine!" said Parker as he led her to the door.

Faith pushed the door hard and got to her car. She started the engine with tears in her eyes, and then began crying so hard she could hardly back up. She looked at Parker one last time as she drove away. He didn't seem to care. She was so hurt and crushed.

After about a week Faith decided she didn't want to hurt anymore. She started dating, but not committing, and really enjoyed not having to answer to anyone. She could go and do as she pleased. One guy she'd been friends broke up with his girlfriend, and she started seeing him for a few weeks. His name was Gary. He came over to Faith's place just as she got off her birth control pills. After about three weeks of seeing each other, Faith found out she was pregnant. Brandi was home at the time Faith took a pregnancy test, and it came out positive.

Faith froze. So many thoughts went through her head, and they were mostly about her dad. She came running downstairs crying, and Brandi asked, "What's wrong?"

Faith handed her the pregnancy test.

"Oh no!" Brandi said. "What are you going to do?"

Even though Faith was nineteen at the time, fear swept over her. All she thought about was how her dad was going to beat her. She imagined her dad punching her in the stomach and started shaking. "Dad is going to kill me!" she shouted to Brandi.

Brandi hugged her and told her to sit and calm down. They both sat on the couch, and all Faith could do was worry about how her dad was going to kill her. Brandi sat with her and comforted her as much as possible. They talked a long time and discussed what Faith was going to do.

"I'm going to bed," Faith said. "I'm physically and emotionally exhausted. I'll see you in the morning. I need some time to think."

"Okay," said Brandi. "I love you. Everything is going to be okay." She hugged Faith and said goodnight, and Faith went to her room. As she laid there with the pregnancy test in her hand, all she could think about was her dad. Images started flashing through her mind. *He'll probably beat me until I lose the baby,* she thought. *He's going to slap me and punch me. He might push me down some steps or slam me against the wall.* The thoughts were getting the best of her, and fear ran through her body. She knew her dad was capable of doing all these things. It was terrifying. She hadn't been this scared in a long time. Trembling, she thought, *What is Gary going to think? What is he going to do?*

Faith put her hands on her stomach. She knew deep inside it was a girl. She could feel it. Thoughts came of her dad molesting her little girl, and then the anger set in. So many emotions ran through her whole body that she just cried herself to sleep. It was a good thing that she was off work the next day. She needed that day to herself so she could figure out what to tell Gary. Brandi worked the early shift and would be home around two.

As Brandi left, she said, "We'll talk when I get back."

"Okay," said Faith. "I'm going to call Gary sometime after you leave."

"Good luck, Faith. I'll see you this afternoon." She left, and Faith sat at the kitchen table in a slight trance.

She worried all day about what her dad was going to do to her and burned off nervous energy by cleaning up the apartment and cleaning up her room. By the time Brandi got home, the whole apartment was clean.

"Wow!" said Brandi. "The apartment looks great! I see you've been busy!"

"I just couldn't sit still," Faith said.

Brandi could see how upset Faith was and told her to come in the living room and sit down and talk. "Have you figured out what you're going to do?"

"Well," said Faith, "I can't tell my dad. He'll kill me, and I'm so scared. The other option is to have an abortion." She felt at the time that was the best thing to do.

"Have you talked to Gary yet?" asked Brandi.

"No," said Faith. "I just wanted to figure this out before I call him."

The girls talked for a long time, and Faith decided to have an abortion. She was too scared to tell her dad. She looked up the number for the clinic nearby and made an appointment. It was for the following week. She called work and took off that day and the next five days and told them it was important. The manager said it was okay, which was a big relief for Faith. The next thing she had to do was call Gary.

She looked at Brandi and said, "I'm so nervous and scared to talk to Gary. I wonder what he's going to say. What if he wants to keep the baby? What if he wants to get married?"

"I don't know," Brandi said. "Just call him and take it from there."

"Will you sit with me while I call him?"

"Of course, I will," said Brandi.

"I can't bear to tell him in person," said Faith.

"This is your decision, and you do what feels most comfortable," she advised.

Faith picked up the phone and dialed Gary's number.

"Hey Gary, how are you doing?"

"Hi, Faith! I'm doing great! What's up?"

"Well, I have something to tell you. Do you have a few minutes to talk?"

"Yes, I do. What's going on?"

Faith could feel herself trembling. She didn't want to tell him, but she knew she had to.

"Gary, I just found out I'm pregnant."

There was silence on the phone.

"Gary? Gary?"

"I'm here," Gary said. "I'm just stunned and don't know what to say. I can tell you that I'm not ready to have a child. I've enlisted in the military and leave next week."

At that moment, Faith made the decision. "I thought that you might say that, so I decided to get an abortion. I made an appointment for next week on Thursday."

"I think that's a good idea," said Gary. "I can't afford a child right now."

Faith felt a little relieved, but sorry at the same time. "One more thing Gary. Will you please give me the money for it? I can't afford to do this so quickly."

"Yes, I will," he said. "I'll drop it by before next Thursday. I have to go now."

"Okay," Faith said. "I'll talk to you later."

Gary hung up, and she could tell by the sound of his voice that he was not happy at all. She started crying.

"I'm going to go upstairs for a while Brandi. Thanks for sitting with me."

"You're welcome! That's what friends are for!"

Faith ran up the steps and went to her room. On the one hand, she felt relieved, and on the other hand, she felt sad. She really didn't want to do this but felt she had no choice. Now she wouldn't have to tell her dad anything at all. She could go and get this done, and he wouldn't know a thing. Those thoughts brought her comfort.

A few days went by, and she heard nothing from Gary. She was beginning to worry that he would not help. She called a few times, and he never answered his phone. Day after day she called, and no answer. Her appointment was just around the corner, and she didn't have the extra money to pay for it. She began to worry. By that Wednesday night, she still had not heard from him and called again to leave a message. She was crying and told him she was going to her appointment tomorrow, and to please give her the money.

The next morning, Brandi drove Faith to her appointment. They got there extra early to give Gary yet another chance to bring the money. Faith called again when she got to the clinic.

"Gary, please, I'm at the clinic and ..."

Before she could finish, Gary picked up the phone and said, "I'm on my way."

"Thank you," Faith said. A huge sigh of relief came over her. She and Brandi sat outside waiting for Gary. He pulled up, and Faith walked out to the car. He didn't even get out and had a blank stare on his face. He stuck his arm out the window and gave Faith cash.

"Thank you, Gary. I'm sorry about all of this."

Gary just stared straight ahead. "I have to go," he said. He then rolled up the window and took off. Faith never heard from him again.

The girls entered the clinic and Faith signed in. After about twenty minutes, the nurse called her. She got up and hugged Brandi, who said, "Everything is going to be all right."

Faith was scared. She went back into the room, and the nurse said, "Put on this gown and lay on the table. The doctor will be in shortly."

Faith got undressed and put the gown on and got on the table. Pretty soon the doctor came in and sat down at the end of the table. He had such a non-caring look on his face, and Faith thought he looked mean. He got out a big needle and told Faith that he was going to give her a shot in her uterus to numb it, and then shortly after he would proceed with the abortion. He said all of that with such a cold stare. It made Faith feel so uncomfortable. He started to give her the shot, and Faith scooted up the table reflexively. It hurt badly.

"Scoot back down here!" the doctor yelled.

Faith had tears in her eyes as she scooted back down. He pushed the needle in, and the pain of it was horrible. Faith could feel the tears streaming down the sides of her face. She felt so all alone and began to wonder if this was the right thing to do. Then the fear of her dad finding out filled her body.

"I'm going to start the procedure now," said the doctor.

As soon as he started, the pain was unbearable. Faith started screaming, "I'm not numb! I can feel everything!"

He didn't seem to listen to her and kept on. Two nurses on each side of Faith held her arms down. She felt trapped and was in so much pain that she started fighting the nurses. The doctor hollered for another nurse, who practically laid on Faith to keep her still. It took all three nurses to hold her in place.

Faith was terrified and had never felt pain like that before. She silently prayed and asked God to let it be over. After a couple more minutes, which seemed like forever, the doctor announced he was done. The numbing never took effect. As she laid eyes on the doctor, he maintained the cold look on his face, as if he had no heart and didn't care one bit of what she was going through. He never did comfort her like she thought he would. He never said a word. He just got up and went on to the next girl.

They put Faith in a recovery room and kept a watch on her for a while to make sure she wasn't bleeding. As she laid there, she could hear another girl screaming and crying. The girl kept saying over and over that she had changed her mind, but the doctor continued the procedure. Faith felt so sorry for her and began to think of herself, as well. She kept telling God how sorry she was. But she was terrified of her dad finding out, and it seemed like something she had to do.

After a while, the nurse came in and gave Faith some antibiotics. "You can go home now. Take it easy for the next few days, and you'll probably have some cramping."

Faith took her pills and met Brandi in the waiting room. They drove home, and Faith went straight to bed. She couldn't believe everything that happened.

"If you need anything, just let me know," said Brandi.

"Okay," Faith said. "Thank you for everything!"

Brandi smiled weakly and closed the door. As Faith lay in bed, she started praying. With the tears streaming down her face she said, "God, please forgive me for what I just did." She started crying even harder. "I know my baby is with you now, and she watches over me. She is my guardian angel." Faith named her Angel and cried herself to sleep.

Chapter 20: A Second and Third Home

"Even if you fall on your face, you're still moving forward."
~ Victor Kiam

Faith did well as the weeks went by and had no physical problems. She always felt like her baby was a little girl. It was a strong feeling, but she tried to put it out of her head and went on with life. Her dad never found out, and that made her feel safe. She continued to work and always had so much fun on the job. It was the one place, other than her apartment, that she enjoyed. It was even more enjoyable when she and Brandi worked the same shift. The customers just loved both of them and wanted to go through their lines just to have a laugh. Parker still came in the store from time to time, and they'd chat. They did become friends and stayed in touch for a very long time.

Brandi was traveling out of town more often these days to see Danny. Due to his job, it was easier for her to go there than for him to come to see her. A couple of weeks after Faith had gone to the clinic, she really felt like taking a trip of her own. She asked for a week off of work and planned a vacation to Florida with her friend Tammy. They drove to Disney World, and Faith was ecstatic! It felt like a dream!

The week they spent there was one of the best times Faith ever had. She enjoyed the theme park, which gave her a renewed sense of childhood. This was the childhood she never had! She didn't want to ever leave! All of the Disney characters and the little river rides were just what she needed! Faith and Tammy even went to a luau. They ordered dinner and drinks and watched the native Hawaiian dancers. It was the cherry on top of the ice cream!

Two days into this adventure, they went sightseeing at a wax museum, visited the beach, and browsed a lot of gift shops. Faith was on cloud nine. She didn't want to go back home after falling in love with Florida and that tropical feel. But soon it was time to head back to reality. The girls made the trip back and talked about their vacation experiences the whole way. Both had such a great time!

Faith went back to work the day after they arrived home, and tried to get back into the swing of things. She thought about her trip and Florida for a very long time and wanted to go back as soon as she could. As for Brandi and Danny, they were getting along great. In fact, Brandi announced that she wanted to talk to Faith, and as they both sat down on the couch, she had the most excited look on her face.

"What's up, Brandi?" Faith asked, wanting to hear what she had to say.

"Well," said Brandi, "last night when Danny and I went out to dinner, he asked me to marry him!"

"Oh my God!" responded Faith. "Really? What did you say?"

"I told him yes! I really love him, and he loves me, and we can't wait to get married! As a matter of fact, we're going to get married in May!"

"May?" Faith yelled. "That's two months from now! What are you going to do? Is he moving in here?" Faith's heart was beating fast.

"That's what I wanted to talk to you about. He's getting a transfer out of town, about two hours from here, and we're going to look for an apartment."

Even though Faith loved Brandi and Danny, her heart sank at the thought that Brandi would be leaving. She didn't want her best friend to get married. She thought she was too young. Brandi was eighteen and had just moved out on her own. Faith felt somewhat abandoned.

"We've only had the apartment eight months, Brandi, and you're leaving in two. What am I supposed to do?" said Faith.

"Well, I was wondering if you could find a roommate. If not, then I'll continue to pay my part until you do," said Brandi.

Faith wanted to cry. She couldn't imagine life without Brandi.

"What about Hope?" suggested Brandi.

"I'll ask her, but I don't think she'll want to move in. I'll check with her first and if she says no, I'll check around."

"Okay," said Brandi. She could tell that Faith was upset, although she pretended not to be. The two girls knew each other well. They could always tell what the other one was thinking, and many times could finish each other's sentences. They had been besties since ninth grade and were as close as any two friends could ever be.

Brandi looked at Faith and said, "Faith, you know we'll always be best friends. Just because I'm getting married doesn't change that. We'll always stay in touch with each other, and anytime you want to come to visit, you're more than welcome."

"Thanks," said Faith.

As the girls hugged, Brandi said, "I want you to be my bridesmaid."

"Oh my God, Brandi, of course, I'll be your bridesmaid!" exclaimed Faith.

They talked for a while about the wedding, and then Brandi said she was going to go to bed because she had a big day tomorrow. Faith stayed up until after midnight and then finally went to her room. She closed her door, got her PJ's on, and went to bed. She cried herself silently to sleep—something she knew how to do from a lifetime of experience. She didn't want to wake Brandi or make her feel bad. She knew the next several weeks would be tough while Brandi prepared to leave.

The next day Faith visited her parents and told them about Brandi. Hope wasn't home yet. Emily couldn't believe that Brandi was going to get married. Soon Hope came home, and Faith told her the news. As Emily went downstairs to finish up some laundry, Faith motioned her to go upstairs when she was done. They met in Hope's room, and Faith closed the door.

"Hey Hope, I wanted to ask you if you'd like to move in with me since Brandi will be leaving. We'll have to split everything down the middle." Faith explained the costs.

Hope said, "I'm still not ready to move out yet, but why don't you ask Richard? I think he wants to leave his house, but I'm not sure."

"Okay," said Faith. "I'll give him a call."

Their brother Richard and his wife Vicky divorced, and the girls were living with their mother. He was interested in sharing the apartment, but Faith wasn't sure how it would work out with him being there. However, she really didn't know anyone else who would want to move in.

"Come over tomorrow around one, and we'll sit down and discuss the bills," invited Faith.

"Sounds like a plan," Richard agreed.

***

As Faith walked through her front door the next day, she could hear the music. Brandi had the music turned up loud and was singing. She looked so happy!

"Hey, Brandi! Turn that down! I'm surprised the neighbors haven't complained!"

"Oh, it's not that loud," Brandi said as she went over to the stereo and turned it down.

"Guess what?" said Faith.

Brandi shot her a puzzled look. "What?"

"Richard will be over here in a little while to check out the apartment. I think he's going to move in."

"That's great!" Brandi said. "I'm so glad that you found someone."

"I know, Brandi, but no one could ever take your place."

The girls hugged, and Brandi was relieved. Faith went upstairs to change clothes. While she was in her room, she heard the doorbell and came down the steps. Brandi answered the door.

"Oh, it's you," she said and closed the door in Richard's face. The girls started laughing as she opened the door back up. Richard was laughing too. He didn't expect anything less from Brandi, who always had a fantastic sense of humor and a quick wit.

Faith told Richard, "Well, here it is!" She began showing him around and explained that the bedrooms were upstairs. "Come on up here," she invited and waved her hand at Richard. He followed her up the steps, and Brandi came up behind Richard.

"You're taking over my room," Brandi said as they walked up the flight of stairs. Faith pointed to the bathroom and told him that they would share it. "You better keep it clean!" she yelled. He just turned his head with a smile and shrugged his shoulders. Faith laughed at the antics.

Richard loved the apartment and said, "Okay, let's go downstairs and talk business."

They sat at the table and went over the bills. Richard agreed to everything and then asked Brandi when he could move in.

"Since we're in the middle of the month, I'll go ahead and move, and you can move in on the first to make things easier. Is that okay?"

"That sounds great," Richard said. "I'll move in then."

They all sat for a while, picking on one another and telling jokes, laughing and having a good time.

"I'm going to go. I'll see you on the first," he said. They all said goodbye, and Richard left.

Faith and Brandi looked at each other because they both knew that this was it. They hugged with tears in their eyes.

Faith grabbed Brandi and screamed, "I don't want you to leave; I don't want you to get married!" The girls laughed at each other. "Oh well," Faith said jokingly, "please change your mind," though she meant it. Brandi was her best friend and Faith felt an impending loss.

The girls went out to get something to eat and brought it back to the apartment. They planned on enjoying the little time they had left there. As they ate, Brandi talked about how excited she was to get married and how things had changed so quickly. Faith was truly happy for her, but felt sad at the same time.

Over the next two weeks, the girls worked and spent as much time together as they could. Every time Brandi went to visit Danny, she took some of her belongings with her, so she wouldn't have so much to do when she finally moved. Little by little, Faith watched as Brandi's things left the apartment, and she could feel the tears well up in her eyes. She knew in her heart that they would always be best friends, but there was still a piece of her heart that was hurting. At the time, it felt like another wound had been added to her overly-wounded soul. She left it there and covered it up, as she did with all the pain she had endured.

Faith's emotions got the best of her, and when Brandi's wedding shower day arrived, Faith made other plans so she didn't have to go. At the time, her heart was hurting so much from her internal pain, that she didn't even think of Brandi and how it would make her feel that her best friend—her bridesmaid—was absent from the shower. All Faith wanted to do was go have fun elsewhere and hide the pain. Many years later as they reminisced, Brandi shared her feelings about Faith not being there. For a moment, Faith didn't remember. After she hung up the phone, she went back in time, and then sat in her room and cried over what she did to her best friend. She couldn't believe how selfish she had been and apologized wholeheartedly to Brandi thirty-eight years later. Brandi laughed, saying it was so long ago. But Faith knew how much it had hurt her.

***

Before the girls knew it, it was Brandi's wedding day! Brandi got married at her mom's house, and plenty of guests attended. As Brandi and Faith stood side by side at the ceremony, Faith whispered in her ear, "Are you sure you want to do this?"

The girls silently laughed, and people could see their shoulder bobbing up and down from giggling. The wedding was beautiful, and Faith was very happy for her friend; she knew that Brandi and Danny were a perfect match.

Richard moved in and had been at the apartment for a little over a week. For Faith, it was hard coming home with her best friend not being there. It felt so strange and out of place. Faith worked as much as she could and hung out at her parents' house a lot. Richard's girlfriend Lisa was over a lot at the apartment, and Faith felt like a stranger in her own home. It just wasn't the same.

One night Faith was home, and Brandi called.

"Guess what?" Brandi said.

Faith answered jokingly, "You're leaving Danny and moving back with me?" Both of the girls started laughing.

"No," said Brandi, and then she blurted out "I'm pregnant!"

"What?" Faith yelled. "That didn't take long! Oh, Brandi! I'm so happy for you!"

The girls chatted for a while, and then Brandi mentioned she had to make more phone calls. They said goodbye, and Faith slowly hung up the phone. She couldn't believe how quickly things changed. *What next?* She thought.

Day after day of coming home, Faith felt like the apartment was her brother's and not hers. He came to Faith one day and asked if it would be okay if Lisa moved in and split everything three ways.

Faith told Richard she'd think about it and would let him know in a day or two. She really didn't want to stay in the apartment anymore and thought about moving back home. The next day she drove over to her parents' house and asked them if it would it be okay to move back home. She told her parents how she was feeling about Brandi not being there. She just wasn't happy in the apartment anymore.

Tom and Emily both said that it was fine if she wanted to come back.

"Can I clear out the den and use it as my bedroom?" she asked since they had bought new bedroom furniture for her room when she moved out. Tom and Emily agreed that would be okay.

"Thanks, Mom; thanks, Dad," Faith said. "I'll talk to Richard tonight and see if he and his girlfriend want to take over the lease. If they do, I'll make plans to move back home."

"Alright," said Emily, "just let us know what's going on."

"I will, Mom," Faith said. "I'm going to go home now and talk with Richard. I'll see you later."

Faith left and drove back home with a sigh of relief, hoping that Richard would take over the lease.

Richard and Lisa weren't home when Faith arrived. She turned on some music and cleaned the apartment. It wasn't until after eight that evening that they came strolling in. They had picked up something to eat and sat down at the table.

"Oh good, you two are home," Faith began. "I need to talk to both of you." She pulled up a chair and snatched some of Richards's French fries. He reached over and pretended to smack her hand.

Faith laughed. "You have to be quicker than that!" she said as she shoved the fries in her mouth. "Okay, I have something to ask both of you, so here it goes." She looked at Richard and said, "I was wondering if you two wanted to take over the lease. I want to move back home for a while and save some money."

Richard looked at Lisa and then looked back at Faith. "Let us talk it over, and we'll let you know," he said.

"Okay," said Faith, "but remember, the first of the month is right around the corner, and I would love to be out by then."

"That's fine," Richard said. "We're going upstairs to talk it over."

"Why don't you all finish eating and discuss it here. I need to get a shower and go to bed shortly. I have to work the early shift tomorrow."

"Okay," Richard said. "We may have an answer for you tonight."

"That would be great," Faith shouted as she went upstairs.

Faith had already taken a shower and was in bed when she heard a knock on her door.

"Come on in," she yelled.

Richard and Lisa came in with big smiles on their faces. "We'll take over the lease," said Richard. "You can go ahead and move out."

Faith jumped up in excitement and yelled, "Thank you! We'll go to the office tomorrow after work and take care of all of the paperwork."

"Sounds good to me," Richard said. "I should be home by two thirty."

"See you then! Good night," said Faith.

Richard closed the door and Faith flopped on her bed with the comfort of knowing that she didn't have to stay there anymore. She figured they must have already thought about taking over the lease since they gave her an answer so quickly. It didn't matter—she just wanted to leave. She picked up the phone and called her dad.

"Can you come over this weekend and move me back home?" she asked.

Tom agreed, and Faith assured him she'd be all packed up and ready to go by that Friday night.

During the week Faith went over to her parents and cleaned out the den and got it ready for her to move back in. In a way, it felt good because she knew that her parents wouldn't charge her for living there, and she could put back some money.

As Saturday rolled around, the only thing left to move was her furniture. Her father came and loaded her furniture, then unloaded it at the house.

***

Now that Faith had been out on her own, it was different living at home. During the first couple of weeks, it felt strange being back home. Tom had not molested her for a couple of years now, and it was finally over. Faith still was cautious at all times, though, and anytime she was sleeping and heard a noise, she'd jump and make sure everything was okay. Even with a locked door, she had trained herself to hear every noise in the night. She had learned how to be a survivor. She was prepared and always watching her dad's every move. After all, she had those thoughts constantly on her mind since she could remember. Thankfully, he had changed and never touched her again.

Faith loved her dad very much—she saw the other side of Tom. He always made sure the girls had pretty much everything they wanted. They laughed a lot and told jokes and had a good time. This was sometimes confusing to Faith, because the mixed signals were haunting her. She always loved her parents despite the dysfunction. She even managed to stay with them for three years.

Hope had a real job by now but traveled from time to time with Tom. Faith knew that he was still abusing her sister. Even though the girls were twins, there was a big difference in the two. Faith wanted to get out on her own and was more responsible than Hope. It seemed all Hope wanted to do was be with guys and get whatever she could. Hope went out to bars with her friends quite often, while Faith didn't like the bar scene.

Faith started seeing a guy while she was at home. She had known him for a while, and it wasn't a committed relationship. He took her out to dinner a lot, and she stayed over at his house from time to time. His name was Chuck. He always had weed and smoked joints when they were together. Even though he always handed the joint to Faith, she refused because she had quit smoking weed when she was seventeen. One time when they were watching a movie, he reached into his pocket and pulled out a baggie. He unrolled it and put some white powder on the table.

Faith already knew what it was, but still asked, "Is that cocaine?"

Chuck said, "Yes," and reached over to the end table for a razor blade. He started cutting lines, about ten of them. He removed a hundred-dollar bill from his wallet, rolled it up, snorted two lines, and then handed the bill to Faith. She had never done cocaine before and thought she'd give it a try. Faith snorted one line and then the next. She sat up and smiled at Chuck.

"Oh, I like this!" she said.

"I kind of thought you would," said Chuck said as he smiled back at her.

He then took the bill and did two more lines before handing it back to Faith. They stayed up almost all night and ended up doing quite a bit of coke. Every time they were together now, they would always do this. Faith was liking it more and more.

The next time Chuck came over to Faith's house, they hung out in her room watching TV. Hope came in, and Chuck pulled out the coke and cut some lines on the table. Hope knew what it was because, without Faith's knowledge, she had already tried it with some friends. Hope had a big smile on her face, and they all sat there snorting lines, watching TV, and talking.

Chuck told the girls he had to go and promised Faith they would talk soon. Faith walked him out to the car, and they kissed goodnight. Faith reentered the house and watched TV until she fell asleep. At this point, she was really enjoying her life. After all, she didn't have to pay rent and was able to store up a little savings account. And the cocaine was a nice little side benefit to having a boyfriend.

***

One weekend, Brandi came to town and visited Faith. Her belly was getting bigger and bigger!

"Boy, you look like you're going to pop!" Faith told her as she gave Brandi a big hug.

They talked for a few hours, and then Brandi headed back over to her mom's house. It wasn't a week later, when Brandi called and told Faith she was in labor and going in the hospital. Faith was so excited for her and Danny!

"I'll call you when I can," Brandi told Faith.

Through happy tears, Faith said, "I'm so excited for you, and good luck!"

They hung up the phone and Faith couldn't wait to hear from her again.

Brandi called the next day and told Faith that they had a beautiful baby boy. Brandi and Danny couldn't be happier! Faith couldn't wait to see the new baby, and Brandi told her she'd be down for a visit soon. During the two years that Faith had moved back home, Brandi had another baby boy. She came to town quite a bit to visit her mom, and then would pop over to see Faith. Brandi and Danny had their hands full with two little boys, and Brandi was such a good mother.

One night, Faith worked the later shift and got home at eleven that evening. She quietly opened the front door and went into the kitchen to get a little snack and something to drink. She was not sleepy and decided to go in the living room and turn on the TV. A particular movie caught her eye. She had already missed the first couple of minutes but watched it anyway. The more Faith watched the movie, the more intense she felt. It was about a lady who got into a horrible car accident with her husband. In the hospital, she found out her husband didn't make it, and that she was paralyzed from the knees down. After she returned home to her family, she began to have healing abilities that she never had before.

Faith was mesmerized during the whole movie. Tears streamed down her face, as a feeling came over her and filled her entire being. She begged God, *I want to be just like that lady in the movie. I want to heal people too.* When the lady touched people, her hands would get hot. She would heal people with her love just by touching them. Faith watched the whole movie on the edge of her seat. It touched her in ways that she didn't understand at the time.

After the movie was over, Faith quietly went downstairs to bed. As she lay there, she gazed at the ceiling and said to God once again, *I want to touch and heal people.* She started crying and meant it with all her heart. She continued crying and thinking about the lady in the movie, but couldn't remember the name of the movie. However, she would never forget how it had impacted her life. What she didn't know at the time was that many years later, God would answer her prayers. Many, many years later, she would remember the name of the movie and come back to it.

***

Faith was a hard worker and knew she would move out again one day. She always wanted to be prepared, which is why she saved her money. She remembered that her mom always told her to "put back for a rainy day."

One early afternoon when Faith got off work, she came home to find Hope in the kitchen. Tom and Emily were still at work. Hope had the day off due to her schedule at a new job, and she wasn't working much with their dad anymore.

"Hey Hope, what do you think about us getting an apartment together?" asked Faith.

Hope spun around and just looked at Faith. She didn't know what to say.

"Ummm, hello?" Faith laughed.

"You just caught me off guard," said Hope. "I wasn't expecting that."

"Well? What do you think?"

"That sounds great," said Hope, "but you're going to have to give me a while to put back some money."

"That's okay," said Faith. "I want to buy some living room furniture, and that will give me some time to start getting my bills straight too."

The girls were ecstatic! Faith went to her room to change clothes and lay out by the pool. She loved the sun and the water, and every chance she got to sunbathe, she did. It was her favorite past time. By the time she got out of the pool and into the house, Tom was home and talking to Hope in the kitchen. Hope was in the middle of telling him that she and Faith were going to get an apartment together. At first, Faith was a little concerned that her dad would get upset, but listening to the conversation, she knew it was going well. He was in a good mood, and the girls had learned to never ask him anything when he was in a bad mood. Faith went downstairs to her room and changed into dry clothes.

When she returned, Hope was still chattering away. Faith sat down and asked her dad if one day next week if he would go with her to the furniture store. She wanted to look at new furniture for the big move. Faith had everything else from her old apartment, but she just didn't want the living room furniture her dad gave her. She wanted brand new furniture and something she could pick out on her own. She started getting excited again. Tom was always helpful in getting the girls whatever they wanted. He really did love his daughters, but just could not control the demons inside of him. It had been six years since he stopped molesting Faith. However, Hope had endured it a couple of years longer.

Faith was elated that Hope would finally get out of there and have a place of her own. Even though the girls were alike in many ways and very different in others, the fact was that they both had a victim mentality. They were both damaged from the emotional, physical and sexual abuse. Faith was more of a homebody, and Hope loved to go out with her friends or boyfriends to bars, restaurants, and dance clubs. She asked Faith to go with her on many occasions, but rarely did Faith accept. She never felt comfortable at bars—it always gave her the creeps. She didn't like dancing because she disliked being the center of attention. She would rather sit in a dark corner somewhere and watch everyone else have fun.

Hope was also blissful about moving out and couldn't wait until the day came. The girls checked out different apartment complexes and prices and finally agreed on one. The next day, Tom and Faith went to the furniture store and looked around. Faith picked out a beautiful pull-out couch and chair. If they ever had company, there would be a place to sleep. She had already bought a coffee table and two end tables that matched the couch and chair perfectly.

Tom had helped Faith out by putting a little money down on her furniture. Faith hugged him and told him, "Thank you!" The salesman said the furniture would be delivered the next day. Faith couldn't wait until it got there. When it did, she stored it in the den and waited until Hope was ready to move. It was about six more weeks until they found the apartment they wanted. Faith had been back at her parents for three years now and was more than ready to go on her own again.

*****

Faith was once again excited about the freedom of being on her own, and so was Hope. They visited the apartment manager and signed a year's lease, and were able to move in on the last day of the month because the previous tenants had already moved out, and the unit was clean and ready to go. Hope was working for a company that let her use the truck to move their things over the weekend. It took two truckloads and both the girls' cars to get everything moved, but through their hard work they accomplished it in a day.

Finally, all the furniture was in, and everything was in place. Hope asked if everyone wanted pizza, and everyone agreed they were ready to sit down and pig out! It was around eight thirty at night by the time everyone left. It was just Hope and Faith now. Neither one could believe that this beautiful apartment was theirs! Hope turned her stereo on, and the girls sat on the sofa talking for a while before going to bed. They both had to work the next day. Faith still worked the night shift. She liked that a lot better because that meant she didn't have to get up early, and she was usually off by eleven at night. Hope worked early in the morning and was usually off by the time Faith had to go in.

The apartment was perfect. Opening the front door, they saw a staircase immediately in front of them, going up to the apartment. The kitchen and living room were in the middle, and to the right was a little hallway with a bathroom, and then a bedroom. The same exact floor plan was on the left side, meaning they each had their own bedroom and bathroom, which was needed. The girls were thrilled to fix up their bedrooms exactly the way they wanted.

Faith did not care that Tom and Emily now had an empty nest, and it would take them a little time to adjust to the absence of the girls. She felt that as long as they were away from Tom, they would be better off. She didn't realize at the time the amount of damage already done to both of them, and that it would result in decades of issues that would sometimes consume one or the other, or both. These deep wounds started manifesting when the girls moved in together.

Though the girls loved each other deeply, it seemed that life was about to tear them apart. Their two personalities collided, and with all of the pain in each of them, sometimes the arguments would erupt like volcanoes. Neither one knew at the time the root of all the anger. If one didn't like what the other one did or said, it usually escalated into a yelling match. They both could see the unruly anger in each other's eyes. They just assumed that the arguing and temper flares were part of adjusting to life in the apartment, but in all reality, it was the result all of the pain and abuse that they both had endured. It bubbled to the surface in all kinds of manners and situations.

It was the beginning of the twins going their own separate ways. Faith would find out much later on in life that they were really never torn apart, but each simply had their own separate journey ... with their own lessons to learn.

So Faith was either at work or at home, and only on rare occasions did the girls go out together. Hope, however, was going out all the time. She always had quite a few boyfriends and friends that she hung out with, and often asked Faith to go along. Faith usually refused, and Hope would get mad and storm out without her.

One time Faith was in the shower, and Hope invited her to go out.

"No, I don't feel like going out," Faith said.

Hope got very angry and opened the bathroom door and yelled, "You never go anywhere with me!" The next thing Faith knew, something flew and hit the shower curtain. It was a bar of soap.

Faith yelled, "Shut the door," and Hope left.

While Faith was alone, she could feel herself getting angry at her sister. Even though they were twins, they had quite different lifestyles. Hope was the flashy, pretty one. She always had her hair and makeup perfectly styled, and the boys loved her. She was a big flirt and set out to always have a good time. Faith took good care of her hair and makeup as well, but didn't like being the center of attention.

It wasn't that Faith didn't want to be with her sister … she just didn't like going out to bars. Almost every time, creepy men would hit on her, and it scared her. She could see the awful look in their eyes and knew what they were thinking. It always felt like that same awful feeling that she felt with her dad. When things like that happened, she would get a friend to walk her out to her car and leave. Home always felt safe to her, away from the crowds. At that time, Faith wasn't in a committed relationship and had a few boyfriends who stayed with her now and then. Hope also had boyfriends over.

Hope had a part-time job for a while as a bartender, and like with most things, she was exceptional. At times Faith would go to see her in action, and Hope would always make the perfect drink. Neither one of the girls enjoyed drinking but would have at least one cocktail. Faith bragged to her friends about Hope's skills, and everyone agreed. She was the perfect bartender! Faith still worked at the same job and had been there for about six years already. Hope blew through many jobs but was always the best at whatever she did.

Although Faith enjoyed staying at home, this didn't mean she was a loner. There were many nights that her friend would come over to cut out lines of coke on the table. Life at the apartment seemed at times like one big party, and Hope often joined in. All in all, they had a good time living together, despite the highs and lows and arguments. As the end of the year drew close, Hope wanted to move to Florida with a friend. Faith was still working and had not decided what she was going to do when the lease was up.

***

One day Faith stopped by her parents' house for a visit. Tom was out in the garage and came in shortly after she arrived.

"Good! I'm glad you're here," he said. "I want to talk to you and your sister about something. Where's Hope?"

"She should be here in a few minutes," said Faith.

"Okay," said Tom. "I'll wait for her then."

Faith was telling her dad about what was happening at work when Hope arrived. She had a big smile on her face and grabbed a glass of Pepsi out of the refrigerator. As she stood beside Faith, Tom announced that he wanted to talk to them about something.

Hope thought she was in trouble for something! She laughed and said, "I didn't do it!"

"No, you didn't do anything, Hope!" Tom said. "I want to run something by the both of you." He sat down on the kitchen bar stool. "The lady next door is planning on moving and selling her house. She said she is just too old to keep up with it and told me that if I wanted to buy it that she would give me first dibs on it."

Right away, Faith was focused on what he was saying. Hope seemed like she was disinterested.

"So, I was thinking that if you girls want to move in and pay the rent, I'll put a down payment on the house."

Before he could finish, Faith yelled, "Yes! That sounds great!" She lit up with excitement.

Tom knew that Faith had held down the same job for a little over six years now. He looked at Hope and said, "What about you?"

Hope was wishy-washy in her answer. "Well, I don't know. My friend and I were talking about going to Florida, and I think that's what we're going to do."

"Well," said Faith, "I'll take you up on your offer and find some roommates to help with the mortgage. I have a little over a month left in the apartment, and I know I'll be able to find a couple of girls to move in with me. Can we go over there and look around?"

"Yes, I think that'll be fine. Let's walk over and see," said Tom.

Faith was really thrilled at the idea of having a house of her own. "Are you coming, Hope?" she asked.

"Yeah, I'll walk over there with you."

The three walked next door and rang the doorbell. The little old lady answered and they all said hi.

Tom spoke up and asked, "Is it okay if the girls look around?"

"Why sure," she said. "You all come on in." She went into the living room and told Tom to have a seat while the girls looked around.

The girls went into the kitchen first. "Ewww ..." said Hope, "look at the ugly paint."

"Shhhh ..." said Faith, "she might hear you!"

The kitchen was crowded with all kinds of old things. Even the refrigerator was from the early 1950's. Beside the kitchen was a separate dining room with a pretty bay window looking out in the backyard. A door led off the dining room to a screened-in porch. Both girls popped their heads out and saw the backyard was loaded with junk. After leaving the dining room and walking back through the kitchen, they entered the hallway and spotted a bathroom on the left, and a bedroom on the right. Everything was outdated in the bathroom, including the pink and green square tiles. Faith and Hope glanced at each other, and then continued down the hallway. The master bedroom was on the left with two closets, a bathroom, and a stand-up shower. The other bedroom was across from the master.

Everything needed fresh paint, and Hope turned up her nose. Faith thought that fresh paint and ripping up all of the old carpet and putting her touch on it would make it look a lot better. As they walked back towards the living room, they noticed a door that led to the downstairs with squeaky steps covered in old carpet. When they got to the bottom, there was a big den and another door that led to the one-car garage. They walked out the door, and there was yet another room to the left. Faith opened the door and discovered it was an old basement about five or six feet underground with concrete walls halfway up and a concrete slab on top of that. It was used for storage and was not a pretty sight. In fact, during heavy rains, the garage would flood.

Hope was not impressed, and all she could think about was sunny Florida, while Faith had ideas about each room she saw. The girls went back upstairs and sat down on the couch for a few minutes.

"Well, what do you think?" asked the lady.

"It's nice but needs a lot of redecorating," Faith said with a friendly smile.

"Yes, I know," she said. "I haven't been able to do anything with it for years."

They all got up, and Faith and Hope told her, "Thank you for letting us wander around."

Tom said they'd be in touch, and they all left.

"I would love to live there," said Faith on the walk back home. She liked the thought of being back in her old neighborhood and right next door to her parents.

Inside their parents' house, Hope said, "I'm really not interested right now, but maybe later." Then she said she had to go for now and meet up with her friend Missy. They were going have lunch and discuss things about Florida. Hope said goodbye and left.

***

Faith sat down with her dad and wanted to get right to the details.

"I really want to move in if you can get the house, Dad," she said. "I'll help with the down payment."

He could see she was serious. "Okay, I'll work out everything with the lady next door and let you know."

"Thanks, Dad!" Faith was thrilled beyond measure. Now she didn't have to worry where she was going after her lease was up. She needed to work on finding a couple of girls to move in with her and already had one in mind who worked with her. She couldn't wait to go to work the next day and ask her. Faith hung out at her parents' house for a while and talked more about the house, getting any information that she could. After a couple of hours, she headed back home.

Faith had to be at work in the afternoon but called to see what time Brenda was working. Luckily, she would still be there when Faith arrived. She decided to go in about an hour earlier and pulled Brenda aside to tell her about the house.

"Want to be a roommate?" Faith asked.

Brenda said, "I'm planning to move out soon, and that sounds wonderful!"

Faith knew that Brenda and her husband were divorcing, but didn't know any other details. "We have plenty of time," she said Faith. "My lease isn't up for about five weeks, and it will take about that or a little longer before the house is ready."

"That's actually good," said Brenda, "because I need some time to get things in order."

"Sounds great," Faith said. "I'll keep you informed."

Brenda said, "Thank you," and got back to work.

Faith went into the break room until it was time to clock in. She now had one roommate and could use two more.

***

A few days later, Tom called Faith and told her that the lady agreed to sell him the house, and they were going to get all the paperwork done.

"Get your money ready and bring it over," he said.

Faith was excited! "I'll go to the credit union tomorrow and get a check ready."

"Okay, I have to work but will be home around three," he said.

"Okay, I'll see you then," said Faith.

The next day Faith brought over the check and handed it to her dad.

"All right, we need to go to the attorney's office so I can sign some papers," he said.

"Okay," said Faith, and they got in the truck and left. "Will my name be on the house?" she asked.

"No, not right now," Tom said, which disappointed Faith…though not enough to challenge her father.

They went to the office, Tom signed the papers, and then back in the car headed home. "When will the house be ready to move in?" asked Faith as they drove along.

"The lady is moving out this week, and there's a lot of work to do. The whole house needs repainting, and all of the carpet needs to be pulled up. Everything needs to be wiped down and cleaned. You need to come over every chance you get and help with it."

"I will," promised Faith. "I wonder what the floors look like under the carpet."

"Well, we'll know what kind of shape they're in when we pull them up."

They got home and noticed the moving truck next door.

"I'll have a key for you when you came over the next time," said Tom.

"Okay, I'll be over on my days off and when I got off work early. I'll see you in a couple of days, Dad," she said.

The next few weeks kept Faith busy. Much to her surprise, when they pulled up the carpet, the floors were beautiful oak wood in almost mint condition. Tom and Faith were both extremely happy about that. Faith cleaned, painted, and scrubbed until she was exhausted. But the thought of moving in kept her energy on high until she went to bed and collapsed. She enjoyed every minute of it. There were almost two weeks left on Faith and Hope's lease, and Hope had decided to move to Florida with her friend Missy. No one knew at the time that they were soon to get some devastating news. Life was about to take another turn that would affect the whole family, collectively and individually.

Chapter 21: Diagnosis and Loss

There is no pain greater than to be helpless in the face of a loved one's suffering.
~ Author Unknown

Tom had not been feeling well for quite a while, but never told anyone. The pain on his left side kept getting worse, but he didn't go to the doctor. He just assumed it would eventually go away. In the meantime, he helped a little with the house and told Faith what needed to be done. Faith continued to work really hard to get her house ready for her to move in.

Faith and Hope moved out of their apartment. Hope moved in with Missy for a while, and Faith moved into the house next door to her parents. She decided to take the den downstairs as her bedroom because it had a door that led out to the driveway. That way, she had her own entrance and could eventually rent out the three bedrooms upstairs. She was always thinking ahead. She got everything moved in, and Brenda moved in about a week later. Brenda also knew a couple looking for a place to stay, and she told Faith about them. Brenda gave her their number, and she called to invite them over to look at the bedroom. They came over and said yes right away. Faith now had three roommates within two weeks.

One afternoon Tom and Emily were at home, and the pain got so bad that Tom asked Emily to take him to the hospital. They ran a bunch of tests, and the doctor told Tom and Emily the news. Tom had pancreatic cancer. Emily looked bewildered, and the doctor could see that they both had questions. He went on to explain that they would get the additional tests back in a couple of days, and to make an appointment with his regular doctor. They said they would send all the tests over to him.

Tom made his appointment. It would be another week before he could get in. Faith was at the house cleaning the next day when Tom walked over to tell her the news. His skin and eyes were already turning yellow, and Faith was wondering what was wrong with him. At the time, she didn't know exactly what pancreatic cancer was or how devastating it was.

Tom went to the doctor and talked about all of the tests that came back confirming he had pancreatic cancer. The worst news was that he had about a year to live. Naturally, Tom was traumatized by the news. The doctor discussed the necessity of chemotherapy and radiation right away. So Tom made the necessary appointments to get started. The treatments made him very sick, and after the treatments, he threw up horrible green stuff due to the radiation. He took off of work for a few days, but then would get his strength back and work until the next treatment.

***

One day Faith was off of work, and Tom called and told her to come over for a minute. Faith walked over, and Tom asked, "Are you working today?"

"No, I'm off," she said.

"Good. I want you to ride over with me to the attorney's office."

Faith looked at him and asked, "Why?"

"I want to sign the house over to you," he said. "You're working and paying the mortgage, and I know you'll take care of it. You're responsible."

Faith lit up. "Thank you, Dad! Yes! I'll take care of it, I promise!"

As they were driving over to sign the papers, Faith couldn't help but think that her dad wanted to get this done because he didn't have much longer to live. On the one hand, Faith was ecstatic about owning the house but felt sad at the same time that her dad was going to die. She could feel her eyes well up with tears. They arrived at the attorneys' office and signed the necessary papers. The house now belonged to her, and she knew in her heart that she'd have to make sure that the mortgage was the first on the list to be paid, and she did.

On the way home, Tom told Faith that he and Emily were still trying to find the daughter they had adopted out.

"It'll be good if you can find her," Faith said.

"I hope to find her before I die," he said, explaining that they had made all the calls they knew how to make, and so far had come up with nothing. "We're going to keep on trying."

Faith could tell that he wanted to know about her and get to see her before he left this world. She could see the sadness in his eyes.

Over the next year, she watched her dad dwindle away to nothing. By the time the chemo and radiation were really kicking in, he had lost a lot of weight and was getting progressively weaker.

"You'll have to come over in the mornings and take care of your dad while I'm at work," said her mother. "I'll be home in time for you to go to work."

So every morning Faith walked across the yard to take care of her dad. Tom was going into nine months of treatments and didn't seem to be getting any better. He got up out of his chair and told Faith he had to go to the bathroom. As he was about to come down the steps, she heard him yelling, "Give it to me Jesus! Give it to me Jesus!" He was wandering the hallway in excruciating pain, screaming out loud.

Faith ran to see what was going on. He looked at her, his eyes and body weak from disease, and said, "Jesus is letting me have it for all of the terrible things I've done!"

Faith knew exactly what he meant, and the feelings of embarrassment washed over her. She just said, "No he's not," and helped him down the steps and back into his chair. "Jesus doesn't make people suffer," she said with conviction.

Even though she felt so sorry for him, she still had all of the past feelings welling up in her again. She got him in his chair and got him some water. His eyes were full of tears that streamed down his face. Faith just wanted her mom to hurry up and come home. She didn't know that at this point, all of the horrors of what he did to her and Hope and everyone else was coming back to torment him.

Tom was getting to the point of being so weak that he had to go into the hospital a couple of times to get an I.V. and hydration so that he was well enough to come back home. Faith would come over early and get her sleeping bag and put it on the floor to go back to sleep. Tom at this point was sleeping a lot. One time while Faith dozed off, Tom coughed, and it woke her up. She glanced up at her dad and started praying. He looked so pitiful, lying there totally helpless.

Please God, don't let my dad die. Please do a miracle and let him live. Faith fought back the tears. Every day when she came over, she prayed that same prayer. Shortly after, Tom went back into the hospital. Emily, the twins, Richard, and other family members visited him all the time. On Thanksgiving 1985, Tom entered the hospital for the last time.

***

One morning, Tom called Faith early and asked her to come up to the hospital. She got to his room and sat in the chair chatting with him. After a few minutes, he motioned her to come over and sit on the bed. As she sat down, he reached for her hand, which made Faith feel uncomfortable. He looked at her in the eyes and said, "Can you ever forgive me for all that I've done to you?"

Faith could not look him straight in the eye, and once again all of those familiar feelings enveloped her. In spite of this, she said nervously "Yes, Dad, I forgive you."

He started crying, and it was the saddest thing Faith had ever seen. Even though she felt sorry for him, she still felt conflicted. Even though she said the words, she didn't feel the forgiveness in her heart at the time. At this very moment, the forgiveness was a decision she required of herself. By telling him this, she was sparing herself huge amounts of pain in the future and help her with closure.

Faith got up, and as she was stood beside his bed, she had no idea what was really taking place. Tom didn't ask Hope or Richard for forgiveness. Why? It seemed that out of all of Tom's many victims, Faith was the one bestowed with the responsibility to reach out and bring healing—not only to her family and some of Tom's victims, but to all those God would bring to her, and to all who would hear her story. The baton was being handed to her. She would be the one to reach out and bring healing to her family, reversing the nightmare.

Tom got weaker and weaker. He had not been able to get out of bed for a few weeks and was down to about seventy-five pounds. The nurses had no trouble turning him on his side because he didn't weigh that much. One day a friend came to see him, the pastor of a church nearby. They had known each other for years. As Pastor Jim walked down the hallway towards Tom's room, he could hear someone moaning very loudly and realized the sound was coming from Tom. He started jogging to get there quickly, thinking that something was wrong. Approaching the door, he saw Tom lying in bed. There was something very different about the way he looked. He seemed to glow.

Jim stood right beside Tom and noticed that he had his eyes closed, but was smiling the most peaceful smile. He reached out and took Tom's hand and softly whispered, "Tom? Are you okay?" Tom slowly opened his eyes, and the smile grew bigger and brighter.

He looked at Jim and said with excitement, "Jim! I finally met my maker!" His confliction, frustration and torment were about to end.

Jim squeezed Tom's hands, and the tears fell. "Yes, Tom! I'm so happy for you!"

At that moment, Tom was able to get out of bed and sit in a chair. He had been bedridden for weeks now without the strength to sit up, yet now he was able to sit in his chair for three days. After the third day, he was back in bed. It was nearing his time to go home, his heavenly home. Over the next couple of weeks, Tom's organs started failing one by one. He was soon on a respirator. The doctor told Emily to gather the family together as soon as she could. They were all there when the decision was made to unplug the respirator. Two days later, Tom died. He never did find his first daughter.

The doctor called Emily at work and Faith at home. Faith went over to the house, and Emily came home and collapsed in the chair. She had only seen her mom cry once in her life, and that was when she was about six years old. Faith was numb. She touched her mom's hand, and Emily didn't move. Faith didn't know how to respond. There were never any touchy-feely moments with her mom, so she removed her hand and said, "It's going to be okay."

Suddenly, Emily cried out, "I don't know what to do! I don't know how to handle all of this!"

Faith told her mom to call the hospital and explained that they would tell her all she needed to know and that the family would help as well. Faith went back to her house and let her mom grieve. By the next day, family members flew in and stayed with Emily and Faith. There was such a strange feeling in the air. Faith couldn't believe that this had happened. When she was alone, she sat on her bed and cried uncontrollably, filled with all kinds of emotions including anger, sadness, despair, love, shame, sympathy, grief, and sorrow. These feelings swirled around all throughout her body. She grabbed her pillow and held it tight and hung her head.

"I love you, Dad," she said as the tears soaked the pillow. She couldn't imagine how life was going to be without him around.

***

After a few days, the wake was set up, and people were allowed to view the body. Faith couldn't bear to go into the room where her dad lay in an open casket. She didn't want to remember him like that. She didn't want that to be the last image in her mind. She stood outside the doors while everyone else came and went. Hope and Rachel, the girls' cousin, came out and saw Faith somewhat hiding.

"Come on, Faith," Rachel said. "He looks so peaceful. It's not what you think."

"No!" Faith yelled. "I can't. I just can't!"

Hope and Rachel continued to persuade her. Rachel took Faith by the arm and told her again, "Come on Faith. Hope and I will walk with you." As Rachel held on to Faith's arm, she finally went in and could feel her body shaking. She really didn't want to go. As they got closer to the casket, Faith finally looked at her dad lying there. He, indeed, had the most peaceful look about him. She glanced quickly and left quickly, Hope and Rachel behind her.

As they got back out in the hallway, Rachel said, "See! I told you he was at peace."

Faith agreed but didn't want to talk about it anymore. After a few more minutes, she asked Hope to take her home.

Two days later was the funeral, the first one Faith had ever attended.

Parker called. "Do you want me to take you to the funeral?" he offered.

"Yes," she said, haltingly.

He arrived at her house and gave her a big hug. "I'm so sorry," he said as he held her tight.

They got ready and met everyone at the church. Brandi was already there, and when she saw Faith, she hugged her. They both cried for a moment. "I'll see you there," Brandi said, as everyone took their places in line to drive to the cemetery. Parker and Faith were about four cars behind the hearse. As they got to the cemetery and made their way around the twisting, turning road, Faith lost it. She watched the back of the hearse and screamed, "I can't believe my dad is lying in a box in the back of that car!"

She was beyond rational thought and started feeling sorry for him. The chemo and radiation had taken a toll on his body. She watched him go from two-hundred-sixty-five pounds down to seventy-four pounds. She felt he was helpless and that he couldn't get out of the closed coffin, and she wanted to go help him.

"I don't want him to be buried in the ground. He's not dead! He's not dead," she yelled.

Parker took hold of her arm while he was driving and comforted her. "Come on now, Faith," he said. "Everything is going to be alright."

Faith knew he was right, but couldn't help the feelings that were engulfing her. She started wiping her tears and held Parker's hand and tried to calm herself down. As they got up to the site where Tom's remains would now reside, Parker held Faith close.

"I just want to leave," she whispered in his ear. "Please, let's go as soon as we can."

"Okay," said Parker, "you just let me know when you're ready to go, and I'll take you home."

"Thank you," Faith said as she snuggled up to the comfort that was being offered.

***

Years later after she had been awakened and healed from her trauma, Faith reflected back to the mess of emotions she had experienced at the funeral—the love/hate relationship she and her sister had with their dad. They were just children who were raised to know nothing else but the pendulum of abuse that symbolized their relationship with Tom. That pendulum swung from nurturing and caring … to rape, threats, and beatings. A hundred highs and lows might happen in one day, and there had been no emotional stability in their lives.

In the midst of this chaos, there was one constant—or "force"—and that was their dad when he was in good-dad mode.

Faith now realized that she and Hope had always "run" to their dad for almost everything, and harbored negative feelings towards their mother. This seems to be typical behavior in childhood abuse—the victims gravitate toward their abuser, often due to psychological coercion, but also to hone in on the abuser's mood and forecast what the next minute, hour, or day might bring.

Chapter 22: Life Goes On

"Grief is in two parts. The first is loss. The second is the remaking of life."
~ Anne Roiphe

The next few weeks were spent adjusting to Tom's death. He died on December 6, 1985. Christmas was right around the corner, and it would be the family's first Christmas without him. Things felt so much different, and it took Faith a little while to get adjusted. Sometimes Faith would go next door to see her mom, and they'd hang out together. Emily seemed to be doing just fine. Faith rarely ever saw her mom show emotions.

Faith knew that her mom must have been lonely at times after Tom died, and took her to lunch often. Emily loved Burger King and Long John Silver's, so that's usually where they went. After dining on fast food, they sometimes did a little shopping. It was always a good time.

About twice a month, Emily picked up Aunt Debbie so they could visit Tom's grave. Then they would go to lunch together, as well. Many conversations took place whenever the two were together, and most of them remained private. Sometimes, Aunt Debbie confided a few details to cousin Rachel about how their day went.

There were a few times that Faith's roommates would ask her to go out, and Faith always said no.

"I just don't feel like it," she'd say, but they could see she was down in the dumps.

Finally, the following month, Faith's roommate Brenda asked her to go out. "Come on, Faith! I won't take no for an answer!"

Faith finally agreed, and they went to a nearby bar. Faith liked the place because it had a restaurant. Through the double doors was a bar that always had a band playing on the weekends. It was pretty nice. Amanda, a friend of Faith's, worked there as a cocktail waitress.

As soon as Brenda and Faith walked in, they noticed the place was crowded. Faith spotted a cute man up at the bar. She looked in his direction, and he turned around and looked right back. Faith smiled as she and Brenda got a table, and noticed that the man kept glancing her way. She thought he was very cute.

Amanda was working that night and spotted Faith. "Glad to see you out," she greeted. "The band tonight is really good. They should start in a few minutes. So, what can I get you two ladies to drink?"

Brenda ordered a rum and coke, and Faith ordered ice tea.

"Oh, come on!" Amanda shouted. "Let me get you a real drink.

"Okay," said Faith. "How about a strawberry daiquiri."

"That's more like it," she said. "I'll be right back."

Brenda leaned over and said to Faith, "That guy to your right keeps staring at you. I've caught him a couple of times." She giggled.

Faith turned to see who it was, and sure enough, it was the same guy she spotted when she first came in. Amanda took him a drink and then headed back towards their table.

Faith asked, "Amanda, do you know who that guy is?"

"Yes, he's with the band," she said. "He runs the lights and sound."

Faith smiled and said, "He's cute!"

Amanda put down their drinks and turned away quickly. Faith saw her go towards the guy again and saw them talking and laughing. Pretty soon, Amanda came back and handed Faith a napkin. "Here you go," she said.

Faith unfolded the napkin and saw a name and number written on it. His name was Kenny. Faith smiled and looked at Amanda.

"He told me he thought you were pretty and wants to meet you," said Amanda.

"Oh, my God," said Faith. "Really?" She felt like a school girl and had butterflies in her stomach.

"He told me he'll come over and talk with you when they get their first break."

"Okay, Amanda, go tell him that will be fine."

Amanda walked over, and Faith could see him light up. He looked at her and smiled. Faith smiled back and leaned in towards Brenda, telling her that he'd be over after their first break. Brenda smiled and felt that Faith deserved some happiness. Ever since Faith's dad died, all she had been doing was working and coming home. For Faith, it was a time of solitary reflection. She still wrestled with thoughts that ran through her head from time to time. When she would get ready for bed, the horrible images danced in her head. She prayed the same prayer she said every night, and at the end added with tear-filled eyes, "Dad, I forgive you." She didn't realize at the time that the forgiveness still wasn't a reality in her heart. But she mouthed the words and sometimes cried herself to sleep. It was easier to say "I forgive you" now that he wasn't around. She didn't have to look into her perpetrator's eyes. She didn't have to be in his presence, seeing both the caring Dad and the abuser. Now, it was only a memory.

***

"Don't you go anywhere!" Faith yelled at Brenda. "I want you to sit right here the whole time he is here, okay?"

Brenda laughed and told her she wasn't going anywhere.

Faith was exhilarated at the thought of meeting someone new. As the band played, she watched Kenny as he worked the lights and sound. She thought that was cool. The band was one of the best she ever heard, and the lead singers were amazing. Soon the lead singer announced that they were taking a break and would be back in thirty minutes. Faith's heart started beating faster. She was nervous meeting Kenny. She saw him finish up with the lights and walk over to the bar and grab a drink. He then was heading to her table. Brenda was grinning from ear to ear.

"Hi, my name is Kenny," he greeted, pulling up a chair next to Faith.

Faith and Brenda introduced themselves to him. "So, where are you from?" asked Faith.

Kenny told her that he lived in a city about two hours away.

"I know exactly where that is," Faith said excitedly. "My best friend Brandi lives there too."

The beginning of that conversation was a good icebreaker, and they talked until he had to go back to work. "Are you two staying until we're finished playing?" he asked the girls. Faith looked at Brenda, and Brenda saw the look in her eyes.

"Yes, I guess we can," Brenda said with a smile.

"Great!" replied Kenny. "I'll talk to you later." He got up and went back to work.

Faith glanced at Brenda and said, "Thank you!"

The bar was very crowded that night, mostly because the band was so good. After they finished playing, Kenny came back over and chatted with Faith. When it was time to go home, she gave him her number and said she'd be back tomorrow night. Kenny was excited and liked Faith's sense of humor.

"See you tomorrow!" Faith said with a smile.

"I can't wait!" said Kenny.

On the way home, Faith could hardly stop talking about Kenny.

"Are you going to come back up with me tomorrow night?" she asked Brenda.

"I work a couple of hours later than you do, so I'll just meet you up there shortly after I get off work."

"Okay," said Faith. She could hardly sleep that night due to the excitement. She really liked Kenny. He seemed like such a nice guy, and he was funny.

The band played for the next few days and Faith went up every night to see Kenny, with or without Brenda. On the last night that the band was playing, Kenny told Faith he would be going home the next day.

"I'll stay in town if you want to go out to dinner," he said.

Faith accepted, and the following night met Kenny for dinner. They had a great time and got to know each other better. It was still early in the evening, so Faith invited him back to her house for a while.

Brenda was home and was glad to see them walk through the door. They all sat around chatting, and then Faith asked Kenny if he'd like to meet her mom who just lived next door.

"Okay," said Kenny, and they walked over next door. Emily was in the living room watching TV.

"Hi Mom," shouted Faith. "I have someone I'd like you to meet."

Emily stood up, and Faith introduced Kenny. They sat in the living room for more than an hour just laughing and getting to know each other. Soon Faith was feeling tired and told Kenny it was time to leave because she had to work the next day. Kenny said goodbye to Emily, and the two went back next door.

Faith stood by Kenny's car and thanked him for dinner and a good time. "I'll call you when I get home," Kenny said.

"Sounds great," said Faith as she walked up the sidewalk. As Kenny pulled out of the driveway, they both waved goodbye. Faith went back inside and talked with Brenda for a moment, and then called her mom and asked her what she thought of Kenny. Emily liked him and thought he was really nice.

"Yeah, he is," said Faith. "I'll talk to you later. I'm going to get ready for bed."

"Goodnight," said Emily.

"Good night, Mom." Faith hung up the phone and got ready for bed. As she was just dozing off, the phone rang. It was Kenny. She woke back up quickly, excited to hear his voice.

"I'm glad you made it home," she said.

"Yes, me too," said Kenny. "I want to ask you something. I was wondering if you wanted to come to my place next weekend and go with me to the bar where we're playing."

Faith was a little nervous, but said, "Sure, that sounds like fun!"

Kenny gave Faith his address, and both looked forward to the weekend. Faith forgot that she was working that Saturday, but figured it wouldn't be hard to find someone to cover for her. The work week seemed to go slow, and all she could do was think about Kenny. She finished out the work week and found someone to work for her over the weekend. She left Friday late afternoon for Kenny's house.

He was very excited to see her, and as she walked in it felt a little awkward because she knew what was going to take place that night, and it did. Kenny treated Faith well, and they got along just fine. The next day Kenny took her sightseeing in the area, and they had a very good time. Later on, they went to the bar where Kenny and his band played. Kenny told Faith she could sit near him while he worked. She liked that idea because she didn't want to be in the crowd without having a friend beside her.

The band was awesome as usual, and Faith had a great time. She still didn't like the bar scene but felt okay since she was there with Kenny. After the band finished playing, Kenny took Faith back to his house. She stayed one more night and then had to leave the next day. On the way home, she felt so happy. As she drove, she cranked the music up in her car and sang almost all the way to her house. She felt good.

Faith and Kenny became a couple, and as time went by, they began creating memories. Kenny drove to her house almost every week, or Faith would go to his.

***

One morning while Faith was fixing breakfast, Kenny called and asked if he could come see her.

"Of course," she said. She thought it was unusual for Kenny to come on a Friday since the band played on weekends. He began telling her that the band was splitting up and that his roommate was moving out in a couple of weeks. He didn't know what to do. They talked for a while, and Faith mentioned to Kenny that he could move in with her if he wanted to.

"You can look for a job here," she suggested.

Before she could finish, Kenny said, "Yes, that would be awesome!" He told her that he was ready to quit the band and move on with his life. "Would it be okay if I moved in when my roommate leaves in two weeks?"

Faith said, "Sure, that would be great." At the time, Faith had five roommates. The three bedrooms upstairs were full. The back room downstairs was occupied by a friend who worked on her house in exchange for rent—basically a handyman. The back room had a separate entrance so that Faith was never bothered by him, and it worked out well. He had done quite a bit of work over the months, including putting in a bathroom and fixing up the room in the back.

Later that evening Faith called Hope and told her that Kenny was moving in. "When are you coming home to visit?"

Hope was having such a good time in Florida and working as a bartender on a small cruise ship. "I hope I can come visit soon."

Faith was excited. She couldn't wait until her sister met Kenny.

***

Faith looked in the freezer to find something to fix for dinner since Kenny would be there later. She finally figured out a great meal plan. She always loved to cook and come up with different ideas, and Kenny loved her cooking.

Faith went about her day until he arrived. They had a wonderful evening together, and he spent the night and stayed the next day while Faith went to work. He kept busy looking through the paper to see what types of jobs were available. After a couple of days together, Kenny went back home to get things organized.

The next day Faith went over to her mom's and told her that Kenny would be moving in shortly. Emily didn't have much to say. She liked Kenny and saw that Faith seemed happy.

As Faith got her room ready for Kenny to move in, she couldn't believe how fast things were going. She started having second thoughts and wondered if she was really ready for him to live with her. It just happened so fast, and before she knew it, Kenny was there and had moved in. It took Faith a couple of weeks to get adjusted to the idea, and then everything seemed to just fall into place.

Kenny had a job within a week, and the people loved him where he worked. It was a family-owned business and Kenny did well there. By the end of summer, he came to Faith and asked her to marry him. She was astounded and didn't know what to say. At the time she didn't want to get married and was scared.

Kenny kept looking at her, and she finally said, "Yes." He was thrilled, but Faith told him she didn't want to set a date yet. He was okay with that. Faith thought that if she didn't set a date and changed her mind later on, it wouldn't be so hard. The concept made her feel a little more comfortable.

Over the winter the couple renting upstairs decided to move out. Faith thought that she'd just fix up that room just in case they ever had company. Now there were only the two roommates upstairs and the handyman downstairs. He was also planning on moving out in the next couple of months, and Faith decided to fix up that room up as well. That would be a perfect guest room because it had its own living room, bathroom, and separate entrance.

As the holidays rolled around, Faith always cooked fantastic meals. She especially loved cooking Thanksgiving dinner at her house. She was a homebody who enjoyed her kitchen and serving dinners at her house, or once in a while at her mom's house next door. One of Faith's roommates didn't have any family in town and always dined at Faith's. He chipped in and added to the meals, and they were always very tasty!

Christmas came—the second Christmas without Tom. Faith was getting used to it, but it still seemed strange without him around. Faith always spent the holidays with her mom. It was sad to see Emily by herself, but she seemed to be doing just fine. Even if she wasn't, Faith would never know.

That winter, Faith's neighbors who lived behind her called and asked her to come over for a minute.

"We've sold the house and are moving out of town. Would you like our fireplace insert?" they asked.

Faith shouted, "Yes! That would be perfect for the cold winters to help heat the house up."

"It puts out a lot of heat, and the people buying our house don't want it. So it's yours," they said.

"Great! Kenny and I will come over after he gets off work. Thank you!" She gave them both a big hug and said, "I'm going to miss you!"

Faith walked back home and could hardly wait for Kenny to arrive so she could tell him the news. They went over the next day to pick up the fireplace insert and installed it. It fit perfectly and heated the whole house upstairs, which was great since a few months of cold weather were still ahead of them. Kenny bought some wood and stacked it up outside against the fence. Faith gathered sticks in the yard and put them in a pile beside the wood. She was very grateful for the insert.

***

One day when Faith was outside and her handyman roommate told her that he was moving out of state and would be leaving shortly. Faith hated to see him go, but she knew he'd been thinking about it for a while. They hugged, and Faith thanked him for all the work he had done on the house. It helped out a lot, especially having another bathroom downstairs. It was much easier walking through the den door than having to climb the steps to use the bathroom.

He moved out over the next three days, and she had an empty room to fix up. Richard was visiting with Emily, and Faith walked over to see them. Richard asked where her roommate was after spotting his truck in the driveway.

"Oh," she said, "He's moving out of state to start his business up."

"Oh yeah?" said Richard with a sneaky smile. "How about if I move in? That will help you and Kenny out with some rent, and I was looking for a new place anyway because my lease is up in two months."

"Why sure," Faith said. "That will be fine."

Richard moved in a couple of months later.

Chapter 23: A New Start

"Nothing in the universe can stop you from letting go and starting over."
~ Guy Finley

Faith was off of work one warm day in March, and it was nice outside. She decided to rake the flower bed. As she bent over to pick up the leaves, she felt a little dizzy and had to stop for a while. She shrugged it off and continued to rake. After a few minutes, she started feeling nauseous and decided to go inside and sit down for a while. *Maybe it's because I didn't eat lunch,* she thought. She fixed herself a bite to eat, and that seemed to help.

The next morning she got ready for work and began to feel sick again. The flu had been going around, and she figured she had picked up a bug. She called into work and told them she wasn't coming in. They told her she had to get a doctor's note before coming back to work. After she hung up, Faith made a doctor appointment for the next day.

When she arrived at the doctor's office, they took her blood and weight and handed her a little cup to do a urine test. When Faith handed the nurse the cup, the nurse told her that they were going to do a pregnancy test just to rule that out.

Faith laughed and said, "Okay," and waited on the table for the doctor to come in. It seemed like she was waiting there forever. Finally, she heard a knock on the door, and the doctor entered. Faith had been going to him for years, and he and his wife lived just a few houses up from her.

They chatted for a while, and he said, "Well, Faith, the good news is that you don't have the flu. However, you have something else, and it's called …" The doctor paused for a moment.

"Yes, doctor?"

He smiled and continued. "It's called morning sickness. Faith, you're pregnant."

Faith was in shock. She wasn't prepared to hear that.

"What?" she exclaimed. "Are you sure?"

The doctor smiled at her and said, "Yes, Faith. I'm sure. It looks like you're about eight weeks."

So many thoughts flew through her head. She didn't know what to think.

"Let's go ahead and do the exam." The doctor stepped out, and Faith got ready. He came in shortly and confirmed that she was pregnant. He told her to make another appointment and from now on would be seeing her once a month until further notice. He left the room and Faith got dressed and went to the desk to make another appointment.

As she got into her car to go home, warm and happy thoughts whirled in her brain. The shock of it was over. She knew Kenny would be thrilled, and she didn't know what her mom was going to think. She wondered what everyone was going to think! On the drive home, Faith felt good. It was a different kind of feeling, and she liked it.

When she got home, she fell on her bed and just laid there getting lost in her emotions. She put her hands on her tummy and lightly rubbed it, knowing a baby was forming inside her. She wondered what it would be, and then suddenly knew it was a boy. She smiled a sweet smile and kissed her hand and placed it on her tummy. Kenny would be home shortly, and she couldn't wait to tell him. Emily wouldn't be home for a few more hours, and Faith couldn't wait to tell her that she was going to be a grandmother again.

Faith grabbed the phone and called Brandi to tell her the news. Brandi was ecstatic! They talked for a while, and Brandi told her to call her immediately if she had any questions.

"I will," said Faith. "I know you're a pro!" They both laughed. "And now I need to call Hope."

They hung up, and Faith dialed her sister. She announced the good news and Hope couldn't believe it.

"I'm going to be an auntie!" she screamed.

"Yes, you are! But don't say anything because I haven't told anybody.

"I won't," promised Hope. "But you better hurry up and tell, or I'm going to!" They both laughed.

"Kenny will be home soon, and Mom would be home in a couple of hours. I better go," said Faith.

"I'm so happy for you!" said Hope.

They hung up, and Faith started walking around her bedroom trying to process this huge change in her life.

***

A short while later she heard Kenny pull up in the driveway and ran outside to meet him.

As he parked and exited the car, Faith said, "Guess what?"

"What?" Kenny asked, kind of puzzled.

"I just got back from the doctor a couple of hours ago, and he said I don't have the flu."

"Then why are you dizzy and nauseous?" he asked.

"Well, Kenny," Faith continued, "the doctor said it was your fault."

Kenny asked, "Why is that?"

Faith looked straight at him and blurted out, "Because you're going to be a dad!"

Kenny's eyes got big, and a huge smile came over his face. He grabbed Faith and hugged her tight. "Wow! I can't believe this!" he exclaimed in pure ecstasy. They held hands and walked into the house.

Kenny paced back and forth, and Faith finally told him to sit down.

"My mom should be home soon. I can't wait to go over and tell her."

"I know," said Kenny. "I'll let you go over by yourself, so you can tell her."

"Okay," said Faith, "I think that's a good idea."

She kept peering out the window watching for her mom to pull up. Finally, she saw Emily driving down the street and got excited. She watched as Emily got out of her car and went into the house. When the door closed behind her, Faith walked over with the doctor's papers in her hand. Emily was sitting at the table, and Faith flung the papers in front of her and said loudly, "Well Mom, it looks like you're going to be a grandmother!"

Emily opened her mouth wide and couldn't believe what she was hearing. "Really?" she said in amazement.

"Yes, Mom. I thought I had the flu."

They both laughed, and Emily stood up and gave Faith a hug.

"Well, Mom, I guess I need to set a wedding date now!"

"Yes, I think that would be good," Emily said with a smile.

Faith went back home, and within a couple of hours, everyone knew. When Faith was finished making phone calls, she told Kenny that they should set a wedding date. They sat down together with a calendar and picked out a date. It would be in six weeks.

"I think that's plenty of time to tell everyone and get things ready," Faith said.

Kenny agreed. As Faith lay in bed that night and said her prayers, she talked a while longer to God saying that she thought that Kenny was going to be a good dad. She also knew that he worked and was always there for her. She kept mulling over the thoughts until she felt comfortable, knowing that she was going to marry him. Faith finally drifted off to sleep.

***

That evening after finding out the happy news, Kenny hardly let Faith lift a finger. He brought her everything she needed. She thought it was sweet that he doted on her.

The next day Emily came over to visit Faith. They were both off of work that day.

"Would you like to go look at wedding dresses?" Emily asked.

Faith said, "Yes, but I really can't afford one right now."

"I want to buy your dress," said Emily.

Faith was so excited. "Really, Mom? Oh, thank you!" Faith gave her a hug, and they got ready to go shopping.

"Be careful on the price," Emily said as they shopped. After picking out the perfect dress, Emily told Faith, "You look beautiful."

Faith was getting excited about everything now—first the surprise pregnancy, and now planning a wedding.

Emily and Faith went up to the counter and paid for the dress. The lady put the gown in a bag with the hanger and handed it to Faith. They left and went out to lunch before going home.

On the drive home, Faith looked at her mom and thanked her again.

Emily smiled and said, "You're welcome!"

When they pulled up in the driveway, Faith hugged her mom and walked back home. She hung the gown in the closet and sat down for a while. She was starting to feel a little nauseous and decided to rest for a bit. As Faith sat back in her chair, she started becoming more aware of being a wife and a mother. Life was changing so very quickly. She thought about how happy Emily was at the thought of being a grandmother again. Faith's eyes got heavy, and she finally drifted off to sleep.

***

Over the next couple of weeks, Faith was busy with wedding planning. They didn't have enough money at the time for a fancy wedding. It was going to be in June and was just around the corner.

Kenny called his parents and asked his brother if he'd be the best man. He agreed. Faith picked up the phone and called Brandi and asked her if she would be her bridesmaid, and she said, "Of course!" It was just going to be the bridesmaid and the best man, and Richard was going to walk Faith down the aisle.

Brandi asked, "Do you still have the bridesmaid gown from my wedding?"

Faith said, "Yes I do, it's in the attic wrapped up in a box."

"Well," said Brandi, "how about I wear it in your wedding?"

Faith thought that was a great idea and told Brandi that would be cool to both have worn the same bridesmaid dress. So that's what they did.

Then Faith called her dad's old friend, Pastor Jim, and asked if he'd officiate.

"Yes," said Pastor Jim. "And you can have the wedding at my church."

Faith gave him the day and time. Next, she got pieces of paper and wrote down the address of the church. She told all of her friends and coworkers, and even some customers who came into the store on a regular basis, all of the details about the wedding day and handed out the address. She decided to make all of the food platters herself. She called Hope and told her what she was doing, and Hope said she'd make the punch. Brandi volunteered to help out with whatever Faith needed. It seemed like everything was coming together!

One evening while Faith and Kenny were watching TV, Faith told him she'd been thinking about quitting work two weeks before the wedding. She also wanted to stay home and raise her baby. At the time, the store was offering union workers a payout to quit and would give them a certain amount of money for each year they had been there. Faith was there for a while and decided to take the offer.

"That's fine," said Kenny. "But things will be kind of tight now and then."

Faith didn't care. All she wanted to do was be with her new baby. She couldn't stand the thought of getting a babysitter or ever leaving the baby and gave her two weeks' notice. When her coworkers heard the news, they all congratulated her but hated to see her leave. After she quit, she got a lump sum of money on her next check, and she put it into a savings account. The wedding was going to be on a Saturday, and some family came in for a couple of days and stayed with Emily. Hope came in from Florida and stayed with Faith. Brandi and the kids came and stayed with Brandi's mom.

***

Faith was excited the Saturday morning of her wedding and went in the kitchen to prepare her deli trays. She didn't realize how long it took. The wedding was at two in the afternoon, and it was already eleven a.m. She hadn't even started to get ready. By the time she was finished fixing the trays and cleaning up, she was exhausted. In fact, she was starting to tire a little more quickly these days, and still had morning sickness from time to time.

Faith got in the shower and had to be at the church an hour before the wedding. Everyone headed over, and Faith and Brandi went to the back of the church to get dressed. Faith felt so beautiful in her gown, and Brandi looked amazing in her bridesmaid's dress. They were having such a good time. Hope came back to join them, and the three just laughed and had a great time reminiscing.

Faith said out loud, "First it was Brandi, and now it's me. Hope—you're next!"

Hope just laughed and said, "Not anytime soon!"

They finally all took their places, and the ceremony began. Richard walked Faith down the aisle, and Kenny's brother was his best man. It all seemed to happen so fast, but the vows were beautiful. The wedding party stayed to take pictures, and Faith asked her roommate at the time if he would go back and take out all the deli trays and get things ready at the house. The photo session took a little over an hour, and when Faith and Kenny got to the house people were everywhere! Upstairs, downstairs—every room in the house and even the front, back, and side yard were filled with people. The deli trays were almost wiped out, and Richard put a keg on the porch. Friends and family ate, drank, and had a great time!

It was almost midnight and Faith couldn't keep her eyes open any longer. She told everyone she was exhausted and needed to go to sleep. She hugged everyone and went to bed. It didn't take her long to doze off, even with all of the music playing and everyone getting drunk and yelling and screaming. She knew they were having a good time, and so she slept through the night without getting up once.

When morning came, Faith crawled out of bed still a bit groggy. She went upstairs to fix some coffee, and the house was quiet. She thought it was funny that her overnight guests were pretty much passed out from the night before. Everyone else had left around half past four that morning. It was a good time for everyone.

Now she was a wife and soon-to-be mother. As she sat drinking her coffee, her life flashed before her. All kinds of memories were taking a stroll through her head. Good ones, bad ones, and thoughts of doing everything in her power to protect her baby. They were fleeting thoughts, one after the other after the other. Pretty soon, Kenny came up and joined her for coffee. The two talked quietly at the table to avoid waking anyone else in the house. They didn't know who all was there until everyone actually got up.

They all had a good time, and all the guests left by that afternoon. Faith and Kenny thanked everyone for coming. Faith cried when Hope told her she had to head back to Florida. She wanted her to stay and be with her the whole time she was pregnant. But she knew Hope had a home and job waiting. Hope was the last one to leave.

It took Faith a few days to get the house back in order. As time went on, her tummy grew larger and larger. She seemed to be doing just fine with the pregnancy and enjoyed being a housewife. She still had two roommates and her brother helping with the mortgage. She called Brandi frequently during her pregnancy to ask questions about this and that. Brandi was always very helpful because she had already had two boys. Faith was grateful for all of Brandi's help.

One day she got a phone call from Brandi. As soon as Faith said hello, Brandi yelled, "You're not going to believe this!"

"What?" Faith asked.

"I'm pregnant!"

Faith about fell off the chair. "You're kidding me!"

"I know, I'm as surprised as you are!"

The two laughed together, and Faith was so happy for Brandi. They would be pregnant together for a couple of months. Faith wished that she lived closer, but Brandi was in town quite a bit to see her mom and family and, of course, Faith.

***

As Faith's due date got closer, Kenny became nervous. He kept telling Faith to make sure she packed her suitcase ahead of time for the hospital. A friend told her to take a long walk to get her labor started. So Faith and Kenny took a walk late that afternoon. By dinner time, Faith kept feeling a burning in her bladder, and it kept getting more intense. By the time she was ready for bed, the burning was worse and kept coming and going, coming and going.

She picked up the phone and called her doctor. The answering service relayed the message, and he called back within a few minutes. Kenny's nervousness was increasing. It was already late at night, and he had to work the next day. Faith told the doctor what was going on. He didn't think she was in labor, but since the burning was coming and going, he told her to go to the hospital. Kenny jumped up and started running around like a crazy man. Faith told him to calm down and that everything was going to be okay. She hadn't packed yet, so Kenny grabbed her suitcase just in case she had to stay at the hospital.

After packing, Faith called her mom and told her they were leaving for the hospital in a few minutes. Emily came running over and was so excited! It took about thirty minutes to finally get everything ready, and Emily hugged Faith as she got in the car to leave. Kenny automatically started driving too fast.

"Kenny!" Faith shouted. "We're not in a hurry!" Faith laughed at him because she couldn't believe how he was acting! They finally got to the hospital, and the lady at the desk said, "Can I help you?"

Faith smiled and said, "I think I'm in labor." The lady told them to come on back and got Faith situated in a room. She continued having the burning sensations in her bladder, and the nurses kept telling her that she was not in labor. Faith knew different. She kept telling them, "Yes, I am!"

They told her, "The doctor will be in shortly."

Finally, her doctor came in and examined Faith. He didn't think she was in labor either, but Faith kept telling him that she was. "I'm always different than the crowd," she said. The nurses went ahead and put in an I.V. and injected a drug without telling Faith what it was.

"What is that?" she asked.

"This will help relax you," the nurse answered.

"Those types of drugs make me sick," Faith announced, and it wasn't long before she started throwing up.

The doctor examined her later and announced she was in labor. He'd be back in an hour or so to check on her.

***

"Try and relax and get some rest before the doctor comes back in," Kenny soothed. Faith was still sick from the medicine and was throwing up every few minutes. After a while, the doctor came back in and examined her. She still wasn't dilating. He gave her some Pitocin to help her along.

Faith was getting sicker due to the medicine. Hours elapsed, and she finally dilated to one. The doctor gave her some morphine to reduce the pain, but that made Faith even sicker. She felt horrible and threw up every few minutes. It was already into the next day, and Faith continued to have the unusual contractions. She stayed sick all the next day into the evening. By now, she was dry heaving. She hardly slept through the night.

Hope was visiting their mother, so the next day Emily brought Hope to the hospital. But Faith was so sick she wasn't able to see them. They stayed out in the waiting room, talking with Kenny. Kenny saw other women coming and going with their new babies, and Faith was still in her room.

Later that evening on the third night, Kenny saw the doctor sitting in the hall near Faith's room. He was bent over with his head in his hands.

"Hey, Doc," said Kenny.

The doctor looked up and said, "I've never seen anything like this!" He got up and walked in Faith's room, and repeated what he had just told Kenny.

Faith laughed and said, "Didn't I tell you that I'm different than everyone else?"

"Yes, you did, and now I believe you," he said with a chuckle. He told Faith that he had done all he could to get her to dilate, to no avail. "We're going to have to do a C-section. I'm going to get you prepared and then the anesthesiologist will put an epidural in your back. When that's ready, I'll start the procedure.

Faith was so sick; she didn't care. She just wanted to get this over with. It was now in the wee hours of the third day. They got her prepped for surgery.

Faith got progressively sicker. She kept grabbing the barf pan that she thought was behind her head, knocking over the anesthesiologist's tools. He was getting upset.

"Please!" Faith yelled, "I'm so sick! I need that pan."

The nurse quickly found her a little pan to throw up in, not that anything was coming up. But Faith felt better having it. She dry heaved every fifteen seconds. She could feel the pain of the epidural being inserted, and what was in it made her even sicker. The nurses put a shield in front of her so she couldn't see the doctor cutting her open. The doctor said she'd feel some tugging, and she certainly did, but no pain. It felt weird to her.

After a few more tugging movements, the doctor said "I have the head," and then he said, "I have the feet!" After one more tug, the doctor held up the baby and announced "There she blows! It's a boy!" Faith could hardly look up because she was so weak, but when she did, she saw the most beautiful baby.

"Look how perfectly round his head is," her doctor said.

One of the nurses said, "Look how big his hands are!"

Faith was staring as much as she could. Her eyes were so heavy, and she noticed she wasn't so sick now. The nurses took the baby to clean him while the doctor started stapling her stomach back together. Faith fell asleep. Her own snoring woke her up several times. She was so exhausted! It had been three days since she came in, and her little bundle of joy was born on Friday at one quarter past five a.m. He was six pounds thirteen ounces and was nineteen inches long. She was too tired and weak to feed him, so Kenny took his little boy and fed him his first bottle.

They named him Mark. Faith was wheeled back into her own private room to get some rest. She looked horrible! Her nurses from the doctor's office came to visit her the next day, and even said she looked like she had fought a battle! Faith laughed and agreed and couldn't wait to take a shower, put on makeup, and fix her hair!

That day the nurse said that they would be bringing the babies to all of the moms so they could feed them. Faith was excited. She couldn't wait to feed her baby for the first time. She heard all of the commotion in the hallway, knowing that the nurses were wheeling the babies to each room. Faith waited and waited. After a while, everything was quiet. The nurse did not bring her baby. She panicked and pushed the button to call the nurse.

When the nurse came in Faith yelled, "Where is my baby?" The nurse looked puzzled and told Faith she'd be right back. She quickly left, and Faith's started worrying that someone stole her baby. She had heard a lot of horror stories about that. Her heart started pounding. After a couple of minutes, the nurse came in with baby Mark.

"I'm so sorry," she said. "He was in the room all by himself." She handed Faith her newborn, and Faith felt sorry for him being back there all by himself. She couldn't believe that no one saw him there. Faith hugged her little one and held him close. She enjoyed feeding him and didn't want to let him go.

Hope and Emily were on their way up to see the new baby. Faith couldn't wait for them to be there. She loved watching her mom hold her new grandson and seeing the look of love on her face. Brandi came in later on and spent some time with Faith and little Mark. Finally, after seven days of being in the hospital, the nurse came in and told her that she was going to take her staples out. "Get ready to go home," she said.

Faith excitedly called Kenny and told him to come get her…now. Kenny came up and helped Faith get dressed. She was in a lot of pain but didn't want any pain meds because they made her sick. Faith just endured the pain and knew it would get better as time went on. The nurse brought in a wheelchair and loaded Faith and the baby. Faith held on tight as the nurse wheeled her down and outside where Kenny was waiting with the car. The nurse helped Kenny secure the baby in the car seat, and Faith rode in the back with him until they got home.

On the ride home, it felt strange being outside. Faith watched the pretty scenery all the way back to her house. When they pulled up, Emily was already waiting outside. She dashed over when she saw the car pull up and helped them into the house. It was nice to be home, and the baby's crib looked so beautiful in her room. Emily held her new grandson and fed him his first bottle at home. Emily stared at little Mark and told him, "I'm your Nanny," and she loved him. Nanny looked so happy as she fed him.

As the weeks went by, Faith and Kenny learned to take care of their new baby. Faith was happy about the choice she made to quit working. After having her baby, she couldn't stand the thought of not being with him all of the time. She put the bassinet by her bed and at times would stay awake all night just making sure he was breathing. She was there to watch over him and protect him. There were many nights she wore herself out by staying up all day and watching the baby sleep at night. He was her pride and joy, and she loved him with all her heart.

Chapter 24: Revelation

"If you tell the truth you don't have to remember anything."
~ Mark Twain

One day Faith went into her room to put the baby down for his nap and smelled cigarette smoke and marijuana smoke. She knew it came from Richard and his friends who were smoking in his room. Since Richard didn't acknowledge Faith's requests to stop, she talked to him about moving out. Richard was angry, but Faith stood her ground. She wanted the best for her newborn baby. Richard moved in next door with Emily, and Faith was relieved.

Just like in their childhood, Emily sided with Richard many times when he and Faith and Hope argued. The hurt and the pain continued to stir emotional havoc in all three of the siblings. Tom had done his job well by tearing the three apart. There was always so much anger and hatred in them for each other. Although there were times when they all had a good time, for the most part, there was no sibling relationship between the twins and Richard. Occasionally Faith and Hope had heated arguments, as well.

The three of them were all hurt in similar and different ways, and their pain would cause them to lash out at each other. All the years of abuse and mind control flowed out of each of them, and all they did was yell out of anger and frustration, never accomplishing anything positive. None of them knew the depths of the pain that was buried so far within them. Their hearts had a hard shell around them as protection of their own selves. One thing was sure—when any of them had disagreements, the tempers flared. They had no idea that it would shape each of them and push them all in different directions, different paths, each on their own journey of learning.

For now, they just lived the way that each of them felt was right for them. Thankfully, Faith and Richard got along a little better since he moved next door. It took a lot of stress off of Faith.

***

One evening Brandi called Faith and told her she was in labor and on the way to the hospital. A while later, Brandi called with the good news of having another boy. That made three for her! Faith was happy for her and enjoyed all the times she went to see Brandi with her baby, or when Brandi came to see her with her growing brood. All of the kids got along great, and it created more memories that Faith and Brandi would always cherish.

On nice days when Emily was off of work, she sat outside in the front yard. Faith looked outside and saw her mom sitting in the shade, and walked over with the baby. They were chatting when Richard came out. They started joking around as usual and laughing.

Then Emily said with a stone-cold face, "If anything ever happens to me, I'm giving Richard the house and everything in it. You girls aren't getting anything."

Faith felt a little stab in her heart, but looked at her mom and said, "That is your house and your things, and you can do whatever you want with it." Although Faith had her own home, she was still upset at what her mom said. She could see the smirk on Richard's face and recalled, once again, that their mother had always treated Richard better than the girls. Faith and Hope were just used to it, even though it hurt them.

Faith stayed a little longer and then went home and called Hope, and told her what their mother said. The girls just shrugged it off like they always did, and buried the hurt in their hearts. After a couple of years, Richard moved out from Emily's house and got his own place. Emily was happy to have her quiet home back.

***

It was a beautiful day. The sun was shining brightly, and white puffy clouds filled the sky. Faith always loved when the sky looked this way. She decided to put the baby in the stroller and go outside for a while. She strolled up and down the street, just right out in front of her yard. Little Mark gazed all around.

As Mark grew, Faith felt it was time for her roommates to leave. She and Kenny sat down and discussed refinancing the house, which would lower the payments. They gave their roommates notice and soon had the house to themselves. They continued to stay downstairs until they got all three bedrooms upstairs fixed up and cleaned, then eventually moved into the master bedroom. Mark had his own bedroom but always slept with his parents. Faith had all of his toys in his room, and he played and sometimes napped there.

Kenny came home one day and told Faith that he was going to get another job that paid more. He wanted to be a firefighter. He had a couple of friends in the department and took all the tests necessary to be hired. This would be a secure job with great benefits, so it looked like things were looking up.

Kenny loved his job, did well, and made a lot of friends. He left the house at half-past five a.m. and would be home the next morning by seven. He worked twenty-four-hour shifts every other day, and then had three days off. On the three days off, he worked at a little shop just at the top of their street in the shopping center.

***

Faith had plenty of time alone at home, and her troubled mind had been working on her. There were many times Kenny would say or do something that reminded her of what her dad did to her. One day, Kenny was sitting in the kitchen, and when Faith walked in, he patted his knees and said, "Come sit on daddy's lap."

Kenny had no idea that his innocent statement was a huge trigger for Faith. But when he said it, Faith felt like she had been punched in the stomach. It made her momentarily ill, but she pretended to laugh and shrug it off. On the inside, however, it tore her up. Once again, there were those feelings that she had to bury without Kenny knowing what was really happening. He had no clue, for Faith had never told him about her past.

It seemed like these kinds of moments kept coming more and more frequently, and she was getting tired of pretending that everything was okay. She continued to focus on Mark, so she didn't have to worry so much about sleeping with Kenny. She was trying to avoid those feelings resurfacing again. Sometimes she'd lay in bed at night, praying about what to do when Kenny would say or do something that triggered a memory. It seemed like she never got any answers.

After a while, Faith started making excuses anytime Kenny wanted to be intimate with her. This seemed to work well, even though she felt guilty lying about it. But somehow the lying felt much better than the unworthiness and shame that continued to haunt her. She didn't want to have those memories popping up every time they were together, so she just wrapped herself in her son and home life, as their sex life began to dwindle. Faith could feel the tension at times when Kenny wanted to be with her, and she would make up an excuse. There were many times that Faith gave in because she knew if she didn't, it would have a profound effect on their marriage. She was also glad that Kenny slept at the firehouse because that gave her time to be alone. Those nights were a relief to her.

One afternoon while Kenny was home, Faith knew she had to tell him. She'd been thinking about it over and over. When Kenny saw her, he knew something was wrong.

"What's wrong, Faith?" he asked.

She began to cry uncontrollably. "I need to tell you something," she began, just barely getting the words out.

Kenny stood up and held her. "You can tell me anything," he said.

Mark was taking a nap, and Faith gained her composure and started talking. "I don't know where to begin," she said. "All I know is that I have to get this off my chest."

Kenny sat down as Faith stood. She looked at him with tears pouring down her face. She lifted up her head and began to tell Kenny what her dad had done to her. She cried the whole time as she told him.

"He molested me since when I was five! He raped me at eleven years old," she cried out. "He continued this till I was about seventeen years old! I'm sorry," she yelled, "but I can't take it anymore, hiding it from you, hiding it from everyone! I had to tell you! I had to tell you!"

Kenny stood and grabbed hold of Faith, and hugged her tight. "I'm here for you," he said as she sobbed on his shoulder. Kenny could feel her whole body shaking. I'm here for you," he said again. "I love you, and we'll get through this together."

Faith hugged him and told him, "Thank you. That means everything to me." She couldn't believe how wonderful he was and how much he understood.

After things settled down a bit, Kenny asked Faith "Have you told your mom?"

"NO!" she shouted. "No! I can't; I won't! I'm too embarrassed!"

Kenny calmed her down and told her that she was going to have to tell her mom. Faith sat down and cried even harder.

"I can't. I just can't." She felt those all-too-familiar feelings welling up inside her. She also suspected that her mom already knew. She had always thought that. That's why Faith had treated her mom, at times, with a cold heart over the years. She really and truly loved her mom, but at the time didn't know how to show it. Faith felt like Emily knew and never did anything about it due to fear of Tom.

Kenny put his hand on Faith's shoulder and said, "Do you want me to tell her?"

Faith said, "No," and then said, "Yes," and then said, "I don't know."

She kept going back and forth, and Kenny said, "I'm going over there right now to talk with her."

"Right now?" Faith asked. "Now?" She thought he'd at least give it a while.

"Yes, right now," Kenny said calmly.

"Okay," Faith said reluctantly.

Kenny hugged her and told her he'd be back after he finished talking to Emily. Faith paced the floor, back and forth and back and forth, and kept peeking out the window to see when Kenny would be coming back. She cried the whole time he was gone, wondering what he was saying and wondering what her mom was thinking and saying. Her heart beat fast as she kept on pacing.

After a couple of hours, she looked out the window and saw Kenny and her mom walking over. Faith's heart pounded faster and faster.

She went into the living room, and Emily came in the front door with tears running down her cheeks. She walked up to Faith and hugged her tight, and then looked at her and said, "Why didn't you ever tell me?"

Faith still thought her mother knew and just said, "I don't know."

Emily said, "You held this in for more than twenty years and never said anything?"

"No Mom, I couldn't. I was too embarrassed." At the time, Faith felt like her mom's tears were not real, even though she was glad to see them. She suspected she knew, and that kept blocking her from feeling any emotion for her mom.

***

Over the next few months, Emily was extra sweet and loving to Faith, and even though she liked it, Faith still felt like it was fake. On the one hand, she appreciated how loving her mom was being, but her heart could not receive it at the time. Still, Faith felt that a ton of weight had lifted off of her, now that her deepest, darkest secret had finally been let out. Life soon began to get back to normal, and Nanny would come over almost every day to visit and play with Mark. They had formed such a beautiful bond, and little Mark just loved his Nanny. The subject was never brought up again.

One day when Faith put Mark down for a nap, she sat in the living room and silently prayed that God would always take care of her son, and to never let anything bad happen to him. She always prayed that God would take care of her family. Faith loved being a mom, and her son was her number one priority. There were times when Hope still didn't understand why Faith just wanted to stay at home. She continued to get mad because Faith didn't go anywhere. Faith had no interest in leaving the house, except for going shopping. Ever the protective mom, she always took her son with her on the few occasions she had to go to the store.

Faith found herself praying more and more, and there were times when Granny (Brandi's mother) would come over and talk about God. Faith loved it. Faith asked her many questions, and she always seemed to have the answers. Pretty soon, Faith was visiting her house every time a minister was there. Faith was like a sponge, soaking up all that was said. Most of the time, she didn't understand what they were talking about, but her spirit knew. Faith's love for God was growing stronger.

One day when Faith was praying in her room, she threw herself on the floor and wept. She cried out to God, saying, "I want to be just like you, Father! Please remove everything inside of me that is not of you!" Faith meant what she said, and over the next few years, she would learn all kinds of things that drew her closer to God during her time with Granny and the group that gathered there.

What Faith didn't realize at the time was the power of her prayer that day. She didn't know that she was actually setting herself up for what would become her life's mission. She would understand those lessons years later. Feeling but not fully grasping her own growth, she simply loved the gatherings at Granny's house and was going regularly.

Faith's bond to her son grew and grew, and she felt that she had to protect him in every way she could. She knew what was out there in the world. Her dad had taught her that first hand, and she was determined to make sure she never left her son alone. Sometimes she would go to church on Sundays or listen to a few TV preachers. Faith continued to pray and learn because she had never been "churched" growing up. It was comforting and important. She was able to discern people who were phonies, and also those who were genuine. When something seemed "not right," she listened to her instincts. At the time, she didn't know that she actually was discerning things and never fully trusted what she was picking up. To Faith, it felt like she was judging, and not discerning. Years later, she would realize she saw things as they were, and that she discerned very well. Over time, she checked out a variety of churches but always felt like she got more out of going to Granny's house than being in a church building. Faith continued to strengthen her faith in a way that made her feel comfortable.

As time went on, Faith thought things would improve once she told Kenny what happened to her. But they didn't. The feelings were still there. Sure, she felt a weight lift off her shoulders once Kenny and Emily knew, so why were the same feelings there when she and Kenny were together? Why were there still trigger words? Faith didn't understand. She thought that maybe these feelings would go away slowly, but they never did.

One thing was certain—Faith's temper never changed. She yelled a lot and slammed cabinet doors, or any door in the house, when she was upset. She just went on with life and coped as best she could, figuring this is how it was going to be. She continued to hide when things surfaced and brought back the past. She was still haunted by her childhood and thought that Kenny would "get it," but it seemed that he didn't. In all reality, he had no clue. He simply said and did things that every man usually does. Faith didn't know at the time that she was the one who had to change on the inside. She would have to heal from her past. She kept looking on the outside for things to change and to feel better. She kept looking at Kenny to change, and he didn't. She thought that change would come from other people, but of course it never did.

**

As always, Faith continued to run into someone who pushed her buttons or said something that triggered a wound. She couldn't seem to get away from it and swept her feelings under the carpet. Thankfully, going to Granny's house when there were gatherings really helped. More and more she loved what she was hearing, and it seemed to help her when not-so-good things arose in her home life.

Her faith was getting stronger, and she just knew in her heart that God was going to heal her of all of her pain and misery one day. The more she shared what she learned with Kenny, the more he'd roll his eyes. Finally, one day he told her that he didn't want to hear about what she thought of God. This really upset Faith because she felt like he didn't care about what touched her. She could feel the tension between them. It was hurtful that she couldn't share what she loved with her husband. She stopped talking to him about it. However, she continued to grow spiritually and could sense a difference in her life. She knew that she could always count on God for everything, no matter what the circumstances were. Kenny just wasn't going in the same direction.

One night Faith had a dream. She was standing in her bedroom, and God spoke to her, saying, "You're the Joseph of your family." Then God placed the coat of many colors on her. She was in awe and folded her arms around the beautiful coat. "Thank you, God," she said and ran upstairs to tell Kenny. In her dream, she came through the kitchen and could see that Kenny and a co-worker were outside talking. She ran out the door shouting, "Look at what God gave me!" as she pranced around in her coat of many colors.

She knew they didn't know what it was, so she explained how God gave it to her and told her that she was the Joseph of her family. She had the biggest grin on her face and was so honored that God had chosen her, even though she didn't know what it meant at the time. Suddenly, Kenny and his co-worker started pointing and laughing at her. She stood in shock, not understanding why they would make fun of her. She ran back in the house in tears, but told God, "Thank you for the beautiful coat of many colors." She believed what God told her.

Then she woke up. Faith lay in bed with her eyes closed and just smiled, saying, "Thank you, God." The next day she looked in the Bible and re-read the story of Joseph. She wondered, *How am I like him? What does God mean by that? How can I be the Joseph of my family when they hardly ever get along?*

Faith never forgot that dream, and it wasn't until years later that the answer was given to her.

Chapter 25: An Answered Prayer

"Raising children is an uncertain thing; success is reached only after a life of battle and worry."
~ Democritus

When Faith had some quiet time, she called Hope. As they talked, Hope mentioned she had been dating a guy named Jason for a while, and Faith asked all about him. As always, Hope told Faith how beautiful it was in Florida and wanted her to move there. Faith loved Florida as well but knew she couldn't move there even though she wanted to. She wanted to at least go and visit Hope but never got a chance. Faith and Kenny had always put their extra money into their home.

As Faith chatted, Hope interrupted and said, "Guess what?" with a happy sound in her voice.

"Oh, it's hard to tell with you!" Faith exclaimed.

With a big blurt, Hope yelled, "I'm pregnant!"

"Oh my gosh!" said Faith. "I wasn't expecting that! Congratulations!"

Hope was so excited, and Faith was excited for her. *Now Hope will realize how a baby changes your life and your heart and the way you do things,* she thought. Faith remembered times when Hope got upset with her because she didn't ever want to go anywhere. Now she'd start to understand.

Faith grinned and couldn't be happier for her sister. "Have you told Mom yet?"

"No, I'm going to call her after I talk to you," she told Faith.

"I've saved all of Mark's clothes, so if you have a boy, I'll send them to you."

Hope was grateful, as Faith had quite a bit of baby stuff and had saved it all.

"Well, I need to go for now," said Faith. "Mark should be getting up from his nap in a minute."

They both said their goodbyes and Faith had a huge smile as she hung up the phone. She was ecstatic for her sister.

***

Winter was settling in, and Faith always made sure that everything at home was perfect. Kenny went off to work, and Faith stayed at home with Mark, as usual. She spent all her time with her son and played little games with him. They read books, especially before bedtime. He was always such a good boy and seemed to smile all the time. He hardly ever fussed. Faith made sure that he had everything that he wanted, and then some.

While looking at her son and seeing how innocent and fragile he was, she wondered how anyone could ever take advantage of a child. She thought about herself being five years old and her dad doing what he did to her. *How could he? How can anyone harm another human being, a child?* Her thoughts got the best of her, and she'd wipe away her tears, even more determined to love and protect her child. Knowing that abuse happens to boys as well as girls in and outside of their homes, she was determined to make sure that Mark had everything at home to make him happy—she wasn't about to let him spend the night at his friends' houses once he started getting older. She had already made that decision while he was a toddler. If she didn't protect him, who would? Faith's mindset was to never take her eyes off of her child, and she was religious about it.

Time went by, and Hope called Faith to say she was having contractions and would be going to the hospital soon. Faith wanted to be with her sister so badly but couldn't afford to go. Soon Hope called and announced she had a little boy, and gave him the name Matthew. Hope was so excited, and Faith cried with joy.

A couple of months later, Hope called and said she wanted to move back home.

Can we come stay with you until we find work?" Hope asked.

"Why sure," said Faith all excited. At this moment, she realized her prayer of raising children together with her twin was being answered. "Just let me know when you'll be coming and I'll make sure everything is ready."

After they hung up, Faith started cleaning the bedroom for her sister. She wanted it to be perfect so Hope, Jason and the baby would feel comfortable. When Kenny got home, Faith told him the news, and he was happy to have them there. They had plenty of room, and Nanny would also be next door to help out.

The next day, Faith was making Mark's lunch when the doorbell rang. It was a longtime friend of Faith's, and she had her little girl, Stephanie, with her, who was a year older than Mark.

"Hey Tiffany," said Faith. "I'm so glad you all stopped by!"

Tiffany came in, and her little girl was excited to be there.

"Stephanie, you and Mark can go play in his room," said Faith, "so your mom and I can talk." They heard the kids squeal and start dragging out toys.

"I was just about to fix lunch," she told Tiffany. "Would you like to join us?"

"Sure," Tiffany said. "That sounds wonderful."

Faith served lunch, and they all sat at the table and had a good time. Afterward, the children went back to Mark's room.

Faith asked, "So, what have you been doing, Tiffany?"

"Well," she said, "I thought I might be pregnant, so I went to the store and got a pregnancy test. Do you mind if I do it here?"

"Of course not," said Faith. "Go right ahead!"

Tiffany went into the bathroom, and a couple of minutes later came out.

"The test is negative," she said, wiping her forehead with a sigh of relief.

"Here," Tiffany said, "it's a two pack. Why don't you use the other one? I'm just going to throw it away, so why waste it."

"Okay," said Faith, laughing. "I know I'm not pregnant, but I'll do it anyway." She took the test and went into the bathroom. After a couple of minutes, she came out with her mouth wide open. "Oh my God! I'm pregnant!"

Tiffany's eyes got big, and Faith's mouth was still hanging wide open. They were both in shock and started laughing, thinking of how Tiffany thought she was pregnant and wasn't, while Faith thought she wasn't, and was! Faith couldn't believe it. She called her doctor's office for an appointment to make sure.

Shortly after Tiffany said, "We have to get home."

"Well thanks!" Faith said with a smirk. "Thanks for coming over and finding out that I'm pregnant!!"

They both laughed and hugged, and Tiffany and her little girl left. Faith couldn't wait to tell Kenny, her mom, and Hope. She got on the phone right away and called Kenny. He wouldn't be home until the morning, but when he heard the news, he was extremely happy. He couldn't believe it either.

"I've already made an appointment, and they're getting me in the day after tomorrow," she said.

As they hung up the phone, Kenny told the guys that he was going to be a dad again. He couldn't wait until Faith went to the doctor.

Emily was at work and would be home later that day, so Faith called Hope. Hope couldn't believe what she heard! They talked for a while, and Faith told her that she was getting her room fixed up and would be working on the house until they got there. Hope was happy for Faith, and they couldn't wait to see each other.

Now, even more, Faith was seeing that she and Hope would be raising their kids together. "Thank you, God!" she said every time she thought about it. Even during prayer time, she gave thanks. All kinds of sweet thoughts came to her mind, like how they could take the kids to the park and how they could all play together. She smiled a sweet smile and started preparing dinner for herself and Mark, while she waited on Emily to get home. Faith was so busy in the kitchen that she didn't even hear her mom come in.

Faith heard Mark scream, "Nanny!" Faith spun around and quickly grabbed the pregnancy test and held it behind her back. Nanny was so busy kissing little Mark all over that she didn't even see Faith grab it. After Nanny had her time with Mark, she sat down.

"Hi," she greeted Faith. "What's for dinner?"

"Well," said Faith, "I have something for you first." She held her hand behind her back.

Emily could see that her daughter was happy and wanted to know right then and there what it was.

"Close your eyes and hold out your hand," said Faith.

Emily could hardly stand it. She was so curious! Obviously, that's where Faith got her curiosity.

As soon as Emily's eyes were closed, Faith said, "No peeking!" She put the test in her mother's hand. "Now open your eyes."

Emily looked, and just for a split second didn't know what it was. Suddenly, she looked up and screamed, "Oh honey! You're pregnant?"

"Well, that test says I am, but I've made a doctor appointment to find out for sure."

Emily was so happy! She was going to be a Nanny again—a grandmother to Richards's two girls, Mark, Hope's baby boy, and now another one on the way.

"You're going to be quite busy," Faith told her.

"Yes, but it will be fun."

Even though Faith had not officially found out for sure, everyone knew she was pregnant. Emily stayed for dinner as she usually did, and then, later on, went home. Later that night, Faith called Brandi and told her the news. Brandi was ecstatic!

"Are you trying to keep up with me?" she said, laughing.

"Well, I don't know about that," said Faith.

They chatted on the phone for a while, and then Faith said, "I'm going to get Mark ready for bed." Her day had been long and full of surprises, and it wore her out.

***

Faith got up extra early the morning of her doctor appointment. She was so curious about how far along in her pregnancy she was. Right before she left, she called Kenny and told him she was leaving shortly and would let him know how things went as soon as possible. She finished getting dressed and headed out the door. When she arrived, they drew blood and got a urine sample. Later the doctor came in and confirmed the pregnancy. Faith was so excited! The doctor told her she was only about two weeks pregnant. She was a little surprised by that because she assumed she was at least five or six weeks.

Now the time will seem to go by slowly, she thought. She began to have those pregnancy feelings that she loved so much again and couldn't wait to get home and share the news.

Chapter 26: Two Baby Girls

"Each daughter of God is of infinite worth because of her divine mission."
~ Russell M. Nelson

Faith saw that Mark woke up, and she pretended to be asleep.

"Wake up, Mommy," he said. "It's time to get up!"

Faith opened her eyes and saw her beautiful blonde little boy and his sweet smile. She put her arms around him and kissed his face all over. He started giggling and tried to get away.

"I'm hungry," he said.

"Well then, let's go in the kitchen, and you can tell me what you want for breakfast."

"Otay," said little Mark as he ran into the kitchen.

Faith closed the door, so Kenny could sleep in a little.

"So, what would you like to eat?"

"Pantates!" yelled Mark

"Pancakes it is!" Faith said and reached down to hug him. "Would you like me to fix you a Mickey Mouse pancake?"

"Yes, Mommy!" Mark screamed.

"Alright then, that's what I'll do."

Mark loved his Mickey Mouse pancakes so much that he usually cleaned his plate. Kenny came in and grabbed some coffee, and Faith already had more pancakes ready. The three sat down and enjoyed breakfast. This didn't happen very often because Kenny worked a lot, but was off that day.

"So," said Faith. "What are we going to do today?"

Kenny said, "I'm going to cut the grass and just hang out at the house."

"Okay," said Faith. "I think after breakfast I'm going to call Hope and see what they're doing."

Before she had a chance to call, the phone rang. It was Hope.

"I was just getting ready to call you!" Faith said.

They had some small talk, and then Hope said, "I wanted to let you know that we're going to pack up this week and will be there this weekend!"

"Oh wow," said Faith. "That's great! Your room is ready, but I'll still tidy up a bit."

They talked for a while longer, and Hope said, "We should be there Sunday late afternoon."

Faith was tickled and couldn't wait to see her and her new little nephew. "The doctor confirmed my pregnancy," she said.

They hung up on that happy note. Past conflict seemed far away.

"They're moving in this weekend," Faith told Kenny. "I have to go to the store and pick up some groceries."

***

The week seemed to fly by, and Faith made sure everything was perfect. She had the whole house cleaned and all kinds of meals planned. Hope and her family finally arrived Sunday around two in the afternoon. Faith got everyone settled in, and Kenny helped Jason unload the truck. It was a fun day. Faith got to hold little Matthew. He was so adorable, and it felt good to hold a baby again.

"It won't be long before you're holding your new baby," said Hope.

Mark touched the baby's head and gave him a little kiss. They ate dinner and settled in for the evening. Jason found work within a few days, and Hope found work after a couple of weeks. She didn't want to leave her baby, but she knew he'd be in good hands with Faith.

Faith took care of him like her own. She loved holding him in the rocking chair and watching his huge brown eyes drift off. He was a good baby. Her day-to-day activities involved staying home and taking care of the boys, while also keeping the house clean, doing the laundry, and cooking all the meals. She also cleaned up after each meal.

Faith tried to keep up the best she could, but it was hard taking care of the boys and three grown-ups. After a couple of months, it took a toll on her. Between all of the house chores and morning sickness, she was becoming exhausted. One day she felt something wet and went into the bathroom. Faith saw some blood in her underwear and got scared. She called her doctor.

"Get in bed with your feet up, and come tomorrow morning," he ordered.

She really couldn't stay in bed the whole time because she had to take care of the baby and Mark. She did the best she could. The next day she went to the doctor, and he examined her.

"For the next two weeks, you have to stay in bed with your feet up. Everything looks okay, but you need to rest. You're doing too much," he said.

Faith was relieved that the baby was okay. When she got home, she told everyone what the doctor said. She knew she had to take care of the children and the chores while everyone worked, but it was beginning to be too much for her because she was the only one doing it all—especially now when she needed to rest for the baby's sake. She called her mom and told her that it was just too much for her to manage.

"Can Hope and Jason move in with you, Mom?" she asked.

"Yes," Emily agreed. "I'd love to have them there."

Faith told Hope her situation, and they moved in with Emily. By then they had been at Faith's house for almost two months. Faith still watched little Matthew, but life was less stressful now that she didn't have to cook and clean for everyone. That took a lot of pressure off of Faith, and she could stay in bed more. She'd only get up when she had to, and Mark stayed with her in her room. Faith made sure he had toys and books so he would be entertained.

As time went on, Faith felt the baby start to move. She enjoyed every second of it and always put her hand on her tummy. "I love you!" she told her unborn baby, just like she had done when she was pregnant with Mark. Faith had a doctor appointment in a couple of weeks and an ultrasound, so she would be able to see if it was going to be a boy or a girl. She and Kenny were excited to find out. It was fun to have everyone guessing the gender.

Faith made the appointment on a day that Kenny would be off work, and they went in for the ultrasound. The doctor had Faith lay on the table and rubbed some jelly-like substance on her belly. He turned the lights out, and Faith's heart started pounding. She could hear and see the heartbeat. The doctor ran the wand over her belly, trying to get the best images. When he did, he stopped and explained what they were seeing on the screen. It was so exciting! Finally, the baby moved, and the doctor was able to get a perfect shot.

He shouted, "It's a girl!" Faith and Kenny were so happy! They couldn't wait to get home and tell everyone.

***

Late that evening as they were getting ready for bed, Faith could not help but think of her little girl. Thoughts flooded her mind, and during her prayer, she asked God to always protect her daughter and son. She wiped the silent tears and started to drift off to sleep.

The next morning Hope called. "Want to go to the zoo?" she asked.

Faith thought it was an excellent idea, and they loaded up the children and spent the day walking around and looking at the animals. Faith and Hope loved going there and always remembered their times together.

When Faith was almost eight months pregnant, she got up about four a.m. to go to the bathroom. As she sat there, she felt something strange come out. She turned on the light, and the toilet was filled with blood and something else. She didn't know what it was and was frightened.

She cleaned herself up and left the toilet "as is," and climbed into bed. Then she picked up the phone and called Hope.

Hope answered the phone in a sluggish voice. "Hello?" She heard Faith crying. "What's wrong?"

"I don't know," said Faith. "I'm scared!" She told Hope what happened. "Can you watch Mark while I go to the doctor? I just called him, and he told me to stay in bed with my feet up again, and to come in first thing in the morning."

"Of course, I'll watch Mark," Hope said. "If you need me, you just call me, and I'll run right over."

Faith thanked her sister and called Kenny. He had to work at his other job, and Faith told him that she could drive herself and would let him know what the doctor said. After she hung up, she could not go back to sleep. She laid there in bed, praying and begging God: *Please, let my baby be okay.*

Hope came over, and Faith showed her the toilet. Hope could not believe how much blood was in there. She was worried.

Faith drove herself to the doctor. He examined her and did an ultrasound. Faith was nervous, and tears streamed down the sides of her face. She watched closely to see the movement of the baby and hear the heartbeat.

After a couple of minutes, the doctor said, "You and baby are going to be just fine. You have a low-lying placenta, and a piece of it had chunked out. That's what you saw in the toilet, along with the blood," he explained. "You have to take it easy for a while and no heavy lifting for the next few days. Bed rest and feet up."

Faith was relieved and silently said, *Thank you, God!* She got dressed and went home and gave everyone the good news. She held her belly all the time now, and rubbed it saying, "I love you." She often wondered if the baby ever heard her and knew what she was saying.

Faith crawled into bed as the doctor had ordered, and kept her hand on her tummy, praying and thanking God for her little girl and that she was okay.

***

On one of her days off, Hope came over and announced that she and Jason were going to look for an apartment closer to where he worked. Faith didn't like that she was not going to be next door anymore, but at least she wasn't living in Florida where she could never see her. Hope was thrilled to get their own place, and when the time came, Kenny helped them move. It was fun watching them get in their new apartment. Faith enjoyed the drive over there with Kenny and little Mark. Visiting them felt good.

Faith was now into her ninth month of pregnancy. One day while at home alone, she kept getting sharp pains that came quickly and painfully, but would only last a few seconds. This kept on happening until Faith thought, *Oh no, I hope this isn't my labor pains!* Sure enough, it was, and the contractions kept coming and going and getting closer apart. Kenny happened to be working that day, so she called him. He started to get frantic, and Faith had to calm him down. He said he'd be home as soon as they found someone to cover for him. He was home in a couple of hours.

Faith had already called the doctor and packed for the hospital. She called Emily and said, "Mom, can you come over and get Mark? I'm in labor and Kenny will be home in a little while."

"Of course," said Emily. She came right over to pick up Mark and a little suitcase Faith had packed for him.

Faith explained to Mark that he was going to spend a couple of days with Nanny. Mark was happy—he loved his Nanny, and his Nanny loved him. Even though Faith knew that Mark would be just fine, she hated to leave him. It hurt her heart so badly because she had never before left him.

She cried as she hugged Mark. "I'll be home soon with your new baby sister," she told him.

Kenny got home and loaded Faith in the car. They arrived at the hospital just before noon. Kenny's work had changed insurance companies, so this was a different hospital than the one she went to for Mark. It was old, and the people were not very friendly. When they walked in, Faith told the nurse she was in labor.

"Right this way," said the nurse and walked quickly down the hall. Faith thought she was getting her a wheelchair like the other hospital but soon found out that wasn't the case. As she walked, Faith had another contraction. She had to stop and lean against the wall. It was that shooting pain again, and it really hurt. She watched as the nurse disappeared around the corner.

The contraction let up, and Faith started walking slowly down the hall. As she turned the corner, she saw the nurse coming out of a door.

"I was wondering where you were," she said.

Faith said, "While you were walking so fast down the hall, I was having a contraction and had to stop."

The nurse didn't really seem to care. "Oh, okay. Follow me." She took Faith to a room where the nurse told her to put on a gown and get in bed. "I'll be back in a few minutes," she said.

Faith did as instructed, and about that time Kenny came in her room. The nurse came back and checked Faith, and told her she was not in labor.

Faith looked at her and said, "I'm not like normal women; my labor is different."

The nurse argued and told her that they were going to send her home in a little while.

Faith got upset. She waited until the nurse came back and told her to call her doctor.

"I'm not going anywhere until I see him," Faith insisted.

After a while, the nurse came back and said the doctor was on his way and should be there in about an hour. Faith continued to have pains, and they were coming closer and closer now. She knew without a doubt she was in labor. Kenny sat with her and looked tired. The doctor finally came in and examined Faith. He didn't really think she was in labor, but after Faith told him the story of Mark's birth, he decided to keep her in. They hooked her up to an I.V., and the doctor came in periodically to check on her.

After a few hours, Faith told Kenny, "Go on home and get some rest. I'll call you later." She knew this delivery could take a while. Faith remembered her thirty-four-hour labor with Mark and hoped that it wouldn't be that long this time.

Kenny went home to get some lunch and sleep. After a few more hours, the doctor came back and announced that Faith was dilating, but her water had not broken. He said he was going to break her water and that she should start dilating quickly. Faith called Kenny and told him to get back to the hospital. The doctor broke her water, left the room, and came back a while later to examine her again.

"It looks like you'll have to have another C-section," he said.

Faith's heart dropped. She looked at the doctor and said, "I really wanted to experience childbirth this time."

He said, "I'll wait a little longer and will let you know." He could see that she wasn't happy about having another C-section.

After a while, he came back and examined her once again. Faith was almost fully dilated, and he said he'd check on her in a little bit and try to deliver the baby. They wheeled her into the delivery room, and the doctor examined her again. She was now fully dilated. They gave her an epidural, and Faith was fine until the medicine started going through her body. She began to get sick and knew from past experience to have a pan ready in case she vomited. Oh, the memories were flooding back!

After twenty-nine hours of labor, little Julie was born. The doctor performed an episiotomy and then used forceps to get the baby out. After much tugging, the doctor finally delivered the baby at seventeen minutes past one a.m. on Saturday. The doctor saw that the umbilical cord was in a knot, and held the baby in his hands with her little face looking right at Faith. Faith was in awe of the love she felt. *This is my little girl,* she thought.

"Do you want to cut the umbilical cord?" the doctor asked Kenny.

"Yes," he said excitedly and cut the connection that had given the baby life while in Faith's tummy.

Faith couldn't keep her eyes of her little girl. She was beautiful! The nurse weighed and measured her. She weighed seven pounds, four ounces, and measured nineteen and a half inches long. She watched as the nurse laid her under a heat lamp and cleaned her up, while the doctor had some stitching to do on Faith. As Faith lay there marveling at her beautiful baby, she couldn't wait until the nurse put her little newborn in her arms. She was so alert and lay quietly under the warm light while the nurse cleaned her off. She kept staring at all the lights. Faith watched her every move as the baby's little brown eyes seemed to be looking everywhere!

Faith noticed this time that after they took out the epidural, she stopped getting sick. Soon they wrapped the baby up and placed her in her arms. Faith stared into her eyes, and looked at Kenny and said, "She's so beautiful!" Kenny agreed, and then he got to hold her. It was an amazing time, one that Faith would never forget. *Now I have two beautiful children who I love and adore.* She couldn't be happier, and life couldn't be better!

The nurses took the baby and wheeled Faith into her room. She was in a lot of pain, and all she kept thinking of was that she was not home with her little boy. She called Emily and said she was in a room.

Emily said, "I'll get Mark, and we'll be right up."

Faith called Hope. "I'll be there tomorrow," Hope said.

When Emily and Mark arrived, Faith called Mark over and hugged him. She sat him on the bed with her and couldn't stand the thought of him going home without her. Nanny and little Mark got to see new baby Julie, and Nanny held her in her arms. Mark bent over and gently kissed her on the cheek.

"That's my baby sister," he said. Faith was happy to have such a beautiful family and felt blessed that Nanny was living right next door and could watch them grow.

It was soon time for Nanny to take Mark back home. Faith's room got quiet. By the time dinner rolled around, she couldn't stand being away from Mark.

She called the nurse in and said, "I want to go home."

The nurse said, "You need to stay a couple more days, but I'll go check and see if you can be released."

After a while, the nurse came in and told her that she could go home in the morning, but not that evening.

Faith was excited and called Kenny. "Come get me in the morning," she said.

She picked up the phone and called her mom. "I'll be home in the morning," she said. "Hand the phone to Mark." Emily put Mark on the line, and Faith told him, "I'm bringing your little sister home tomorrow."

Then Faith laid back in the bed and was in a lot of pain, but didn't tell the nurse. She was worried they would not let her go home. She just couldn't stand being away from her little boy.

The next morning came, and Kenny picked up Faith and got the baby snuggled in the car seat. Emily and Mark were already waiting at the house. Kenny got the baby out of the car seat and brought her in, and Faith hugged and hugged Mark. Now she felt complete.

Nanny sat down and fed Julie her first bottle. Faith marveled at her mom's face. Little Mark stood right beside her, kissing his baby sister on her cheek. It was picture perfect! Kenny had taken the week off from work, and it was a good thing because Faith was in a lot of pain.

"You should have stayed in the hospital a little longer," he kept telling her.

Kenny had to take care of the baby that whole week—feeding her and getting up in the middle of the night. Faith could hardly walk because of the pain. It took just over a week before Faith started feeling better. She was glad Kenny had taken off to help her and could not have done it without him.

***

As Faith was having her morning coffee, Hope called to say that she and Matthew were coming over to see the baby. She hadn't seen the baby yet because she had been too busy. When Hope came in, she picked up baby Julie and couldn't believe how little she looked. She hadn't held a baby in a while. By this time, Mark was four years old, and Matthew was a year old.

That Christmas Hope invited them over for Christmas dinner. They drove to Hope's house and had such a fun time. Faith and Hope were in the kitchen cooking away while Kenny, Jason, and the children played in the living room. Faith loved cooking with Hope. She was such a great cook, and it was a joy doing things together with their families. *God has granted my heart's cry about us raising our kids together,* she thought. They helped the kids open their gifts under the tree, and then enjoyed a fantastic dinner. They were all stuffed and had a great time.

It started to get dark, and Faith told Hope that they were going to head back home. They got all bundled up and said their goodbyes, and headed out the door. It was a nice drive back to their house, and Faith and Kenny talked about how much fun they had.

***

It was cold that winter, but they didn't get the snow that they had hoped for during the holidays. Faith got the children ready for bed, and then sat back and relaxed for a while. She loved being a mom, and it seemed like everything was going well. She and Kenny were getting along great and never really had any arguments. However, Faith was still troubled by the same issues every time she and Kenny were intimate. The thoughts of what her dad did to her would come rushing in, and she would have to fight them. In her head, she kept telling herself, *This is my husband. This isn't Dad,* and fought back the images that flashed in her mind. Faith always wondered if this is how it was going to be for the rest of her life. She hoped that one day it would all disappear. By now, the intimacy was getting even less frequent. Faith just wanted peace in her heart and did not want to ever think of those memories again.

The weather remained cold over the next couple months, and Faith loved making winter recipes. She had just finished baking homemade bread when the front door opened. In walked Hope and Matthew. Hope smelled the fresh bread in the air and told Faith that she wanted some.

"Get it yourself!" Faith said, laughing.

Hope looked at Faith and said, "There is a reason why I'm here, other than eating your bread."

"Oh yeah?" Said Faith. "Why?"

Hope looked right into Faith's eyes and said, "I'm pregnant!"

Faith's mouth hung open, and she shouted, "Congratulations!"

"I just got back from a doctor appointment, and he said I'm about six weeks along."

"That's wonderful," said Faith. "You should have a girl this time."

They sat for a while and snacked on fresh bread and butter while the kids played in Mark's room.

Hope got Matthew and said, "I'm going over Nanny's to tell her. You want to come?"

"No, that's okay," said Faith. "You go tell her your good news, and if you want to come back over, you can."

"Actually," said Hope, "I have a lot of running around to do, so I'm going to run next door and then head out."

"Okay," said Faith. They said goodbye, and Hope went out the door.

***

The cold days of winter were coming to an end. Spring was right around the corner, and Faith loved feeling the warmth and seeing the buds on the trees. She enjoyed all four seasons. Each had special memories in their heart. She and Hope spent time together at the park and on shopping adventures. Hope's belly was growing, and during her last few weeks of pregnancy, she stayed home a lot.

When Hope was close to delivering, she felt that something wasn't quite right. She had not felt the baby move in quite some time. She called the doctor, and they instructed her to get to the hospital. The nurse examined her and picked up a very faint heartbeat. She called for the doctor right away and told him Hope needed an emergency C-section. The doctor told the nurse that everything was okay, and to just wait a little while longer. The nurse yelled at him, and told him again that he needed to come in, and needed to do it now. He finally agreed and came in to examine Hope.

He called for an emergency C-section. When he delivered the baby, she was lifeless and so tiny. They did all they could to get her to respond, and after a while she did. The little girl weighed only four pounds. Hope gave thanks to the nurse that day. If she had not demanded the doctor come in, the baby would not have made it. They found out that the placenta had gone bad about the seventh month of pregnancy, so the baby was actually starving. Hope's doctor at the time told her she didn't need another ultrasound in her seventh month.

They got the baby all cleaned up and placed her in Hope's arms. Her baby girl was the first baby to be born at the hospital that year…a New Year's Day baby! To Hope and Jason's surprise, the local TV crew came in to welcome her special baby. Hope was exhausted and didn't really want the camera crew in her room. They entered anyway, so she made the best of it. She found herself and the baby on the front page of the local newspaper. It was exciting. Her faith in God had been growing since she gave birth to Matthew, and now found herself thanking God over and over for saving her little girl. She stayed in the hospital for a while until the baby was strong enough to come home. She named her Angelica.

***

Faith loved staying at home and raising her children. She became very obsessive about having everything at her home that would make her kids happy, so they didn't want to go to anyone else's house. Faith and Kenny bought a swing set and put it in the backyard. Kenny built a sandbox for the kids to play in. Even though the backyard was fenced in, Faith never left her children alone outside.

Even when inside, she would make sure all of the doors were locked. As time went on, she became more obsessive. She watched over everyone's children who came to visit, making sure they were safe at her home. All of the kid's friends loved coming over. Faith made sure that they had almost every toy and game to keep them busy. She baked all kinds of treats, and sometimes they'd do crafts together. Hope brought her children over to play as well. It was the perfect place, guarded by the ever-vigilant Faith.

Little Angelica was always a small baby. When she was about eight months old, she didn't eat as much and was losing weight. Hope took her to the doctor, and when he examined her, he could hear that something was wrong with her heart. Through the stethoscope, he heard the blood swishing. He decided to do open heart surgery when she was ten months old. When the time came, Hope was worried sick. She stayed at the hospital while Faith watched the other children. The surgery was successful, and the doctor sewed a patch on Angelica's little heart. She had to be watched closely over the next few years.

After little Angelica celebrated her first birthday, Jason announced that he was going to reenlist in the military again. He had served five years previously and thought that it would be a good idea to get back in and make a career of it. It would provide better benefits and more money, so he re-enlisted and was told that they would be stationed in Kentucky. Faith was upset that they were going to move a few states away. Jason told Hope that she could stay at the apartment until he found a place to live, and then they could come up. Hope agreed and was happy that they could stay for a little while longer.

Chapter 27: Loss and a Long Lost Sister

> *"People who come from dysfunctional families are not destined for a dysfunctional life."*
> ~ Bo Bennett

One day while Emily was off of work, she received a phone call from the attorney who worked on the adoption of her little girl years ago. Emily and Tom had given up the child several decades prior, so hearing from the attorney was quite a shock. It turned out to be the news that she had long awaited.

The attorney explained that the adoptive parents said it was okay for Emily to have contact with her daughter. When she was given a number to call, Emily was ecstatic and nervous at the same time. That day when she reluctantly decided to give her firstborn daughter up came flooding back. She began thinking all kinds of thoughts: *How does my daughter feel about it? Is she hurt or angry?*

It took Emily a while, but she called the number and talked to her daughter for the first time. Her name was Erin. They made plans for her to come and visit, and when Emily was finished talking to Erin, she went over to Faith's house. Faith could tell that something was going on by the way Emily looked. Emily told Faith the good news, and Faith was so happy for her mom. She could see that Emily was very nervous.

Emily said, "I hope Erin doesn't hate me for giving her up."

Faith comforted her mom. "All things happen for a reason, and I'm sure Erin won't hate you. Why would she come down if she hated you, Mom?"

Emily smiled at those words of reassurance and stayed for lunch with Faith and the kids.

***

Erin would be there in two weeks, and everyone was excited! Faith, Hope, and Richard could not wait to finally meet their older sister. As Faith contemplated on her sister over the next days, she couldn't help but think again of how lucky Erin was for not enduring what the rest of them had gone through. She wondered how Erin felt about being adopted. When the spiritual gavel came down that fateful day, it was decided that Richard and the twins would be with their parents. For they were the ones who had that particular path to walk. Erin had a different journey and all the lessons that came with it.

The day came when Erin pulled up in the driveway. She brought her youngest daughter Daniela with her. Everyone ran out of the house to meet and greet their new sister and niece. Hope was the first to run up to Erin and give her a big hug. Emily fought back the tears as she saw her daughter for the first time. She looked a lot like Emily's sister Jennifer. Everyone talked and talked and shared stories, all getting to know each other. Erin spent the night, and the next day was on her way back home. She visited a few times thereafter.

Richard made a trip up to see Erin as well. It seemed that Richard and Erin hit it off, and Faith assumed that Richard welcomed a new sister—one that didn't come with all the horrors he had experienced, along with the twins. By now, Richard was able to talk about the abuse and how it affected him. However, his perception of the twins was tainted because of what Tom made him believe. It played a major role in the anger, bitterness, and judgment that he carried for them, not realizing that Tom's intent all along was to pit all three against each other.

The time came for Hope to pack up the children and head for Kentucky. They were able to find a home in Tennessee close to Jason's base. It was a sad day for Faith. She thought they'd be raising their kids together well into the future, and now Hope was leaving. After a while, Faith got used to them being gone and was happy that Hope settled in well in Tennessee. They called each other quite a bit and talked for hours. Faith really missed her sister.

It wasn't long after Emily met Erin for the first time that she started not feeling well. She kept telling Faith about her lower back pain. Her job kept her on her feet eight hours a day, and her doctor gave her a list of back exercises. Faith reminded her mother to do them.

***

After a while, the pain got a little worse, and Emily's voice sounded hoarse. Faith had a bad feeling about it. She thought that her mom might have throat cancer. Emily had always smoked quite a bit. One day Faith was at home, and Emily came over. She looked scared.

"What's wrong, Mom?" asked Faith.

"I just went to the bathroom, and blood was in my stool," said Emily. Faith could see that her mom was worried.

"That's it!" Faith said. "I'm calling my doctor and getting you an appointment. He is really thorough."

Faith made the appointment for Emily that was scheduled in just a couple of days and went with Emily to the doctor. He asked a million questions and then ordered some tests. He then told them to set an appointment in four days, when the tests would be back. Faith took her mom to get the tests done, and then waited a few days for the results. She took Emily back to the doctor so he could explain the findings. It was what neither one of them wanted to hear.

Emily had colon cancer.

The doctor told her that he'd have to operate to see how far the cancer had spread.

Surgery day came, and Faith and Richard sat in the waiting room. After a few hours, the doctor appeared—and his face was grim. Faith could tell he was about to deliver some bad news, and he did.

"I took out what I could and also removed her ovaries," he explained. "However, the cancer has spread to her intestines. There was no way I could remove it."

Faith and Richard were devastated even more when the doctor said, "By the looks of things, I give your mom about fourteen months to live. I'm so sorry. It looks like this has been spreading for about three years. She'll have to come in and see me, and we'll get started with chemo as soon as possible."

Faith was numb. She looked at Richard and felt like she was in a dream—she wasn't able to talk. "Can we go see her now?" Faith asked the doctor.

"Yes," he said. "She's in a room now and will still be pretty groggy, but you can go see her for a few minutes. She needs to get some rest."

Faith and Richard went to her room and stood there in silence. There were no words. Faith held her mother's hand and could feel the tears sting, but she wanted to be strong.

Emily slowly opened her eyes.

"Hi Mom," Faith said. Emily looked so frail and exhausted. "I'm going to let you get some rest. I just wanted to let you know that I was here, and I'm going home and will be back later."

"Okay," Emily said with a very weak voice.

Faith told Richard, "We should go so Mom can get some rest."

Richard said his goodbyes and told her he'd be back later, and they both left.

On the way out of the hospital, Richard told Faith he was going to move back in with Emily so he could help her.

"I'm right next door," Faith said, "and I'll help her, too."

Richard spoke out. "I don't like where I'm living right now. My lease is up in three more months, and then I'll move in."

Faith called Hope and told her the news. Hope cried and cried, and said she'd try and get down to visit as soon as she could.

After Emily was discharged from the hospital, Faith took care of her. Emily spent more time over Faith's house than her own. Emily was so strong. She never showed any signs of weakness. No one would ever know that she was sick because she held it all in. She eventually went back to work part-time and had always loved her job. If she was feeling good, she went to her appointments by herself. All the other times, Faith took her.

***

Autumn was just a couple of months away, and Mark was starting kindergarten that year. He was quite shy and a bit scared to start school. But he took the bus the first day, and Faith and Julie hopped in the car to meet him at the school. They walked him to his class and mingled with some of the other children. When they met his teacher, she made Mark feel completely at ease and for him she was the best teacher ever.

The teacher asked if Faith would stay that first day and help. After a few days of helping the teacher, the kids fell in love with Faith. She became one of the teacher's helpers and visited every day. She did fun things with the class and loved the notion that she didn't have to be away from Mark all day. Faith was really in her element and thought up of all kinds of activities for the children, and especially loved when the holidays were near. She went to the store and bought crafts for the children, and Mark was proud that everyone loved his mom.

It was fun for Julie as well, because she could play with all the classroom toys.

Richard made plans over the weekend and moved in with Emily; Faith hoped that Emily would get her much-needed rest now. Even though Faith and Richard talked at times, she could feel the anger in his heart toward her. It was a pent-up rage that had been steadily building since childhood, unresolved. She never hated Richard, but she hated how he could be at times.

There was a time that Richard, Hope, and Faith sat down outside and had a short conversation about what their dad did. They each shared just a few things about how they felt. Richard told both the girls that when he was little, Aunt Jennifer's first husband was crazy. He recalled how Hope and Faith were about a year or so old, and Richard was five. He re-lived how their uncle used to hold him down and tell the twins to pull his hair, spit on him, hit him in the face, and jump on him. There wasn't anything he could do, except endure the two little ones being mean to him. He told them that he always hated them for doing what they did.

He went on to express that it really wasn't until he had children of his own, that he knew Hope and Faith didn't know what they were doing. How could they? They were just a little over a year old. The girls knew that Richard carried deep-seated anger for that, and what their dad did as well. Faith hoped that Richard would one day heal from those wounds.

As they finished up talking, Faith told Richard that he needed to seek help for all that happened. He told her she was crazy and that he didn't need help at all, and that he was just fine. But Faith knew otherwise. The three of them ended their conversation that day. Nothing ever really became of it. But at least they got to air out a couple of things.

***

Emily was still working and getting weaker. She finally talked to her manager and told him she was going to retire. She hated to leave her job, but it was getting more and more difficult to stand on her feet. Faith watched as her mom started losing more weight.

Faith was scrubbing dishes when she saw her mom through the kitchen window walking up the deck steps in the back. Her mom took one step and another, with an excruciating look on her face. Faith knew she was in pain.

When Emily opened the back door, her mom pretended to be just fine. She greeted Faith with a big smile and asked where her babies were.

Faith hollered, "Nanny's here!" Mark and Julie came running. Mark was seven by now, and Julie was almost three. Julie liked to hug Nanny's legs, and Emily always thought that was so cute.

Emily sat down, and Faith got her some tea. "Would you like to stay for dinner, Mom?"

"Sure," said Emily, "that would be nice. What are you fixing?"

"I'm making meatloaf, mashed potatoes, and corn—your favorite."

"Yum, I love your meatloaf!" Emily said, smiling through the pain.

Emily stayed and dined with Faith and the kids, and then later went home.

Faith could see that her mom was deteriorating, and bought her a brass bell. "If you need anything, ring the bell so Richard can hear it and check on you," said Faith. There were many times she had to use the bell.

One night while at home, Emily woke up and couldn't catch her breath. She had the bell by her bed and started ringing it. She kept ringing and ringing, but Richard didn't appear. She managed to get out of bed, but as she walked, she couldn't breathe and fell to the floor. When Richard finally came up the steps, he was annoyed that he had to stop what he was doing and go up to his mom's room. Then he saw her lying on the floor and ran to her.

"Mom? Are you okay?"

"I can't breathe," Emily said with a strain.

Richard helped her up and drove her to the hospital. He felt terrible that he didn't respond sooner. The doctor said she had fluid in her lungs and had to drain it.

Richard called Faith early that morning and told her what happened. He brought Emily home later that night, and she went to bed exhausted.

***

As usual, Emily spent most of her time at Faith's house and stayed most of the day. Faith was juggling the two kids and taking her mom to her appointments. She knew the fluid was not a good thing. She remembered that when her dad started getting fluid in his lungs, it wasn't long before he passed. Emily steadily lost more weight. One late afternoon about two months later, Emily said she felt like the fluid was back, and asked Faith to take her to the hospital. Kenny was home to watch the kids.

After a while, they admitted her. The doctors said they had to drain a lot of fluid. Faith figured she'd be done in a few hours, but they wanted to keep Emily overnight. The next day, Faith went to see her mom, and it looked like she was not getting any better. Faith felt in her heart that she was not going to come out of the hospital.

When she got home, she called Hope and told her. "Hope," she said crying, "I don't think Mom is going to make it, and you need to come down right away."

Hope was very upset. Jason took a leave of absence, and they were at Faith's house in two days. By then, Emily was extremely weak. When Hope arrived, she and Faith went to see their mom while Kenny and Jason watched the kids.

One morning, Emily's doctor called. "I'm sorry to bother you, Faith, but your brother is at the hospital yelling at your mom and demanding that she make a will. Is there any way you can tell him to be quiet or leave, or else I'm going to have to call security and have him removed."

Faith was infuriated at her brother for doing this while their mom was in such a fragile condition. But she knew he was bound and determined to get their mother's house. Faith called Richard. He didn't answer. She called the doctor back and was informed that Richard had just left. Faith assured the doctor that she'd talk to her brother when she saw him and apologized for his outburst.

After a few days, Faith and Hope could see that Emily was taking a turn for the worse. When they walked into her room, they were shocked to see her lying in bed with her head back and her mouth wide open. She was unconscious. Hope tried drizzling a little water into her mouth, to no avail. The nurse said there was nothing more they could do. It hurt Faith's heart to see her mom in this terrible situation. She felt so helpless, and her heart was breaking.

The next couple of days, Faith stayed with the children and let Hope go see her since she had been away for a while. It also gave Faith an excuse not to go. She knew her mom wasn't going to make it and couldn't bear the thought of being there.

Everyone was tired, and Faith and Hope fixed a light dinner. Shortly after dinner, the phone rang. Faith knew that she'd be getting a call soon, and was a little hesitant to answer. She picked up the phone and heard Emily's doctor.

"Faith," he said. "You need to make plans for your mom to come home and get hospice to come to your house."

Faith screamed, "No! I can't do that, doctor!" She was crying so hard it was difficult to talk. "I don't want my mom dying in my house in front of my children. I can't bear the thought. Please, I'm begging you to please keep her in the hospital!"

The doctor told Faith that he would do as she wished, but only for a couple more days. Then her mother would have to come home.

"Thank you," said Faith and hung up the phone. She ran outside to be alone and pray on the porch. With her face in her hands, she begged God to please take her mom so that she didn't have to suffer anymore. *Please, God, I don't want my mom to die in my home. My heart can't take it, and I know Mark would be upset. Please! Please!* she begged God over and over again. She was crying so hard; she could hardly breathe.

Soon Faith wiped her tears and went back into the house. She told Hope what the doctor had said. Hope went up that evening to see her mom, and Faith stayed home with the kids. The next morning around seven a.m., the phone rang and woke Faith. Everyone was sleeping. It was the doctor.

"Faith?"

"Yes, doctor."

"I just wanted to let you know that your mom passed about an hour ago. She wasn't in any pain."

The tears rolled down Faith's face. "Okay, doctor. Thank you for calling."

She hung up the phone and quietly woke up Kenny, hugging him as she told him that her mom had just died. Kenny held her and told her he was sorry.

"God answered my prayers," she said, getting choked up. "I didn't want her to suffer any longer or die here."

She got up and knocked on Hope's bedroom door. "Mom just died," Faith said, her face wet with tears. Hope began to cry, and they hugged each other before Hope went back in to tell Jason. It broke Faith's heart to have to tell Mark because he loved his Nanny so much. She told him later that Nanny went to be with Jesus and would be watching over him. She knew Mark didn't really understand, but he knew that Nanny wasn't going to be around anymore. Julie was too little to understand.

Richard and Hope took care of all the funeral arrangements and decided to have a closed casket. No one wanted to look at Emily's emaciated body lying in a coffin and remembering that last image. Faith was numb but felt such a huge peace all over her that she couldn't cry if she wanted to. She had never felt a peace like she was experiencing. It was like her mom was right there with her, holding her hand and letting her know that everything was all right. She knew that this peace came from God.

Over the next couple of days, Richard thought Faith was being cold and didn't care about their mother's passing. Faith ignored his remarks because she was confident in what she felt. The funeral was a very quiet one. Even during the funeral, Faith felt this wonderful feeling. She noticed it just stayed with her and didn't leave. This peace lasted for about six months, and then one day while she was alone, she cried out to her mom and told her how much she missed her. She still felt that peace, but was able to shed tears now. Even when she cried, it was only for a moment, and then that loving, peaceful energy filled her entire being. She loved every minute of it and knew her mom was there with her.

Faith found out that Emily never made a will. The house belonged to all three of them. Faith called Hope and told her, and Hope was just as surprised as Faith. After talking to Hope, she sat on the couch and wept, knowing that her mom was grateful for taking care of her while she was sick. Emily could have made a will, as she threatened for years, giving everything to Richard. But in her last weeks, she had a change of heart. For the first time in Hope and Faith's life, they felt like their mother really loved them too. It was very healing.

Hope and Jason left a few days after the funeral and went back home. Faith hated to see her sister leave. Her house was quiet again, but they spoke quite a bit on the phone, catching up with things.

***

Erin, their older sister who had been given up for adoption, made plans to come down to visit, so Hope made plans to come as well. Faith was glad to see everyone.

Sunday morning came, and Erin was getting ready to leave. Hope went over to say goodbye while Faith was making some goodies for Erin to take back with her. Hope was gone for just over an hour, and then came back and told Faith that Richard was putting her down and making up lies about her to Erin. She said she couldn't take it anymore, and that Erin believed everything that Richard was saying.

Hope was very angry as she reported this news to Faith, and Faith felt flooded with pain. All the years of all of the lies hit her like a ton of bricks. She made a quick decision at that moment. Erin was leaving shortly to go back home. Faith didn't want to start a new relationship with her sister based on lies. Richard was very good at manipulating these types of situations.

Faith told Hope to leave for a while with her kids and come back in a couple of hours. Hope had some shopping to do, so it suited her fine. She went over to say goodbye to Erin and left. Faith locked all of her doors. She heard Erin ringing the doorbell a few minutes later, but didn't answer. This was the last straw for Faith. She hated lies and didn't want to look into Erin's eyes with her possibly believing the drama. Faith was always the one who everyone lied about. *But no more,* she thought. *I've had enough.*

Erin left that day, and it would be more than twenty years before they ever spoke again.

***

There were many tough days with Richard living next door. Faith coped as best she could, and they didn't speak much to each other. Hope called with news that Jason was going overseas, and she was thinking about moving in with Richard instead of staying in Tennessee with no family. Faith was excited all over again. Richard was not happy. There were many arguments between the two, and Hope couldn't take it anymore and made plans to move back to Tennessee.

The girls made the decision to sell the house and not let Richard buy them out like he wanted to do. Now, the only thing to do was convince Richard to go along with it. It took a while, but he finally agreed, and they put the house on the market. All the while, the girls prayed for the sale. Hope was moving out the following weekend and had everything packed and ready to go. It was sad to watch her and the kids pull out of the driveway. Faith wiped her tears as she saw the U-Haul truck steadily go up the street until it disappeared.

About a month after the house went on the market, Faith and Kenny were awakened by the phone at two a.m. Faith answered to the sound of Richard yelling that the house was on fire. Kenny threw his clothes on and ran over, yelling for Faith to call 911. The call went to the firehouse that was just two miles away. Kenny had worked at that station many times, filling in. The call also went to the firehouse where Kenny worked, as well. Richard told Kenny that the fire was in the laundry room downstairs. Kenny turned on the water hose at the front porch. As soon as Kenny opened the front door, he got on his knees and crawled through the living room and downstairs to the laundry room. The black smoke had already come down to two feet off the floor.

Kenny sprayed water everywhere, putting the fire out before the firetruck got there. When Kenny came out, he was choking. The oil furnace had caught on fire, and he had breathed in a lot of black smoke. He coughed and coughed, walking to the front yard as the firetruck was pulling up. Kenny almost fainted. The guys got him to come sit on the back of the firetruck and gave him oxygen.

The next day, Faith called Emily's insurance company and told them what happened. They said they were going to send an agent out to assess the damage and would let her know. The lady called back and asked if Faith could come in and talk to her. Richard was working, so Faith went in to see the insurance lady. They sat down and talked, and Faith told her that her husband had actually put out the fire. The agent said that she would send a check for the damage so they could fix what needed to be fixed at the house. All in all, it wasn't too bad, but it did have a lot of smoke damage that needed to be cleaned, which the insurance covered. This was another hold up on selling the house. The insurance check was made out to Richard, Hope, and Faith. After damages were paid, the rest would be split three ways.

After a few months on the market, the house finally sold, which removed a lot of stress from Faith's life. When Richard left the house, they didn't speak. It would be close to twenty years before they would speak again.

Hope was happy because she could put that money down on a house in Tennessee. Faith hoped that her sister would be back again soon, but it never happened. Life happens. Even though they were twins, they each had a different path...a different journey. Neither one knew at the time how those paths were going to change their lives and tear them apart. It would be sixteen years before they would ever see each other again.

After the house sold, and before the new owners moved in, Faith found herself on her deck in the backyard overlooking her mom's front yard. As she stood there, visions of her mom, Aunt Debbie, Rachel, Hope, and Richard came flooding back to her. *Those were such good times,* she thought as a smile came across her face. Recollections of everyone cutting up and laughing caused her to pine for those days. *Why couldn't it be that way all the time?* Faith wondered. But she knew why. Even after Tom's death, the abuse impacted them because it was instilled in each of them and shaped their personalities. Even through this, Faith had many good memories, and during her alone time would close her eyes and reminisce.

Once during a conversation with her cousin Rachel, they started sharing the memories. They talked for a while, bringing up other memories and laughing out loud. One thing led to another, and then Rachel disclosed something Faith had never known. Rachel told her that the day Faith confided in her mom about what her dad did to her and her sister, Emily never went to his grave again. Faith was taken back by the news and told Rachel she was surprised to hear that. According to Rachel, Aunt Debbie said that Emily took a lot to her grave, and no one ever knew the pain and agony she kept inside.

After the phone call ended, Faith hung her head and silently thanked her mom for having her back. After all these years, Faith wished her mom was standing in front of her so she could hug her so tight and never let go. Faith knew that her mom could see her thoughts, and for a moment, felt her presence. She quietly said, "Thank you, Mom. I love you!"

***

Faith continued to go to visit Brandi's mother, Granny, whenever she could. Her religious views were going in an entirely different direction than Hope's. This was the core of what tore them apart. The differences in beliefs caused many arguments. Faith told her sister that it was okay to have different beliefs, but Hope didn't see it that way. She wanted Faith to believe everything she did, and when Faith didn't, Hope went into a rage.

Hope called one day and told Faith that Jason got stationed in Germany and that they would be moving there for three years. *That's a long way from home,* Faith thought. The girls didn't talk much anymore, and when they did, most times it ended up in an argument over religion. Faith tried to avoid those conversations, but somehow it usually ended up that way. There were many times they got into huge battles, and Hope told Faith that she never wanted to talk to her again.

While in Germany, Jason invited Kenny to visit. Kenny had never been out of the country and made plans to go, and brought along a friend. It was wonderful to see Hope, Jason, and the kids, but after four days Hope went on a rampage about Faith's beliefs. Kenny and his friend couldn't take it anymore and booked a hotel for the next three days before going home.

Over the years, the twins walked their different paths and kept drifting further and further apart. After Germany, Jason was stationed in Puerto Rico, and Hope lived there for three years as well. The calls now between the girls were fewer and farther between. Hope became more obsessive with religion and even told Faith to stay away from her children. She didn't want anything to do with her. Faith cried many tears over it, and the thought of raising their kids together vanished. At times, Faith remembered how her dad had separated the children since they were little. *He did a great job,* Faith thought, with deep cynicism.

Chapter 28: Ministry

"God moves in a mysterious way, His wonders to perform. He plants his footsteps in the sea, and rides upon the storm."
~ William Cowper

Summer was coming to a close, and Faith could feel autumn in the air. She loved the smell of the leaves covered in the morning dew. It was that time of year. School would be starting shortly, and the holidays were right around the corner.

Kenny was working at his second job up the street, and Faith was busy taking Mark and Julie out to buy new school clothes. She enjoyed shopping and buying things for the kids. They had such a fun time out. Faith always stopped by Toys R Us and let the kids look around and play with the toys.

After shopping, Faith came home and put Julie down for her nap. Mark was tired as well, and he watched TV while Faith got on the computer. For some reason, she felt that she should check Kenny's email. He had told her the password a long time ago, and he had actually forgotten all about that. She logged in and noticed a couple of emails from a girl she had never heard of. She opened and read them … and started shaking. Kenny had made arrangements to meet this woman at the mall. Faith knew in her heart that he was cheating on her.

When Kenny returned home from his second job, Faith confronted him. He made all kinds of excuses, none of which Faith believed. She knew. She felt it. There was nothing Kenny could say to make her think otherwise. They got into a huge argument.

"How could you?" Faith asked. "What about the kids? Did you ever stop to think about that? What about our family? Why would you do this to me and the kids?"

Kenny stuck to his story. All the trust she ever had for him went out the window that day. She didn't want to stay with him, but she didn't want to get a divorce because of Mark and Julie. They loved their daddy. Faith wondered if she could ever be intimate with Kenny again, knowing that he had been with someone else. The thought just sickened her.

Several weeks went by, and Kenny was extra nice as if nothing had ever happened. Faith could see he was keeping his cool, but in her heart, she knew he was having an affair. Knowing a divorce would be devastating to the children, she finally told Kenny that she forgave him. Kenny continued to stick to his story. She remembered a statement he made when she first met him: "Never, ever admit to anything." That statement swirled around in her head for a long time. During their intimate moments, her mind wandered, and tears streamed down, but she never let him know about her tears. Faith had that part down to a tee. She knew how to cry at night without anyone ever knowing.

She couldn't help but wonder who else he had slept with. It was really hard on her, but she figured she could get through it because of her children. She decided to stay with Kenny, and it took about a year to start getting over how she felt. Even though she never forgot it, things seemed to get better.

***

Faith was still a stay-at-home mom and took good care of her children. She made sure they had what they needed, and Julie was fast approaching her first year at school. Julie was excited! She loved going to the school with her mom to visit her brother, and also to participate with the other children. She knew the school well.

Soon both kids were in school, and Faith focused on cleaning and having dinner prepared. She was also still helping out at the school with activities in both Mark and Julie's classes. Many times, she'd swing by a fast food place and buy lunch for all of the children, and surprise them by knocking on the door just before the lunch bell rang. They loved it!

One day a friend, Katy, called and asked if Faith could help her clean a house the next day. It was a paying job, and Faith agreed. Faith had helped Katy on occasion, and it was nice to get out of the house and also make a little money. Soon Katy was asking her to help two or three times a week. Faith liked cleaning houses, and the money was great. She decided to put out flyers to pick up a couple of jobs of her own, since she could finish work and be home before the kids arrived from school.

When Faith got home from helping out at the school, a lady called about having someone clean for her. She asked Faith to come by and give her a quote. Faith drove over to the lady's apartment for a tour. They talked for a while, and Faith was hired to clean twice a month. One job led to another, and after a few months she had picked up six cleaning jobs per month. The extra money was used to buy the kids more things and was also spent on the house.

After a while, she had her own cleaning business. The kids were getting a little older, and other than holiday parties, Faith wasn't needed as much in their classes. So her career was perfect, and her cleaning business began to grow with more jobs and higher quotes. When she got a higher paying job, she'd give a lower paying one to someone else. Soon she had all high paying jobs and was cleaning five to eight houses a week. She even had a few real estate agencies that hired her. She saved a certain amount to make sure she had enough to buy her kids everything they wanted for their birthdays and Christmas.

Enjoying the outdoors one day, Faith decided she wanted to put a pool in the backyard. She missed the one at her parents' house and knew it would be great for the kids. The summers were quite hot, and having a pool would be a lot of fun for Mark and Julie and their friends. When Kenny got home, they discussed having to cut three big trees to accommodate the pool. They couldn't install an in-ground pool because the whole neighborhood was built on river rock. Excavation would involve blasting underground, which would be too expensive. So they opted for an above ground pool and surrounding deck.

Faith and Kenny wanted an idea how much it would cost for the pool, the deck, and the tree cutting. Faith called different tree cutters in the area, and it was very expensive. One company wanted a thousand dollars for only one tree, and that didn't include cutting it into firewood. It was disappointing. Faith prayed every day for God to find a way for her to get a pool for the kids.

One day as she was talking to Katy about the trees, Katy mentioned a friend who could cut the trees. Faith asked him to come over and give her a price, and to her surprise, he said he would cut all three trees into logs for just under five hundred dollars. She couldn't believe it! She told him she'd get back to him later after getting bids on the pool and deck. She called Kenny, who was astounded at the price, but told Faith not to get her hopes up until they knew the total project cost. But she kept the excitement in her spirit and knew that it would all work out somehow.

As Kenny pulled into the driveway that evening, the neighbor, Carl, stopped by to say hello. Both Kenny and Carl came in the house and sat down as Faith was fixing dinner. Kenny began to tell Carl about their plans to put in a pool and deck. They had actually gotten the idea from Carl because he had one as well.

"Well, if you buy the deck material, I'll build the deck for you," said Carl. He had built a few decks in his time and was really a Jack of all trades.

Faith spun around and said, "Oh, my gosh, Carl! Thank you!" She was in the middle of asking how much he was going to charge when he interrupted and said he wouldn't charge them anything. Faith could feel the tears well up in her eye as she hugged and thanked him.

"Let's go outside and start measuring for deck material," said Carl to Kenny. They spent some time outside, and Carl gave suggestions on how to build it. Faith was exhilarated! She kept saying in her mind, *Thank you, God!* It seemed like it was all coming together. They found someone to cut the trees down for a phenomenal price, and Carl wasn't going to charge for his labor. Now all they had to do was price the pool and the decking material and the company that would level the pool area.

Everything seemed to go in their favor, and Faith and Kenny decided to get their pool. Faith saw how God was bringing everything together. They got started right away, and everything was finished in the late fall. Their pool would be ready for use the following spring. It turned out even more beautifully than Faith had imagined! She wanted everything at her home to be perfect, and her heart's desire was for her family to always be happy.

***

Faith had remained close to Brandi's mother, Granny, and was now starting to help bring different ministries to Granny's house. There were a few times when Brandi visited, and Faith always loved it when she was there. They hung out and laughed, and the kids played together for the weekend. Faith always hated to see Brandi go back home.

Faith's thoughts about life were beginning to change the more she attended these gatherings. Her love for God continued to grow. She began to see things she never saw before, and her heart was becoming full of love, understanding, and forgiveness. At one gathering she met a lady from out of town named Sylvia. Faith noticed she had such loving eyes. Sometimes when they chatted, it felt like Sylvia was looking right through her. After a while, they became friends. Anytime Sylvia came to a gathering, Faith invited her to stay at her house.

"The first time I laid eyes on you, I saw light all over you," Sylvia told Faith. "I know that there's something very special about you." Faith listened in awe but didn't fully understand it at the time. Sylvia also said, "You have a very loving heart, and God is doing something special in you." As time went on, they talked by phone and kept in touch when Sylvia wasn't in town.

One evening Faith was at home on the computer, looking at the website of a minister named Ted. She really loved Ted and his ministries, and told people that he had the purest heart of anyone she had ever known. He had been to Granny's a few times, and the whole group loved him. As Faith searched his website, she saw just how huge his ministries were. She also noticed a minister named Monty and his wife on the site who lived only four hours away. Faith thought she'd give them a call and see if they did home gatherings.

After the first ring, she heard, "Hello?"

"Is Monty there?"

"This is he," Monty said.

Faith explained that she was a friend of Ted's, who had come a few times to minister at Granny's house. She asked Monty if he ministered at home gatherings. They chatted for a while and really hit it off. They got along so well; it was as if they had known each other all their lives. After talking for a while, Monty said that he'd love to minister at Granny's. He went on to say that he had a wife and five children, and would be able to visit sometime in the future.

"Great!" said Faith. "I'll call Granny to see which weekends work best for her, and let you know." They hung up, and Faith called Granny right away.

"Hey, Granny! I found a minister on Ted's website and invited him to come and minister at your house one weekend. I need to know which weekend will work for you."

Granny asked a few questions and gave Faith a couple of weekend dates.

"That sounds great, Granny. I'll call him tomorrow and get it set up."

The next day Faith called Monty. They had a long talk and got along wonderfully. He had such a great sense of humor, and they laughed and laughed. Faith couldn't wait to meet him. They set up a date for a weekend for him to come down. Granny said he could stay at her house—she often had various ministers stay with her.

"You can come by my house and chat for a while, and then follow me over to Granny's house," she told him.

Monty was excited to meet a new group of people and couldn't wait to drive down. He'd be ministering in two weeks, which gave Granny enough time to call her group and let them know. Everyone usually brought a covered dish for the weekend lunches. Faith talked to Monty a couple of times before he finally arrived in order to coordinate things, and they had such informative conversations about the Bible. Faith was full of questions and wanted to know more about God. She was like a sponge, soaking up all he said.

Monty got into town on a Friday. The doorbell rang, and Faith knew it was Monty. She ran to answer the door and greeted, "Hi!"

"Well, hi to you Faith, nice meeting you!" responded Monty. Faith gave him a big welcome hug and had appetizers ready. She poured him a big glass of water, and they sat at the table and talked for a couple of hours getting to know each other. Faith thought he was awesome. He was the first person who actually answered every question she had about God. He was a lot more experienced and could see the light in her eyes.

Kenny came home with Mark and Julie, and Faith introduced Monty to her family. The kids stayed for a minute and had some appetizers, and then went downstairs to play. Kenny sat down, and they all enjoyed lots of laughter throughout their conversation. Faith was happily surprised that a minister had such a great sense of humor. She had pictured them all as serious and drab… but that was not Monty. His sense of humor matched up quite a bit with Faith's, and he was surprised at how well she kept up with his.

After a while, Faith called Granny. "I'm on my way, and Monty will be following me over to your house," she said.

Granny said, "I'm ready, and I can't wait to meet him!"

Granny just lived two minutes away. When they pulled up, Faith walked in with Monty and then left while Granny got to know him a bit. The meeting would be the next day, Saturday, followed by another on Sunday, with lunches served afterward. Later on that evening, Faith made a baked spaghetti casserole to take with her. She loved eating at Granny's house because everyone always brought something, and the food was so good.

The gathering that weekend was one of Faith's favorites! She learned so much, and Monty was an awesome speaker. He took time out to answer any questions people had. They all loved him. He had the ability to lift people's hearts and even prophesied over a couple of them. Sylvia was at the meeting that weekend and loved the new minister. She said that he was deep and had a special message to give. Faith and Granny agreed. At the end of the meeting on Sunday, they couldn't wait to reschedule and have Monty back.

It was time for Monty to leave, and everyone said their goodbyes. Faith told him she'd be in touch to set up another meeting whenever he had the time, and did so later in the week. Monty said he delighted to come back! They spoke over the phone for a long time.

"Can I bring my wife and five children?" he asked.

"Why sure," said Faith. "You all can stay at my home this time if you want to. I have plenty of room for everyone."

Monty agreed, and Faith couldn't wait to meet his wife, Trudy.

***

It was summer, and the kids were out of school. When Monty and his family came down, all of the children loved playing in the pool. Faith let Monty's family have the downstairs. She and Kenny had just bought new den furniture and a big screen TV with surround sound. They had a sectional sofa with two reclining chairs and a queen sleeper in the other end of the sofa. The back bedroom had a queen-size bed and another sectional sofa. Monty, Trudy, and the kids had plenty of room, and they loved staying at Faith's house.

The following weekend, one of Faith's favorite ministers was going to be in town. This time he'd be at a hotel conference room instead of at Granny's because there were a lot of people who were going to attend. Faith loved him and his wife and made plans to go. She loved how he'd prophesy over people at the end of each gathering, and she was always ready to hear a word from God for herself. As she sat and listened to this wonderful man, she soaked up all she could. She remembered a time when she didn't have a clue what he was preaching, and now she could understand almost all of it. It showed her how much she had grown over the years.

At the end of the gathering, Faith prayed that the minister would prophesy over her, and he did. He finally got around to her and said:

"God hasn't forgotten you, that's for sure, and He's not going to leave you in the place where you've been. He's going to bring you farther beyond that which you've yet seen in Him. I see you standing as it were at the edge of a terrain, and you're saying, 'God, should I go or should I stop? Should I go or should I stop?' And Gods says, 'Just don't make any hasty decisions and watch what I'll bring. For I'll make clear your path, I'll make plain your way. Changes are coming, and when they come you will know because it will be as bright as day! And suddenly the terrain before you will change, and it will be different than it's ever been because you're going to find yourself locked into a place that will open up this ministry within. God's called you; He's chosen you, and yet you feel like you've been kind of stuck on the backside of the desert and can't get anywhere. And God says I haven't forgotten you; I know right where you are, and I've put you there! And in my time, I'll show you a new step you must take. There won't be any questions, haha! And I'll bring you forth, not for your sake, but for the sake of others about thee that must receive of that I'm doing in you. So be encouraged, be strengthened and watch and see, changes will come, but not too hastily."

The gatherings were usually recorded, and whoever recorded it asked Faith if she wanted a copy of her prophecy. She said yes, and felt it in her heart to listen to it when she got home, and transcribe it word for word on paper. This minister over the years had spoken over her quite a few times, but for some reason, Faith felt like she needed to keep this one. She remembered a time at Granny's when he spoke over her and asked her if she wrote songs. Faith told him that she didn't write songs, but she wrote poetry. He went on to tell her that he sees her writing, but this time it will not come from her hand, and that Spirit will be writing through her. Faith never really gave it much thought. She just assumed that one day she'd be writing poetry again.

As time went on, Faith and Monty and his family got close. There were times when Faith would go to their house and help with Monty's ministry. As they all got to know each other more and more, Monty and Trudy could see that Faith had some inner wounds. They could tell by the way she acted. For instance, when she felt irritated or in a bad mood, her tendency was to slam cabinet doors. One day, they all sat down and had a talk. Monty and Trudy confronted Faith and told her what they were thinking, and Faith told them what happened to her while she was growing up. Faith was curious how they knew. She thought she had hidden it well, which was true for most; they were just more experienced in seeing the truth within.

They told Faith that her actions clearly spoke to them that she had been wounded. The little bursts of anger, the slamming of doors and cabinets, and the yelling were all telltale signs. This intrigued Faith, and she wanted to know more. In fact, Monty told Faith that his mom died when he was five, and then he was put in foster care where he was beaten and abused badly. Faith felt the connection with

Monty stemming from the similarities in their early lives. Trudy told Faith of all the horrors that Monty suffered at the hands of his foster mother. It was awful; she knew his pain.

After a short time, Monty was coming to Faith's house quite a bit. They shared childhood traumas, and Monty explained to Faith the wounds that were inside her. The more she heard, the more she wanted to hear. Faith wanted to be healed of everything she had buried throughout her life. She listened, but there were many times she didn't understand what Monty was saying.

By now, Faith had become Monty and Trudy's ministry secretary. She helped with some of the meetings and helped put together Monty's little booklets and brochures. She mailed them out all over the country. This took a load off Trudy, who homeschooled their five children. Faith loved helping, and it made her feel a part of the ministry. Anytime they were together, they continued to talk about the abuse that Faith had suffered and helped her see things in a new perspective. Their friendship grew very quickly.

Faith went to many gatherings and saw firsthand how Monty preached and how the people loved him. She always said that Monty brought down the house! Faith heard quite a few people over time tell Monty that what he had prophesied over them had come true. She saw the tears streaming down people's faces when he got up to preach. This really touched Faith's heart and demonstrated what a powerhouse Monty was. She was amazed and wished she could touch people the way he did. She looked up to Monty and his gifts.

After a few months of going to Monty and Trudy's house to help with the ministry, she noticed that a lot of people were giving her dirty looks. These were people she had met before, and she didn't understand why they were acting this way. She pulled Monty aside and asked him why people were ignoring her and giving her dirty looks. Monty reassured Faith that everything was okay. It was that they were very jealous of her. Faith still didn't understand why they would be jealous of her. It made her feel very uncomfortable. All she did was give one hundred percent while she was there, and served in any way she could.

After Faith returned home, it wasn't long before Monty came down and spent a day or two with her. He told her that God was going to use her in a very special way. Anytime Monty said something like that, it got her really excited. She wanted to obey God and do His will. To think that God was going to use her was icing on the cake! However, the more Monty came to Faith's house, the more she saw that he would change into a completely different personality, like that of a child. It was happening more and more. Every single time he went into this childlike state, he clung to Faith and wouldn't leave or let her go anywhere until he came out of it.

Faith didn't know what to do. It just made her angry at him, and the angrier she got, the more he turned into a child. It was so confusing. After a while, it would seem to let up, and he'd go back home. It started taking a toll on Mark and Julie, and they started not to like him very much. They thought he was crazy. After a while, even Kenny didn't like it when Monty visited.

On the other hand, Faith felt very sorry for him. She called Trudy one day and asked her about his personality changes, and told her it was really making her mad and upsetting her family. Trudy told Faith that if Monty heard a trigger word from someone close to him, it sent him back to when he was little. Back to when he found his mom dead, and then the horrible abuse he suffered from then on. Faith had no idea then what a trigger word was.

"What do I do?" asked Faith.

"When he gets like that, you have to reassure him that he is loved and he is safe. You also have to talk in a low voice, because if you raise your voice, it will scare him and take longer."

Trudy reminded Faith about her outbursts that were due to her own abuse, and so it was with Monty—but just in a different way. Faith started recognizing the times she became angry with her son, Mark, and yelled. Mark got such a scared look on his face. Faith would see that look and sometimes keep yelling. She couldn't help herself. It was stemming from the abuse of her father. Now she was beginning to see that her yelling was having an effect on her son. However, at the time, Faith didn't know how to control her angry outbursts. She felt horrible afterward and recognized that the anger inside her was out of control. She lay in bed at night and wept silently. She never wanted to scare her son. She loved him very much, but somehow that ugly side of her would come out at times.

***

As autumn and winter rolled around, Faith found that every time she answered her phone when Monty called, she would somehow say a trigger word that set him off. She had no clue what the words were that upset him. But she could tell by his voice that he changed, and then she'd get mad. If she didn't say the right thing to help him, he'd hop in his car and drive down. This really started to upset both Faith and Kenny. The kids were also noticing that something was not right with Monty. But they were too young to discuss such personal things, so Faith tried to keep them busy when Monty turned into a child. It was starting to disrupt the family quite a bit.

Kenny told Faith that he wanted to call the police on Monty to get him to stay away from the house. He even said he wanted to get a restraining order, but never did. However, Faith felt compelled, for some unknown reason, to try and help Monty. She felt sorry for him, even though sometimes he made her so mad that she wanted to throw the phone against the wall and bust it into a million pieces. Kenny started keeping his distance from Monty, while Faith was just getting more confused.

One night while Kenny was working, Faith asked God what she was supposed to do. She went on to tell God that she was no psychiatrist, psychologists, or counselor, or ever had any training to help someone emotionally. She just couldn't figure out what to do, and it was getting her more and more angry. She began to cry very hard. *I'm not healed either and have wounds that are deep. I need help too. What about me?* Faith thought to herself. *What about me God? You're making me help this person, and I have no idea of what I'm doing, and you're not helping me!!* Faith was extremely upset. She felt that God had left her all alone. But Faith had a big heart, and even though she was angry, she felt compelled to continue to do what she was doing. It was like there was no escape. It was so strange.

Monty began telling Faith, little by little, of how God was bringing her to a higher place in Him. Faith enjoyed Monty when he was being an adult. When they had talks like this, it excited her. She always wanted to know more, but sometimes Monty said he'd have to pray to get more answers. So Faith waited until Monty told her something else. Then one day, Monty told Faith about his best friend who was a huge ministry icon and famous Christian singer. He told her that he could not reveal his name to Faith or his purpose at the time, but he had given his friend Faith's email address and said he would be in touch soon. Faith was excited and curious about this mysterious man. It wasn't until later that she found out his name was George. The more Monty talked about God doing something amazing in her life, the more excited she got.

When Faith went to bed that night, she prayed and thanked God for all that He was getting ready to do, even though she didn't know what it would be. Faith just trusted, and then she had a dream. She found herself in her Uncle Greg's house walking out the back door to talk to her dad. He was out in the backyard talking with Greg. Faith approached them, and suddenly Tom got angry at Faith. She took off running so he couldn't get her. She ran through the house and knew that her dad was close behind. She ran out the front door, into the driveway, and hopped in her car so that she could get away.

As she approached her car, it became an electric golf cart. She got in and started down the driveway. She turned her head to see how close her dad was, and then slammed on the brakes. She couldn't believe what she was seeing—her dad was floating down the sidewalk. His arms were folded across his chest, as if in a Spiritual straight jacket. His feet were about a foot off of the ground, and he looked so helpless.

He was literally floating down the sidewalk. Faith looked at him in disbelief because she still couldn't process what she was seeing. She felt like evil spirits were carrying him along. As she looked at her dad's face, he couldn't speak but mouthed the words *I'm so sorry!* He had the most remorseful look on his face. Faith backed out of the driveway and headed home. For some reason, she had a key in her hand but didn't know what it was for. She got home, and then she woke up, lying in bed crying.

At that moment, Faith knew that all of the evil he had done in his life was because of the evil spirits in him. Through her tears, she said out loud, "I forgive you, Dad." That night she really meant what she said. Faith forgave her dad. This time, it really came from her heart. Such a wonderful feeling came over her that she couldn't get back to sleep for a couple hours, but when she did, it was a very peaceful sleep. When she got up the next morning, she called Monty and told him of the dream. He sounded so happy and told Faith he was proud of her for forgiving her dad. Faith felt good. He reminded Faith, once again, that it was a sign that God is working in her life, and later told her that the key in her dream represented her being the key to her family's healing. And this was just the very beginning.

Chapter 29: Messages

"Look at every path closely and deliberately, then ask ourselves this crucial question: Does this path have a heart? If it does, then the path is good. If it doesn't, it is of no use."

~ Carlos Castaneda

It was late spring, and Faith and Kenny's fifteenth year anniversary was coming up. Faith wanted to surprise Kenny, so she called two very good friends, Ashley and her husband Doug, and told them what she had planned. She asked if Mark and Julie could stay with them for the week. They happily agreed and told Faith to let them know which week it would be. Faith was excited. She could trust Ashley and Doug to keep her kids safe and made plans the week of her anniversary. She bought two airline tickets to the Florida Keys. It was a done deal. She couldn't wait to surprise Kenny!

One weekend prior to the anniversary surprise, Monty came down to visit Faith. Kenny and the kids were at home playing in the pool, and Monty pulled Faith aside.

He said in a stern voice, "We need to talk, it's important."

Faith could tell he was serious. She poked her head out of the door and told Kenny, "I'm taking a walk through the neighborhood with Monty and will be back shortly."

Kenny told her, "Take your time."

As Faith and Monty started walking, Faith asked, "What's on your mind?"

Monty got serious. "What's the matter?" Faith asked.

Monty began to talk. "I have to tell you, Faith, that during a prayer God spoke to me and then gave me a vision, a knowing that something serious is going to happen in your life."

As soon as he spoke the words, Faith quickly glanced at him with a scared look in her eyes. It was like he was reading her mind, and said, "No, Faith, no one is going to die."

Faith was relieved and figured she could handle anything that he was going to say now.

Monty continued, "Something is getting ready to happen, and your life will take a drastic turn. There are some things I can tell you, and some things that I cannot at this time."

Faith's heart was pounding. She knew that Monty heard from God and was mesmerized at what he was going to tell her.

"You are about to inherit a huge ministry. God is going to use you in ways you never thought of. There is also going to be a man who is part of this ministry."

Faith was puzzled and asked, "What do you mean, Monty?"

"That's all I can say about that part for now. Just trust God in how all of this is going to unfold. You're being called, Faith. God is going to shake you up and bring you to where He wants you."

Faith didn't know what that meant at the time but still she was excited. "God is going to use me?" she asked.

"More than you know," Monty said. "Just remember that your life as you know it is about to change."

They continued their walk, and all kinds of ideas were coming across Faith's mind about how God was going to use her. She was pleased knowing that God saw her and knew her. She never thought in a million years that she would have or be part of a ministry, but she always sought after God and always had a compassionate heart.

By the time they were walking towards the house, Faith could hardly wait to see what was going to happen. Her mind was running rampant. Monty told her that it would all come about in God's timing. Faith wanted to continue talking about the things that he was sharing, but Monty told her that it was enough for now, and as God spoke to him about it, he would share it with her. At the time, Faith didn't know what Monty meant when he said her life was going to be shaken up and changed. In her innocence, she thought that everything would lead to a beautiful life with her and her family.

They walked across the front yard and went inside, Faith still glowing at what he told her. Monty stayed for a few more minutes, and Faith asked, "Do you want to stay and have dinner before you go home?"

Monty said, "I want to get home before dark," and then told everyone goodbye. Faith walked him out to his car. She could not stop thinking about what he had told her during their walk and was all smiles. Kenny even asked her what was going on because she looked so happy. She told him that they just had a great walk and talked about God, and it put her in a good mood. She didn't feel like she should tell Kenny what Monty had told her because Kenny never wanted to discuss God with her anyway. So she kept it to herself.

Faith asked Kenny to light up the grill and said she'd get the hamburger patties out of the refrigerator. "Why don't we eat out by the pool tonight for dinner," she suggested.

"Sounds great to me," Kenny said and went out to light the grill.

Faith got everything ready and told the kids that dinner would soon be served on the deck, but that they could stay in the pool until it was time to sit down. Faith loved eating outside. It always felt like her own little beach area. After they finished, the kids got back in the pool. Faith went inside to get her surprise and show it to Kenny.

"I'll be right back," she said and came through the door with her hand behind her back. She looked at Kenny. "I have a surprise for you," she announced with a huge smile. "Close your eyes and hold out your hands."

Kenny did as he was told, and soon felt something in his hands. He opened his eyes and saw two plane tickets. He opened it up and saw that Faith booked a week in the Florida Keys. He was very happy. "Wow! Really?"

"Happy almost anniversary," Faith said.

Kenny stood up and hugged her, and responded with, "Thank you and happy anniversary! What about the kids?"

"I've already talked to Ashley and Doug, and they're staying with them for the week."

"That's great!" said Kenny. "Thank you so much!"

Faith just smiled and knew they were going to have a good time, even though she didn't want to leave her children. But she knew that she and Kenny needed some time together.

***

The weekend was over and the week ahead was filled with things to do before the kids had summer break. The following Monday morning started out pretty much the same as always. The kids were in school, and Kenny was at his other job, just right up at the top of the street. Faith got the house cleaned and decided to get on the computer for a while. When she turned it on, she noticed a little yellow smiley face at the bottom of the screen. She didn't really know what it was, so she clicked on it. It was Yahoo Messenger.

She knew what Yahoo Messenger was, but had never used it before. She saw Kenny's screen name on it—a screen name she had never heard of. Her heart started pounding. She knew. She noticed that a couple of women's names were offline, but there was one that was online. Faith started shaking. She decided to say hi to the girl, who would think it was Kenny. By now, Faith was seriously shaking.

She typed the message: Hi, how are you?

The girl answered back and said: Hi Kenny! Why haven't you called me?

Faith continued to pose as Kenny to get information: Sorry, I've been busy and couldn't get away from my wife to message you.

She typed back: You're married?

Faith typed: Yes, does that matter?

The girl answered: Yes it matters! You never told me you were married!

Faith could hardly type because she was still shaking so badly. She decided to expose herself and tell the girl that she was posing as her husband.

I'm Kenny's wife, and I apologize. This isn't my account. But would it be okay if I ask you a couple of questions?

The woman said: Sure.

Has Kenny been seeing you?

He was supposed to call me and meet somewhere, but so far has not.

The woman repeated that he never told her that he was married. Faith got all the information she needed and thanked the woman for helping her learn the truth. The woman said she was glad to help. Faith highlighted and copied the transaction and sent it to her email. She also noticed Kenny's email address—one she knew nothing about—and typed it in, and hoping he was using the same old password. Bingo! She was in his email.

Faith's heart was pounding out of her chest. There, in the email, she saw that Kenny had been talking to a few women. This caused her to weep uncontrollably, and she was very thankful that the kids were in school, so they didn't witness her shock and grief. She copied everything in the email and sent it along with the conversation she had with the other woman. She thought she was going to have a heart attack because her heart was beating extremely fast and her whole insides were shaking like they had never shaken before.

She picked up the phone to call Brandi. Faith couldn't even push the buttons because of shaking. She must have dialed at least thirty times to get in touch with her dear friend. It took more than thirty minutes to dial a seven-digit number.

At last, the phone rang, and Brandi answered. Faith couldn't even talk. All she could do was wail.

"What's wrong?" Brandi kept asking her over and over.

Faith finally got out one word at a time. "I, I, I ..." she stuttered. "Kenny is ... is ... is cheating on on on meeee." It was all the words she could to come out.

Brandi talked to her for more than an hour and did all the talking because Faith literally couldn't talk. Brandi finally told her to go lie down and breathe and call her back later. They hung up the phone.

As Faith sat in the chair dumbfounded, she started remembering what Monty had told her just last week. The words rang in her head. *Your life is about to drastically change.* She heard the words over and over.

Oh, my God, Faith thought. *I wonder if this is the beginning of what Monty was telling me! No wonder he couldn't tell me then.*

Faith went back to the computer and printed everything out. She put their airline tickets on top of the papers and got in her van to drive up the street to where Kenny worked. Then she rolled the passenger window down and motioned Kenny to come over. Her heart was still beating out of her chest.

As he walked out to the van, Faith handed him the stack of papers and said, "Here are the airline tickets along with all of the emails of the women you've been talking to, and you can shove them up your ass!"

She spun off before he even spoke. She didn't want to go back home because she knew he would be there shortly. She drove down the end of her street by the lake and parked for a while, knowing he wouldn't come down there. Then she got on her phone and called Monty.

"Hi!" Monty said with delight, until he heard Faith's voice. "What's wrong?"

Faith told him what she had found and then asked him if this is what God showed him. "Is my marriage over? Is this what God showed you?" Faith asked, choking on her tears.

Monty was silent for just a moment and said, "Yes, Faith. It is."

She began crying even harder, not so much for Kenny, but for Mark and Julie. They loved their dad, and Faith couldn't see the family split up. She talked to Monty for a while and then went home. She was glad to see that Kenny wasn't there and went back to the computer. A couple of minutes later, Kenny came walking downstairs. Faith confronted him with everything as she sat plunking on the computer. Kenny denied everything. Faith spun around in the chair.

"You are a liar. Just admit what you did."

***

Kenny kept denying everything, even with the proof right there in front of him. She remembered, once again, that he said years ago: "Never admit to anything." She reminded him of that, and he still kept on denying. As Faith sat at the computer, she decided to use the search key and see if there was anything else there. She typed in the word "me" and then hit search. Suddenly, Kenny's emails were coming up that he had written to other women. As soon as Kenny saw what was coming up, he ran over to the computer and shut it down. Faith knew right then and there that this was something he didn't want her to see.

She yelled at Kenny. "Sooner or later, you'll have to go back to work. And if I have to sit here until hell freezes over, I will, because I'm going to see what's in the computer."

Kenny stood back and knew there was nothing he could do, and finally admitted to some of his misdeeds.

Faith cried and screamed, "Do you realize what you've done to your family? I really hope it was all worth it!"

Kenny was speechless. There was no way he could continue to lie now with all the evidence in front of him.

"Get out and go back to work," she said. "I can't even look at you right now!"

Kenny left, and Faith went upstairs. *God, please show me if my marriage is over.* She found herself on the floor with her face buried in the carpet, begging God not to take her marriage. All she kept thinking of was Mark and Julie and how this was going to hurt them badly. She couldn't imagine the family being torn apart, and how different things would be if that happened. She cried and begged God some more. Her face was soaking wet. Then she got up, wiped her tears, and said out loud, "God, I trust you with your decision, whether you take my marriage or not. It is really not my marriage, it's yours, and I trust what You to do with it however it turns out."

Faith walked around the house numb. She felt so betrayed and felt she had given all of herself to Kenny and the children, and always focused on having a happy home. She couldn't believe what she was going through right then, and more importantly, she dreaded how a divorce was going to affect the kids. Her heart was crushed. Their anniversary was just two weeks away, and she had to decide if she was going to keep the plans or not. She prayed again for God to reveal if her marriage was over. No sign appeared.

Faith decided to go on the trip, thinking maybe that would help find answers to her prayers. Their anniversary came and off they went to the Florida Keys. Kenny was as nice as nice could be, but it wasn't the same. After arriving and getting settled in, Faith went out to the pool to try and relax. It did feel good to get away, but she couldn't stop thinking of what Kenny did. Now all she could do was worry about Mark and Julie, and found that her heart was holding so much pain she thought it would burst.

Faith could hardly look at Kenny. Going into the next day, Faith decided to at least try and enjoy herself while she was there. She had always loved Florida, and now she would be there for a week. They went to dinner a few evenings later and headed back to the hotel. Later when they went to bed, Kenny tried to get intimate with Faith, and it almost made her sick. The feeling just wasn't there. All she kept thinking about was how he betrayed her and the children. "Really?!" Faith said, "I don't think so."

They stayed for a week, and Faith tried to enjoy herself as much as she could. When they got back home, things were different. She couldn't stop thinking about the divorce debate raging in her head. She thought about the first time she caught him, and his promise that it would never happen again. One of Kenny's problems was that he always thought he would never get caught. But Faith had a saying of her own, one that her dad used to say.

She looked at Kenny and said, "Six days for the thief and one for the master."

"What does that mean?" he asked.

Faith told him, "You can cheat and cheat and cheat, but one day you're going to get caught, and you did."

***

For the rest of the summer, Faith went on with life as best she could, and still kept asking God if she should ask for a divorce. She never seemed to get an answer. Later on, Monty and Trudy came down and wanted to know if they could all four talk about what was going on and maybe help Faith and Kenny's marriage. They all sat in the living room, and Kenny didn't like anything that they were saying. He really didn't seem to care. Faith could tell that he wasn't putting forth any effort, and after a while, they all got up and went about their day. Kenny went outside to do yard work, and Monty and Trudy stayed for a while.

The subject changed and Trudy started going into more detail about some of Monty's childhood that still affected him. He still needed much healing. She explained that his foster mother used to beat him and his little sister, and would also starve them.

Faith looked at Monty as he hung his head. She felt sorry for him.

"What all happened?" Faith asked.

Trudy spoke up and said that the woman was very hateful, making Monty eat big tablespoons of cayenne pepper and then laughing when he choked with his mouth on fire. She teased him with some water that she never gave him. She also kicked his little sister down a flight of steps, breaking her arm. The foster mother made his sister wear shoes that were two sizes too small for her, giving her the crippled feet that she has today.

Faith felt so sorry for Monty. Her heart was breaking. She grabbed Monty's hand to comfort him, and then he said, with tear-filled eyes, how he found his mom dead in a chair when he was five years old.

"I tried to open her mouth to see if she would talk, and she never did. I crawled up in her lap and started hugging her and talking to her, but she never responded. After a couple of hours someone stopped by and saw that she had died and called the hospital to come get her," Monty explained and hung his head again. He looked pitiful as he relived the moment.

Trudy could see that Faith was really not in the mood to listen to this right now, due to her plight with Kenny. She took Faith's mind off Monty for a while by quickly changing the subject and talking about how God uses everything for His purpose. After about an hour, Monty and Trudy said they were going to head home. Faith thanked them for coming down to try and help with her situation. They soon left, and Faith went to check on the kids to see what they were doing.

Every time she looked into their eyes, all she could think about is what Kenny did. She just didn't know what to do. She didn't want to hurt Mark or Julie, but on the other hand, every time she looked at Kenny, the thoughts of him being unfaithful were more than she could handle. It tore her apart. She cried herself to sleep every night and cried any time the kids were not around.

One night while Faith was sound asleep, she had a dream that she and Kenny were in a car, driving by a river. Kenny was driving fast, and it was storming out. Faith yelled for him to slow down as she watched limbs fly from trees and hit the windshield. She kept telling him over and over to slow down. He just continued driving fast, staring straight ahead with a mean look on his face. When Faith looked in front of her, she saw a huge boulder at the top of the street. She yelled again for Kenny to slow down. As soon as they were about to hit the boulder, Faith was lifted out of the car through the top, and the next thing she knew, she was flying over the river. It was flooding, and the water was silver. Then she felt someone grab both of her wrists, one by one.

A voice spoke out loud and said, "I GOT YOU!"

Faith knew it was God speaking to her. She then floated over the water very peacefully for a while until God spoke again and said, "I'm going to put you in the water with Hope, and I want both of you hold on to the branches." Faith was scared of the rushing waters. Before she could say no, she was there in the silvery water with Hope, and they were both holding on to a huge limb that had branches. Each of them held on and looked at each other.

Then Faith woke up. She sat up in bed and was wide awake, wondering what the dream meant.

The next day, she told Monty about the dream. Monty told her that many things were coming, and to remember that God would be with her. Faith felt comforted because, in her dream, the voice was loud and clear. She could feel God holding her wrists tightly and letting her know, with a loving stern voice, that He had her.

Chapter 30: Divorce

"Change is inevitable. Growth is optional."
~ John Maxwell

After about three months, Faith needed to get away. She called Brandi and asked if she could stay with her for a week or so. Kenny had a vacation coming in September, and Faith figured he could take care of the kids. Brandi said yes and couldn't wait until Faith came to visit. Faith booked her plane ticket and told Brandi what time she would land. Staying with Brandi would give her time to think and also share all the heartbreak she was going through.

Brandi picked Faith up at the airport and was very supportive. Faith, however, didn't tell her about the things she and Monty spoke of. Monty said that God was speaking to Faith and no one else. He also told her that God was doing a work in her and that no one else would understand, because He was not doing the same in them. She never uttered a word of what Monty told her that day on their walk.

The bottom line was that Faith trusted God and didn't want to disobey Him. She sensed that Brandi was upset because she wasn't being told the whole story. Brandi also mentioned that she didn't agree with Monty being at Faith's house all the time and that they seemed inseparable. Faith tried to comfort Brandi without telling her all the good stuff that Monty had been telling her. But she knew in her heart that this was her time and that God was going to do many works in her. She hoped Brandi would accept that Faith loved her, and just stick with her until God released her to say something. It was such a pull on Faith's heart not to tell Brandi everything, but her trust in God was stronger, and she knew she had to keep quiet for a while.

While Brandi and her husband went off to work, Faith was alone at the house. It gave her time to think and pray. It also gave her alone time to cry before Brandi got home. Faith was still distraught and continued asking God to show her if her marriage was over. She prayed and prayed every night as she fell asleep, begging God to provide an answer before she returned home. As she lay in bed one night, she started to drift off. Suddenly, God showed her everything that was going to happen in her life. She felt a peace and a blissfulness that she never felt before. The feeling overtook her. She was exhilarated as she lay in bed viewing what looked like an amazing movie and watching all that God was showing her. She saw things that made her extremely happy and knew all was going to end well.

As she opened her eyes, she could hardly believe all that she had just seen. She was overwhelmed with gratitude and bliss. Then without warning, everything disappeared from Faith's mind. "No!" she yelled. She had been basking in what was happening, and then it was all taken away from her. She lay in bed, trying the best to recall all that was shown her, to no avail. *God please,* she begged, *please bring this back to my memory!* But He didn't. However, she knew in her spirit that what was revealed was beyond exciting, and she would always remember that night.

The next day when she awoke, she ran downstairs to tell Brandi. Brandi told her that the memory would come back to her when God wanted it to. She could see how lit up Faith was and was happy to see her friend smiling again. Brandi went to work, and Faith had the whole day to herself. She called Monty about the vision. He was very supportive and assured her that everything would come to pass, even though she didn't remember it right now. Faith was on cloud nine!

When Brandi got home from work, Faith told her she was leaving in the morning but didn't want to use the return flight. On the way down, the air travel had made her sick, and she decided to drive the twenty-two hours back to her house, and explained that the road trip would provide some much needed "alone time." She asked if Brandi could drop her off at the car rental place on her way to work. She packed everything up the night before, and Brandi drove her to the car rental place that morning.

They hugged each other goodbye, and Faith thanked Brandi for the hospitality.

"It's all going to be okay," Brandi said as she smiled at Faith.

"I know," said Faith, "it will work out the way it's supposed to."

***

Kenny called while Faith was waiting on her rental car. She told him she was going to drive until it started to get dark, and then get a hotel and drive the rest of the way in the morning. He told her that he'd be working at his job at the top of the street that day and that the kids were across the street at the neighbor's house until he got off work at four. She told him she'd be home sometime the next day. Faith's rental car pulled up, and she put her suitcase in it and took off. It was a nice drive, and she loved looking at all the beautiful scenery. Sometimes she rolled down the window and let the wind blow her hair all around. She couldn't help but think of the mystery of what God had shown her a couple of nights ago. She was still excited about it, even though all details were taken from her memory.

After about ten hours of driving, the sun began to set. Faith exited the freeway to look for a hotel room for the night. She found one just a block away and booked a room. It felt so good to be by herself in the hotel. Of course, as always, she looked for holes in the walls or bathroom. It was a habit. The coast was clear, and she felt comfortable. She decided to go down the street and get something to eat and bring it back. She lay in bed, enjoying her meal, and watched a little TV. Then she took a long, hot shower and felt renewed.

Even though Faith was still in awe of what God showed her that night, she still worried that she had not received an answer about getting a divorce. It took her a little while to fall asleep, and before she knew it, the alarm went off. She got out of bed and fixed her coffee. She sipped it and got dressed and ready to go. Once everything was stowed in the car, she drove through a fast food line and got some breakfast. Then it was back on the road. She was really enjoying this long drive and the peacefulness she felt. She cranked up the music as loud as it would go and sang in the car. It was fun, and she felt free, like a teenager again just for a little while.

The time flew by, and before she knew it, she was only about an hour away from home. Faith finally reached Kenny's workplace and parked right in front. As she entered, Kenny was not up front, but another other guy yelled back and told him that she was here. After a few seconds, he appeared. When Faith saw Kenny, she was stunned. She couldn't believe who she was looking at! She wondered if her mouth was hanging wide open as she stared into the face of her husband and saw a totally different person! He did not look like himself at all. Faith couldn't explain it, but suddenly all the hurt and pain that he caused drained from her in an instant. Then the love that she once had for him as her husband wasn't there. This all happened in just a few seconds, and Faith was speechless. She had to get out of there. She told Kenny she just stopped by to tell him she was home, and then got back in the car and drove to her house ... all the while not believing what she had just seen and felt.

Once inside her home, she sat down and grappled with feelings of confusion and disbelief. She asked, *God? What just happened?* As soon as she asked that question, a knowing came over her that her marriage was over and that she was going to ask for a divorce. It was strong. Faith knew that God had answered her prayers in a way that she had never considered. She had never experienced anything quite like it. She picked up the phone and told Monty what happened. He told her that God was giving her the answers she had been praying about.

***

Faith was home for about a week and was still awe-struck by all that transpired. That night, she dreamt that she and Kenny were on a large platform overlooking an ocean, with tables, umbrellas, and chairs. People were out enjoying the day. She and Kenny walked over to the edge and looked at the water, and in the distance, Faith saw huge dark clouds forming in the sky. As she watched, they grew bigger and started heading toward them. The wind picked up, blowing some tables over. People ran towards the building for cover. As the wind was whipping Faith's hair all around, she realized the storm clouds were a message from God and felt they symbolized her marriage.

As Faith kept looking upwards, the clouds became more and more ominous. Kenny took off running, and Faith was the only person out there. Somehow, knew she was okay. She finally started running towards the building, but never caught up with Kenny. Then suddenly, she woke.

The next day she called Monty and told him about her dream. He told her that God was taking care of her, even in the midst of what looked like a storm. Faith loved how Monty could always interpret dreams.

It took a couple of days for Faith to process everything that happened, and figure out how she was going to approach Kenny. She thought about what she was going to say. *How will I tell the kids, and what were they going to think, and how are they going to respond?* These thoughts whirled in her mind as she continued to focus on her current situation. Her heart sank as she knew, without a shadow of a doubt, that she had to break the news to her husband and children soon. She ran into her bedroom and wept. *My babies!* she thought. *I won't be able the bear the look in their eyes when we tell them Mommy and Daddy will no longer be together.*

Faith waited until Kenny was off of work one day and the kids were in school. She shook like a leaf and couldn't believe what she was about to share with him. She looked him right in the eye, knowing he wasn't expecting what she was about to say.

"I want a divorce."

"Don't you think you're being a little rash?" he said.

Faith just looked at him in disbelief. "Really? You think I'm being rash?" She told him that he was the one responsible for this mess. He was the one who created it, and he was the one who said, the last time, that this would never happen again.

Kenny never argued with her. He just said, "Okay," and admitted it was his fault. He said that when the kids got home, together they would tell Mark and Julie.

Faith walked away and waited for the kids to get home from school. It was Friday, and that would give them the weekend to adjust before they were back in school on Monday. Just the thought of hurting her children tore her apart. She kept praying silently that Mark and Julie would be okay. When they arrived from school, Faith's heart began to beat exceptionally fast because she knew what was coming. They waited until after dinner and then sat the kids down. Kenny began to explain to them that mom and dad were not going to be together anymore. He said that they loved each other very much and that they loved them very much, but just couldn't live together anymore.

The kids' faces were blank. Faith jumped in and told them that everything was going to be okay, and made sure that Mark and Julie didn't see how badly she was hurting. She put on a good show and was all smiles to make sure their hearts didn't break any more than necessary. All the while, she felt ripped apart piece by piece, especially when Mark and Julie started crying. Faith held Julie and Kenny held Mark, and they all hugged. Kenny kept telling them that everything would be okay and that they all still loved each other. That would never change.

It took a little while to calm them down. All the while, Faith's heart was torn by the pain her children were experiencing. She hated it, but there was nothing she could do. She felt totally helpless and really depended on God to help all of them through this tough time.

***

Later on that evening, Kenny told Faith that he'd give her money every month to help with Mark and Julie. Faith told Kenny that he didn't have to move out—he could take the downstairs bedroom and still be there with the kids. Kenny said no very quickly and announced he was moving in with his co-worker friend.

Faith was surprised. "Why wouldn't you want to still be here with your kids?" she asked.

"It would just be too weird," he answered, and said he'd be moving out the next day.

Faith couldn't believe what she was hearing, but Kenny did exactly what he said. The very next night, she called to check on him, and he was already out with another woman. Faith was horrified. Her pain from her finding out he was cheating on her all came rushing back. On top of that, she had to hide her pain from Mark and Julie. It was shocking that he was already on a date, and she assumed he had been doing this all along.

After a couple of months, Kenny told Faith that he wasn't going to give her any more money to help with the kids and that he was going to get the divorce papers drawn up and let the court decide how much he needs to pay each month. That's exactly what he did. When he brought the papers to her to sign, she never looked at them. Kenny told her that everything would be split down the middle, but told Faith that she could give him what she wanted to when he got his own place. Faith agreed and signed the papers.

After that, Kenny got an apartment and Faith gave him everything that he needed to get set up. Once Kenny got everything he wanted, he began to treat Faith badly. He told her he made sure her name was off of his pension, and that if anything ever happened to him, she would not get anything from him. He told her she was responsible for all the credit cards, the house payment, and all the bills, and that all he would do was pay child support. Faith was shattered. *How could he? After all he did to me, and now he's just twisting the knife in my back.*

Faith yelled, "I'm not going to pay any credit cards," and she didn't. They argued all the time now, and Faith knew the kids could sometimes hear them fussing. She felt helpless. There was no way to afford the house and pay all the bills with her cleaning jobs. She didn't want to sell the house. It was all the kids had ever known, and leaving their home would hurt them even more. Faith had no savings because she always put her money into her home. Kenny was getting worse on a daily basis, and Faith didn't even know him anymore. This wasn't the man she married at all. Or maybe it was. His true colors were being exposed.

Faith was learning how to raise her children by herself now and continued to work and cross her fingers that the house payment and bills were paid. During this time, she called Monty and Trudy, and it seemed like Trudy didn't want to talk to her. She always had an excuse. It was bad enough that the people who came to the gatherings were ignoring her and giving her dirty looks. But now, Trudy wasn't speaking to her. Faith was hurt and confused. After a while, she asked Monty what was wrong with Trudy. Monty said that she was busy and tired lately.

As time went on, Faith put on a happy face for the children. She wanted them to feel safe, secure, and loved, even though she was falling apart on the inside. As usual, every time Faith called Kenny, he argued with her. He was so full of hatred for her, and she couldn't understand why. One day she called him at the firehouse. She knew the crew he worked with held her in high regard. When they handed the phone over to Kenny, Faith asked if he was going to pick the kids up that weekend. Suddenly, Kenny started yelling and saying things that didn't make sense.

"Oh, well you just go ahead and do that, Faith. You're so mean to me and the kids."

"Kenny, what are you talking about?" she asked.

Kenny said something else that was completely out of context, yelling and screaming, and then hanging up the phone. Faith was totally confused for just a moment, and then finally realized Kenny was saying things in front of the guys to set her up. He was turning everyone she knew against her!

The next time she talked to Kenny, she confronted him about it, and he just kept telling her she was crazy. He lied more and more, and had a plan. It was to make him look good and for Faith to look bad. The sad thing was, everyone believed him. *But why not?* Everyone already had it out for Monty, so Kenny saw the chance to make matters worse.

Everyone fell into his trap. Even the children started to believe their dad, and Mark began to treat Faith with disrespect. Sometimes he shot her very hateful looks, which broke her heart. Faith knew what Kenny was doing, but no one listened to her. Kenny even called Hope and told her the same lies, and was very sweet to her. Although she was Faith's twin, she fell for it too, hook, line and sinker.

Chapter 31: Turning Their Backs

"Above all be the heroine of your life, not the victim."
~ Nora Ephron

Granny was hosting another gathering at her house one weekend, and Faith took the kids with her. They liked visiting, and especially enjoyed all the wonderful food people brought. Faith was still soaking up everything she heard, and it gave her hope and trust in the messages she was receiving at that time. Afterward, the people had lunch and chatted amongst themselves.

A woman who had known Faith for a very long time told her to come and sit by her and said she could hardly take her eyes off her the whole time when the minister was preaching. She said that she saw Faith all dressed in white in a beautiful dress, surrounded by a bright white light all over and around her. Faith lit up when she heard that message. The lady also told her that God was doing things in her and that all she could do was trust. With everything going on in Faith's life, she really needed to hear that message. The lady smiled as Faith got up to mingle with the others. She felt such a beautiful, loving presence all around her. She was learning, little by little, about the amazing things of the spiritual life, and she loved it.

After lunch, Faith and the kids went home. When Faith went to bed that evening, she thought about what the lady had told her and felt such joy. As she lay there, she had yet another dream. This time, she was standing on the back porch of her mom's house, which was right next door. As she looked up, she saw Jesus standing on a big straight limb about fifty feet above her. Jesus told her to come up. Faith noticed that he didn't use his mouth to speak, but she knew what he was saying. He was speaking to her telepathically. She found herself floating up to Jesus, and stood beside him. He turned and looked at her and smiled, and once again told her without moving his mouth, *Good! Now go back down.*

Faith started floating back down and stood back on the porch. Now, Mark stood in front of her with her arms around him. He seemed to be about five years old. She looked up, and Jesus told her once again to come up. With her arms around Mark, she started floating back up. As soon as she got near the limb, Mark stuck his foot out, and they started falling backward. As they plummeted toward the ground, Faith thought, *Jesus is not going to let us fall.* As soon as she thought those words, they started floating back up and stood beside Jesus again on the limb. He smiled at Faith and said, *Good, now go back down.* Faith landed on the porch safely with Mark, and then she woke up.

She lay in bed wondering what the dream meant. Perhaps it meant that she was to have faith at all times. Maybe it meant that Mark might do something later in life that would make him fall, but Jesus would help him make his way back up. The bottom line was that she would need to trust God at all times, no matter what a situation might look like.

***

One day as soon as Faith got home from work, Monty called and was crying.

"What's wrong?" she asked. She could hardly understand what he was saying. She calmed him down, and he began to speak.

"Trudy just told me she's in love with another man and wants a divorce."

Faith was astonished. "No way!" she said, not quite believing what she was hearing. "Where are you?"

"I'm sitting outside in the garage," he told Faith, sobbing. "She wants me to leave, and I have no place to go. I don't know what I'm going to do. I love her. I don't want a divorce!"

"Come stay with me and the kids. You can have the downstairs," she offered, feeling sorry for him. Plus, she could relate because she was going through the same thing. "We can help each other out."

Monty finally accepted Faith's offer and came the next day. He helped with the groceries and a bit with the mortgage payment. When

Faith told Kenny that Monty was staying with them for a while, he got very angry. Faith explained what happened and that Monty didn't have a place to go. She felt sorry for him, and he could also help out a little with the bills. Kenny didn't agree at all, but Faith didn't care what he thought at this point.

She still enjoyed conversations with Monty, and he kept giving her little tidbits of insight about how God was going to use her. He told her once again that a huge ministry icon and famous Christian singer—George—would be in touch very soon. Sure enough, as she sat down at the computer, a short email from George had arrived. He introduced himself, saying he was there to help with her and Monty and get them where they needed to be. Faith didn't quite understand what he was saying at the time but was so excited just to hear from him. She wrote back and thanked him for all the help that he was going to provide, and couldn't wait to hear from him again.

Faith ran upstairs and told Monty that George had made contact, and Monty seemed happy. She read him the email, and Monty told her that God sent George to help with this special situation between the three of them.

"The ministry?" asked Faith.

"Yes," said Monty, "and much more. As time goes on, things will open up to all of us."

Faith learned to trust God no matter what things looked like in the natural, and no matter if anyone was upset with her. Monty told her that friends and family would fall away during this time, until God brought her to the place He wanted her to be. Even though she saw everyone turning against her, she knew in her heart that God was in control of it all. After God brought her out and into her new life, everything else would fall into place.

It hurt Faith deeply that Brandi was extremely upset with her and said that Monty could not be trusted. Everyone was seeing something entirely different than what was really going on, and Faith could not tell anyone about it. She remembered that Monty warned her that people would not be able to see what God was doing. There were many days and nights that Faith cried because everyone in her life was either not talking to her, or talking about her. She just continued to have a strong faith in God and knew He would bring them all back to her in his timing. All she could do for now was dry her tears and trust God.

Faith thought that having Monty under her roof would bring financial assistance so she wouldn't have to sell the house. Kenny kept pressuring her to do so, and Faith got upset with him. She told Kenny that this is where Mark and Julie grew up, and she was not going to sell their home. She did everything in her power to keep her home. It held so many memories—not just of being married and raising Mark and Julie there, but how her dad helped her get the house and all of the hard work she put into it. But Kenny did not care in the least.

Meanwhile, Monty was still reverting back to his childhood at least three or more times a week. It was all Faith could do to keep her cool. She had no idea then that Monty was perhaps suffering from a dissociative disorder brought on by severe childhood abuse. She had so much going on with Kenny and taking care of the children, that sometimes she let her temper get the best of her and yelled at Monty. It never failed that when she yelled, things got worse. Then Faith would get even angrier, and then Monty would get worse off yet. At times it was just a downward spiral that lasted for a few days.

Faith always tried hard to get Monty back to himself before the kids got home from school. Sometimes Monty wouldn't be quite back to normal, and Mark and Julie saw how he was acting. With them being so young, they didn't understand what was going on. They just got mad and told their dad, which always turned into an argument between Faith and Kenny. There were many times that Faith cried out to God and asked why He was not helping her. It seemed that Monty got all the attention, and she was the one trying to help him.

Then one day Faith received an email from George. He explained that God sent Monty to her so that she could help him and heal the little boy who was abused and abandoned. George told her that when she got angry, raised her voice, or said something to hurt Monty's feelings, he reverted back to the little five-year-old. His mind and his actions would be that of a little boy. George said that when she saw Monty in this state of mind, she needed to actually see him as a little five-year-old and treat him as such. She needed to assure him over and over that he was loved, and that she would always be there for him. She also needed to talk in a very low, loving voice, because if she didn't, it would remind him of horrible things, and he would stay in that childlike mindset.

As Faith read the email, she didn't quite understand it all. She asked George about her circumstances and all that happened to her. She wanted to know if God was going to heal her. George replied that it would all come in due time, but for now, she was to help Monty. Faith tried the best she could to do what George said. But when Monty went into this frame of mind, sometimes she handled it well, and other times it was a disaster. Faith found that if she was not in a very good mood when Monty fell into the childlike mindset, it made her feel frustrated ... and then Monty would get worse. Faith felt like she had so much on her shoulders trying to keep everyone happy, especially her children. She told George that she was glad he was helping her through these challenges because she knew nothing about Monty's emotional and psychological needs. She told him that she was a victim herself, and felt so left out. She felt like God was abandoning her for Monty.

***

After a while, Faith found out that Kenny retracted what he told her about the divorce being his fault. Now he was going around telling everyone that Monty was to blame and was the cause of the divorce. He had everyone believing him. No one believed anything Faith had to say. She didn't understand, after all these years of her friends knowing her and her heart, that they would believe Kenny rather than her. This tore her apart even more. By now, everyone she knew was against her. All kinds of rumors floated around, mostly started by Kenny. He had the perfect alibi. He could hide his affairs from almost everyone, and now have someone to put the blame on. It worked out perfectly for him.

Faith was tired of Kenny's not telling the truth of their divorce. She decided to write Hope a long email about what Kenny did to her. It took a long time to type out the message because it was still fresh and hurt her deeply. She cried and cried and could hardly type. By the time she was done, she had exposed everything to Hope. Faith waited patiently for Hope's response, knowing that she would have her back and send her love. The next day Faith opened her email and saw a message from Hope. She smiled, just waiting to read what her sister said.

But the message was not what she expected. Kenny got to Hope, as well. Faith put her hand over her mouth and cried even harder at the harsh words she read coming from her sister. She blamed everything on Faith and told her that she was the cause of the divorce. Faith could not believe what she was reading. She cried so hard that it took her a long time to read the rest. Hope, in her religious mindset, told Faith that what Monty taught was of the devil. Word after word was so far from the truth. Faith was numb. She thought that by sharing her heart and the truth of the painful divorce, as well as the hurt that Mark and Julie were going through, Hope would have some kind of love and understanding for her. But she didn't. Not one word.

Faith reached over and shut the computer down. It felt like her heart hit the floor. *Why? Why, God, is everyone turning against me? Why won't they believe me? You know my heart God! Why is everyone stomping on it and tearing it apart?* It took her a while to let it go, or at least she thought she let it go. What she did was bury that hurt and pain along with the rest. She decided not to talk to Hope for a while, even if she called. Hope's words cut her deeply. After every crushing blow she'd been through ... now this. It was as if the people she loved most were shunning her. No one was there for Faith during her divorce and all she endured. Everyone was so focused on Monty that everything else fell by the wayside.

The next day as Faith was getting the kids ready for school, Monty could tell something was bothering her. She let it all out—how everyone had turned against her. How Kenny was telling lies, and everyone believed him. It just hurt. Even her own sister, who wasn't even in the country, listened to what everyone else was saying and made a wrong judgment against her. Monty saw how much Faith was upset and began to tell her again that this was bound to happen because God was bringing her to a higher place in Him. He told her that the others were not included on her journey. All Faith could do was trust that God was going to take care of everything.

Chapter 32: Special Purpose

"There's no way to be a perfect mother and a million ways to be a good one."
~ Jill Churchill

It was Sunday night, and Faith was getting ready for the work week. Right after dinner, she got a phone call from one of her clients who said she was no longer needed. This was her highest paying client, and Faith was upset that she would no longer have that job. At the end of the week, yet another client informed her that they couldn't afford her any longer and would have to let her go. Faith needed this money to take care of the bills.

One night as she was getting ready to go to sleep, she heard someone in the hallway. She kept her eyes on her bedroom door and saw Monty walking slowly towards her bedroom. In an instant, Faith saw her dad. She started shaking and memories flooded into her mind of the things he did to her. As Monty walked closer and into her bedroom, he asked if she was asleep. By now Faith was crying. Monty asked her what was wrong. She was crying so hard that he couldn't understand her. He knelt by her bed and started to comfort her.

Faith began to tell him that she felt her dad's presence when he was walking towards her room. She started telling Monty a few things that her dad did to her that she hadn't told anyone before, crying the whole time. She said that when he was coming down the hallway and stopped at her door, she remembered her dad doing the same thing. Faith began to open up for the first time. Monty was very supportive and told her how sorry he was. The conversation went on for about an hour. When Monty felt like Faith was calm enough to go to sleep, he left her room and went back downstairs. As he left, Faith felt a sigh of relief. Even though he helped her by listening, she couldn't get over how her dad's presence was in Monty that night. She finally drifted off to sleep.

Over the next few days, Faith just let things slip by and went on about her daily life as usual—taking care of the kids, keeping up with the house, and trying to find more jobs. The following week, Faith and Julie went to the store. As they were sitting at the stoplight, the van just stopped running. Faith tried to start it, and there was nothing. People began blowing their horns and acting rude. Faith begged God to help her. Suddenly, two guys came to her window, and Faith explained that she couldn't get her van to start. They told her to put it in neutral and pushed her into the parking lot. She rolled down her window to thank the guys, but they were nowhere to be found. She looked all around and in every direction, not ever seeing the men.

Faith knew that God had sent her two angels. She called a tow truck to take her van to the dealer right down the street. They said it would be four or five days before it would be ready. The tow truck driver dropped her and Julie off at a car rental place so she could rent a vehicle until her van was ready. Expenses seemed to be adding up little by little. It seemed like the more she lost jobs, the more other things would come up for her to pay. She also had Mark in a private school and wanted to make sure he stayed there.

***

When Faith got home, she put a couple of ads out to try and pick up more clientele. Kenny was of no help. Anytime Faith would call, it would always end up in an argument. He told her he wasn't going to do anything to help her, even though he knew it was for the kids' sake. Things were starting to pile up. After five days, her van was ready. Monty took Faith over to drop the rental car off and to pick up her van. Then he had to go out of town to minister and would be back in two days. Faith put what she owed on the rental car company and the bill from her van on her and Kenny's credit card—just over twelve-hundred dollars. Faith drove home and got dinner ready for the kids. She was glad to have her van back.

The next morning she got the kids ready and drove Mark to school, which began an hour earlier than Julie's school. So Faith took Mark first and then looped back around to take Julie to the bus stop. Julie usually hopped up front when Mark was dropped off, but this time she wanted to sit in the middle seat in the back.

"Strap in!" Faith said. Julie buckled up, and they headed home.

Faith was sitting at the stoplight at the top of her street. The light was green, and Faith pulled out into the intersection to make her left turn. Traffic was a somewhat heavy, and by the time the cars went through, the light turned red. Faith had to make that left turn, or she would block traffic. She started to make the left turn, and without her even noticing, a car ran the red light at high speed, T-boning Faith's van. It hit so hard that it knocked the van up on two wheels before it rocked back down on the road.

The next thing she heard was Julie crying and yelling, "Why did he do that?" Faith must have been knocked out for just a second, and she had to gather her thoughts.

"Are you okay honey?" she asked. Julie was scared, but she said she was okay and that her ribs hurt.

"Just sit still, baby," Faith said with a reassuring voice. "I need to pull the van out of the road."

When she parked, she noticed the passenger seat was shoved closer to her and that the floorboard was buckled. If Julie had been sitting there, her legs and feet would have been crushed. Faith got out of the van and looked it over. She could see that the sliding door was pushed in and the top was pushed out. As she looked through the window, she saw that the floorboards from the passenger seat all the way to the end of the rear wheel tire were buckled about eight inches up. Faith closed her eyes for a moment and thanked God for saving Julie that day.

No one stopped to see if they were okay. Faith called the police, and they came in about five minutes. She told the officer what happened. The guy that hit Faith lied and said the light was green. Faith took the officer out to the light and showed him how the traffic flows when the lights are red or green. The police officer told Faith that she still ran the red light. Faith argued with the officer and told him she had no choice. But the man who hit her ran the red light as well. The officer didn't write anyone a ticket that day and told both of them that they were responsible for their own vehicles. Faith was very upset. She just paid close to eight hundred dollars to get her van fixed the day before, and now it was totaled. She didn't have the money to fix it or get another vehicle. Faith had told the officer that Julie's ribs hurt, but he never called for an ambulance. He just left her there at the scene with no assistance at all.

Faith called Kenny and told him what happened. Even then he had a nasty attitude. She told him she didn't have a vehicle now, and to come take Julie to the hospital to make sure she was okay. He finally agreed and drove to the accident site, and then took her to the hospital. Kenny called Faith and said Julie was fine. The doctor said that her ribs were sore from the seatbelt. Faith then called the insurance company and was told they would only give her what the van was worth. She had paid almost twenty thousand for it just two years ago, and now they said they could only give her seven thousand for it.

The tow truck came and gave Faith a ride home, and took her van back to the same place where it had been worked on the day before. The guys there couldn't believe what happened.

When Faith got home, she collapsed. *What now?* she thought. She needed another vehicle because she had to work, and she had to have one by tomorrow. She picked up the phone and called her client and told her she would have to cancel work today. The lady told her not to worry, just come back in two weeks. Faith lost money that day, which upset her. She called Monty and told him all that happened, and then later checked her computer to see if George had written. Sure enough, there was an email from him.

She opened George's email quickly. He always made her feel better and helped her in ways that she would never have thought of. She now depended on George for help. George told Faith that God was doing things in her life that she wouldn't understand at this time, but to continue to trust in Him. He said that God had already known about the accident, and told her that God kept Julie safe by putting her in the back seat. Once again, she was amazed at how God let George see things so he could help her. He reminded Faith to keep her good energy up, so when Monty got home, he'd feel safe and happy. The thought came to Faith of how, once again, it was all about Monty. Faith wrote an email thanking George again for his help.

***

Monty came in the next day late in the afternoon and took Faith to find a car. She ended up getting a two-door Pontiac. It was okay for what she had to do. At least she had transportation. The very next week she lost two more jobs. Everything seemed to be falling apart right before her eyes. She was hysterical! She didn't want to lose her home. She did everything she knew to do to keep it, and Kenny was of no help. He kept telling her to sell it, which made her even angrier.

That weekend, Mark and Julie went to stay with their dad. Friday night Monty and Faith talked about the things that had happened the past week, and how God was setting everything up. Faith got up to fix a drink. She always kept a little something in the cupboard, just in case she was in the mood. She fixed herself a mudslide and sipped it. Monty told her to come downstairs in his room and chat. Faith grabbed her drink, and they went downstairs to sit on the futon and talk. Suddenly, Faith started feeling her dad's presence again in Monty. She felt nervous that he might try to kiss her, and scooted away. Monty saw the change in Faith's attitude and asked her what was wrong.

Once again, memories started coming to her mind. She started crying again, and then yelled at the top of her voice, "Why did he do all these things to me?"

"It's okay," Monty said and reached over to grab her hand. "Just tell me what's on your mind."

Faith opened up again like she never had before, and told Monty yet a few more things that happened. She cried and held her face in her hands. She never told anyone these secrets before and felt so dirty. She couldn't believe that she was saying things that had been buried for so long. As she got more and more upset, she tipped her glass and swallowed the rest of her drink. Then she stood and threw the glass at the wall, putting a dent into it.

Monty got scared and turned into the little boy. This made Faith even angrier.

"Oh sure, God! Let's just help Monty here and not worry about Faith," she screamed. She was crying even more, and Monty was getting worse. Looking around and falling apart herself, Faith had no other choice but to bury her feelings and help Monty. It took her a while to settle down, and then she began to help Monty as much as she could. She put all of her feelings on hold because she knew that she would never be able to sleep until he was back into reality.

Faith told him she had to go to the bathroom. While there, she dried her tears and begged God to help her. *I don't know how to do this,* she said to God. *Please, help me to help him.* She continued to pray. *God, please help me as well. I'm in such a bind, and everything is getting to me. I trust you, but I need some help.*

Faith opened the door and went into Monty's room. She remembered what George said about lowering her voice and telling him how much she loved him. She had to hug him and hold him for a while. It took almost three hours before Monty was satisfied and felt safe. It was two a.m., and Faith was exhausted. She made sure Monty was okay and told him goodnight, and that she loved him and would see him in the morning. She headed up the steps and went to bed. It didn't take her long to fall asleep.

The next morning, the first thing Faith did was get on the computer to see if George had written, and he had. He told her how proud of her he was for helping the little boy. He never mentioned what she was going through, and Faith didn't say anything about it. Once again, it always seemed to be about Monty. However, Faith was glad for George's help, because he and Monty were the only people who had her back.

***

There were many times that these episodes happened to Faith. She'd see Monty as her dad, and they'd talk about it. Faith shared a little more each time. Usually, it ended up with Monty reverting to a child again. Even in her time of trauma, she helped him. She started learning the art of using a soft voice. All of her life she was around yelling and screaming, and it was embedded in her. She'd always get an email from George the next day, talking about it and telling her more and more of how she could help Monty. But she couldn't help but think that all of the attention was going to him, and not her.

Many times she felt like God was abandoning her feelings and what she had gone through.

A couple of nights later, Faith had a dream that a woman was sitting in a chair and holding a baby. She got up and put the baby in Faith's arms and asked Faith if she'd take care of her son. Faith said yes. The woman thanked her and walked away quickly. Faith tried to find her, but the woman was nowhere to be found. She looked for her everywhere, and could not find her. She was now holding this baby boy wearing a cute little blue outfit. She looked at him and smiled, and then woke up.

Faith went to her computer and wrote to George about her dream. George said that he wanted to chat with her on Yahoo Messenger, and for her to set it up. He said he'd contact her in a day or two. When she had Yahoo Messenger ready, she emailed her screen name to George, and he was now able to chat with her. This made it a lot easier. George went on to tell Faith that God gave her that dream. In the dream, Monty's mother handed her son to Faith to take care of him.

"In other words, Monty's mother knows that God has put Monty's life in your hands to heal him," said George's message. He went on to say that when Monty is in the childlike mind, he was looking to Faith as his mother. "That's why you have to have a low voice when speaking to him, and make sure you tell him he is safe and loved."

Faith cried. She couldn't believe that God was using her to heal someone else. After she finished talking to George, she prayed and told God, *Thank you. I feel honored, and please give me patience through all of it.*

The weeks went on, and it happened that one to three times a week "5-year old Monty" needed Faith's help. It got to the point that no matter what she said, it threw Monty into the little child mode again. Sometimes it was unbearable, but she remembered what God had told her and showed her in her dreams. Sometimes she'd forget, and Monty would plummet downhill. It took all of Faith's energy to bring him back up. It took a toll on Mark and Julie as well.

One day while the kids were in school, Monty came in and chatted for a while. Monty felt they needed to get quiet for a while and pray. They sat on the sofa in the den, and Monty started out with a prayer, and then sat in silence for a while. Faith kicked back on the sofa and got comfortable, and just started thanking God for everything. Then she was silent. Staring at the wall of the den, she began to have a vision. As she sat quietly, she saw herself at what seemed to be the bottom of a coliseum. It was filled with hundreds of people from all walks of life. It was very quiet and orderly, and she held out her right hand as she stood at the edge. Everyone who walked by her touched her hand and moved on so the next person could do the same. She knew that these people were touching her for healing.

As Faith looked in the distance, she could see two men were trying to work their way up to the front. It looked like they were carrying someone, but she couldn't see who it was. As they got closer, Faith started walking slowly toward them. In her heart, she knew these men were bringing someone to her to heal. As people continued to walk by and touch her hand, the men got closer. When they were almost in front of her, they put what looked like a stretcher down. The crowd in front of it parted, and Faith saw who it was. She put her hand over her mouth and yelled out loud, "Oh my God! That's my sister!" Hope was lying on the stretcher dressed in white, with her eyes closed and her head turned to the left side. As soon as she said those words, the vision vanished.

Faith gasped and was startled, which made Monty sit up and ask her what happened. She told Monty what she had just seen. She'd never had a vision before, and now God gave her one. At the time she didn't know what it meant. Monty didn't know either, even though he gave Faith some ideas of what it could have meant. Faith had always thought of that vision and the meaning of it. It was strong and clear, and she would never forget it. At night and over the years when she went to bed, she'd ask God to reveal the message to her in that vision. It would be many years later before He did.

The weather was turning cooler, and Faith was out on the deck looking at the beautiful trees that surrounded her backyard. The clouds were puffy and gray. As she stood on the deck just looking all around at nature, she suddenly got an eerie feeling. About that time, Monty came out and asked her what she was doing. She continued to look at the sky and told Monty that this was going to be a bad winter. She said she wasn't talking about the weather, but she felt like things were going to be in an upheaval. He looked at her and asked her what she meant.

"I don't know," said Faith. "I just feel it. I see it in the sky, and I see it in the trees. It's almost like I know." The feeling was so strong that she knew it was true. She just knew, without a shadow of a doubt, that some very troublesome times were ahead. Faith didn't realize that at the moment she had an inner knowledge, and she was right.

Faith went inside and got dinner ready for when the kids got home, still thinking about what she felt earlier. She always loved cooking for them and making them things that they loved. She really wanted to make them as happy because she knew they were hurting too. She knew in her heart that she'd have to sell the house. She kept thinking about how everything was going downhill for her. She was now down to just one or two jobs a week, and Kenny wasn't helping at all. If she sold the house, she could use that money to rent another one. She finally made the heart-breaking decision to put her home on the market. She had no other choice.

Her home had so many memories. Her dad helped her get it when she was twenty-four years old. She got married and had children in that home. Downstairs on a concrete wall were Mark and Julie's painted handprints from every birthday. It was going to kill her to sell her home. Kenny left her with no other choice. She had to do what was good for the kids. She couldn't make the full mortgage payments. She always thought Kenny would help her, but he had turned into someone she didn't recognize. She could never get over of how he was treating her. About a week later, Faith called an agent and got the sale sign up in her front yard. The sign crushed Faith. Whenever she looked at it, she cried as all of the memories of her home flooded her mind.

***

One day before the kids got home from school, Faith went outside and sat on the bench by the pool. She found herself staring through the trees past her mom's house. She sat quietly and peacefully. Suddenly, she began to see herself standing with her back towards her. Once again, it was like watching a movie. She was having another vision. In front of her was a line of people standing in single file line that seemed to go on for a long way. It looked as if there were hundreds of people.

Then she heard a voice speak loud and clear: "Only tell them what I tell you to tell them." It was a strong voice. The vision ended, and Faith was in awe. She knew God had spoken to her and gave her another message. However, she didn't know what it meant. At that time she was just beginning to realize that she could hear messages on her own. She sat outside for a while in total amazement, thanking God and asking Him to reveal what He meant.

Later on, she picked the kids up from school and came back home to fix dinner. When Monty arrived, she told him about the vision.

"God is going to use you to speak to people, and He's giving you the gift of insight to help others. God will let you know when," he said.

Faith spoke up. "I have to remember to tell them only what God tells me to tell them. Not to add or subtract from the message."

Faith was overwhelmed with joy. Later on, she ran to the computer and told George about her vision. He told her that God would be giving her messages and that this was some of what God was going to do with her and the ministry. This confirmed Faith's belief that no matter what was going on around her, God was doing something in her. It helped her at times when her life was changing right in front of her. She remembered that every time she thought of Brandi, their relationship changed. She couldn't wait until God was finished doing what He wanted to do, so she could finally tell Brandi everything.

***

One day as Faith sat at her computer just messing around, a Yahoo Messenger message suddenly appeared in the top corner of her screen. Her eyes quickly focused on the "Mom1000" handle. Faith's immediate thought was, *Who the heck is this?* She opened up the message and read words that made her face squint with curiosity.

The message said: *Faith, I know this might be very hard for you to believe, but this is your mom.*

While Faith knew her mom was in spirit now, it wasn't hard for her to believe this was possible. Over the past years, Faith had heard how people communicated with loved ones through radio waves, TV, and other electronic devices. Faith and Monty had seen the movie White Noise a few months prior, which was about how spirits used electronic devices to talk to their loved ones.

Faith continued reading, and her "mom" went on to say: *There are a lot of changes coming up for you, and I'm here to help you. I know I wasn't a very good mother while I was on the earth plane, but now I can help you. God is going to use you like never before, and you will be able to help many people when it is time.*

Faith put her hand over her mouth in disbelief, but something inside her knew it really was her mom's spirit communicating with her. She typed back quickly with tears in her eyes, telling her mom how much she missed her.

"Mom" typed back: *I'm more help to you now than ever before. You need to trust God with all of your heart because there will be some hard times ahead and your trust will be needed more than ever before.* After that, "Mom" was off the messenger.

Faith could hardly believe what just transpired. All kinds of thoughts flew through her head. *Can this really be happening to me? Is this really my mom?* Faith didn't say anything to anyone. She wanted to think about it for a while. The very next day "Mom" messaged her again. *It has to be her*, Faith thought. "Mom" was telling her things that only she would know. After that second message from "Mom," Faith knew it really was her trying to help her through the computer.

Faith called Monty to discuss it with him. He could hear the excitement in her voice and asked what was going on. Faith wondered if he'd believe what she was about to tell him. She told him what happened while she was on the computer. Monty listened. After Faith was through, she waited for his response.

"Well? What do you think?" Faith asked. She thought Monty might assume she had finally lost it! But he didn't. He was very encouraging and even helpful. He told Faith of others he knew who had experienced this, as well. Monty also reminded Faith of the movie White Noise. After their conversation, Faith felt relieved, excited, and a little confused. However, as time went on she saw how her "Mom" was there to help Monty and her with the ministry and the things to come. Faith was glad of that. Now she had both George and "Mom" helping, and boy did she ever need the extra help, especially in these hard times.

Over the next few weeks, Faith and Monty looked at houses to rent. Faith couldn't find one that suited her. All of the houses that Monty had picked out were old and needed a lot of work. It just didn't feel right to Faith. She wanted the best for her kids, and she wasn't about to settle for anything less. They had been through enough, and she wanted them to be happy with their new home.

***

After the kids went to school one morning, Faith got on the computer and noticed a new email. It was from George! He told Faith he was there to help her through the tough times, and that he was led by God to help in times of trouble and to encourage her. Faith loved the way this man talked. She was always amazed that a rich, famous Christian singer was there to help her. He went on to say how everything is on God's time, and not to worry about what things looked like in the present. God was putting all the puzzle pieces together, and she had to walk it out step by step. He also told her that George was not his real name and that he couldn't give Faith his real name yet. But in due time, he would. His mission was to help her and Monty.

Faith felt a lot of encouragement from this man. She sent him an email back thanking him for all his help. She really needed it. She told George she was never churched, so a lot of this was very new to her. But she knew she could trust Monty because he heard from the Lord and received messages about what was going on. Faith was now getting messages from George one to three times a week, and was always excited to read those emails.

Faith had not paid the mortgage for two months and prayed it would sell quickly. One night, she had a dream that the doorbell rang, and when she answered, there were about five Asian people at her door. They just walked right in. It was a mother, father, and some teenage kids. They just started sitting on the furniture and walking all around the house like it was theirs. Some of the kids were playing on the couch upside down as the parents walked all through the house. When Faith woke up, she thought it was a silly dream and told Monty about it.

"Faith? Don't you see?"

"See what?" she asked Monty.

"God is showing you that Asian people are going to buy your house!"

"Really?" Faith said.

Two days later, the real estate agent called to say she'd be showing Faith's house that day. Faith had to make sure no one was at home. The kids were in school, and Faith went out for a while until the showing was over. Later on, the agent called and told Faith that the couple was interested in the house. They made an offer and Faith took it—a bit lower than Faith expected, but at least she could make plans now to get another home. The people that bought the house were Asian! They had a small restaurant just up the street. Faith was excited at how God showed her in a dream who would buy her house.

She quickly called Monty to tell him.

"See, I told you that God is bringing you to where He wants you. Step by step, you just have trust in Him," Monty told her.

"I do!" said Faith. "I do trust the Lord with all my heart!" Faith was able to see how God had been working up to this point. Even with everyone against her, she knew that God was bringing her to a different place in Him she had never known before.

Now that the house sold, it would take about thirty days before Faith could move. She started packing everything she could in boxes, and stacked them downstairs so she would be ready. It seemed that with every box, a tear rolled down her face. She just couldn't believe how her whole life was changing. She never thought in a million years that she would ever get divorced. Now she was leaving her home of twenty years. She worried how it would impact her kids and wanted to find a nice house to rent.—one the kids would love and enjoy.

After a couple of weeks of packing, Faith came across a house that she thought was beautiful. She called the agent and made an appointment. A couple days later she took Monty with her while the kids were in school and went to see the house. When they pulled up to the front, Faith couldn't wait to get inside. As the agent let them in, she fell in love immediately! It seemed to have a light all around it, inside and out. As she walked around the house, she could envision living there and knew this was the house she was going to rent. It was perfect with five bedrooms, four bathrooms, and three floors. There were times when Monty's kids came to visit, so Faith wanted to make sure she had plenty of room. It was beautiful! She couldn't wait for the kids to see it!

She asked the agent when it would be ready. He said it needed to be cleaned first and would be ready about the middle of the first week. Faith told him that she needed to be out of her house on the thirtieth and really needed to move in on that day. Faith also told him that she had a cleaning business and asked if she could go ahead and do the cleaning. The agent agreed and told Faith that he would charge half the first months' rent since she was cleaning it. Faith was astounded! She made plans with the agent to clean it before she moved in.

The agent told her to come by and fill out the paperwork. After a couple of days, the agent called and said she was approved. She finally sold her home and had to give Kenny half of what she got for it. She had wished now that she would have never put his name on the house, especially after how mean he was treating her. Faith took most of that money she got from the house and set it aside for the new house. The rent was pretty high, but Faith loved the home and knew Mark and Julie would too. The rent was paid for the next five months, which would give her more time to pick up cleaning jobs.

The agent also told Faith that she could clean the homes he had available, and Faith agreed happily. At this time Monty wasn't helping out with the bills at all. He was using what money he had to do his ministry, which included traveling out of state. So Faith was pretty much on her own.

While he was in town, she and Monty drove over while the kids were in school and spent most of the day cleaning, and returned the next day to finish up. It was a big house, and even though it wasn't dirty, Faith wanted it to be perfect for Mark and Julie. The next day Faith and Monty finished cleaning, and when the kids got out of school, she loaded them up in the car and took them over to pick out their rooms. Julie flew up the steps and quickly picked out her room, and then Mark picked out his. They looked excited, and Faith loved seeing the smiles on their faces. *This could be a new start for them,* Faith thought.

The day came to move out of Faith's home and into the new one. She went through so many emotions as she packed up. She still couldn't get over leaving her home. It was heart-wrenching. Faith tried to put on a smile the best she could for the kids. She knew they were going through a tough time as well. She understood but had to follow what God was doing in her. She knew that through God, all things were possible. Even though she and her children were being torn apart at the time, she trusted God with all her heart.

With the children and Monty helping with the move, they finally got everything in the new house. At the time, Faith brought what she needed, and there were still a lot of boxes in the garage that had not been opened. She had already filled the four bedrooms and used the other as an office. They all got settled in.

Chapter 33: An Uncertain Future

"No matter what the situation, remind yourself, 'I have a choice.'"
~ Deepak Chopra

By now, Kenny, through the courts, was paying child support. He hated every dime that he gave Faith and kept accusing her of giving it to Monty. That was not true. He never knew how much Faith needed that extra money to help put food on the table and pay a bill or two.

Things seemed to get worse with Mark. He was pulling away from Faith. He couldn't stand Monty and kept telling his dad that he wanted to live with him. There were a couple of times when Faith and her son got into arguments, and then Mark would call Kenny and ask him to come get him. It ended up that Mark went to live with his dad. This broke Faith's heart.

Kenny called Faith one day and told her he was going to take Julie away from her. Faith was horrified. She couldn't understand why he wanted to hurt her after all she had done for him. Mark and Julie were her life, her every breath, and she couldn't stand the thought of not having her children with her. Kenny took Faith to court, and in the courtroom, the judge called for Mark and Julie to speak to him in the back room. The judge decided that Mark could live with his dad because he was old enough to make that decision. However, Julie could stay with Faith. When the children were walking back to their seats, Mark gave Faith a hateful look that she'd never forget. She was fighting the tears back. *Why would my son do this to me?* she wondered. It ripped her heart in two. He had a stare of pure hatred.

Then Kenny told the Judge that Faith made more money than he did, and the judge believed everything Kenny said. The judge cut the child support very low, and it was all Faith could do to keep from bursting out in tears. Faith had walked in without an attorney because she could not afford one, and Kenny's attorney chewed Faith up and spit her out. It was one of the worst days of her life. By this time, Kenny had everyone on his side believing the lies that he told. They all judged her because of Monty. She felt so all alone, and now her own son was turning against her. Everyone seemed to hate Monty, and they hated that Faith was listening to everything he said.

However, Faith knew that God was pulling her away from the familiar. She trusted God with all her heart. She could see the turmoil, and even though it hurt her, she always prayed and told God that she was His. God knew what was best, and that all she could do was trust. There were several times she felt a red flag regarding what was going on and would bring these thoughts to Monty and discuss them with him. He always reminded Faith that God had her and was taking her to a higher realm, one that even she couldn't see right now. Then they would pray, and sometimes Monty would prophesy, and then Faith would feel better.

That night when Faith went to bed, she had another dream. She dreamed that she was in her doctor's office and went up to the window to sign in. The lady didn't open the window. Faith knocked on the window, and the lady ignored her. She tapped on the glass again, and still, the lady ignored her. Faith looked all around the doctor's office, and it was pretty crowded. It seemed that no one noticed her. She tapped on the window one more time, and still nothing. Suddenly, a dark-haired lady, maybe in her early thirties, came bursting out of the door that led back to the doctor's office. She was crying uncontrollably because she found out that she wasn't pregnant again. She ran through the waiting room and out the door.

The very next second, Faith found herself outside in the parking lot behind a van door. Faith saw the same lady closing her door. "Don't worry, you will get pregnant, but not in your timing … in God's timing," Faith said. The words just came out of her mouth without any knowledge of what she was saying. But she knew they were true words and something she had to tell the lady, who just stared at her like she had seen a ghost.

After Faith spoke those words, she found herself back in the doctor's office in the back room. Then she woke up. Faith knew that in spirit she was giving someone a message who needed to hear it, and a wonderful feeling came over her.

***

Kenny had been dating a woman for several months, and the kids came home one day with surprising news. They told Faith that Janiah was pregnant. Kenny was going to be a dad again.

Faith was working very hard and trying to keep the bills paid and food on the table. She made sure her kids came first. She had lost all of her jobs before she moved, and now picked up three in the new area and couldn't seem to pick up anymore.

It seemed like anytime there was turmoil happening, George emailed Faith and reminded her that all was well and going in the direction that God wanted it to. He always gave Faith instructions on how to handle everything. Monty seemed to be getting a lot better and wasn't falling into a childlike state as much. It was few and far between now. Faith was relieved. George was so much help—always there when she needed him, and always calming her down with his loving heart. Faith found herself falling for this mystery man, and he appeared to be falling for her, as well.

Faith saw George as a great man of God. He could see things that no one else could, and Faith was mesmerized at how he miraculously knew things that happened to her or Monty and would email her and talk about it. He always showed so much love and compassion, and Faith checked her computer many times a day for his emails.

She spent most of her time with George on the computer because he always led her in the right direction. She was amazed by his insights. After a while, George told Faith that they would be together soon and she would help with his ministry. Faith was beyond elated! She thought about the day she and Monty went for a walk, and he told her that she was going to be a part of a ministry. She thought that she and George would eventually get married, and she would be a part of his ministry. This excited Faith beyond everything. It made the tough times not seem so bad, and when it was all over, she would be with George!

She thought about George nonstop, and Monty told her little tidbits of information, just enough to keep Faith excited. Then he would say that the time wasn't right yet, but soon would be. Faith could hardly wait until she would meet George! There were many times that she begged Monty to share any information with her, but he said that he couldn't at the time.

The next day Monty went to apply for a job at a car dealer selling used cars. He got the job. Faith was happy, as this would help with bills. After a week of working there, Monty told Faith that God spoke to him about a certain car. He asked Faith if she could put the vehicle in her name, since her credit was better than his. Faith told Monty that she could try and see if the application would go through. The newer used car was priced at eleven thousand dollars. Monty told her that if she put it in her name, he'd take care of the payments. She figured that would be great since they could use a second vehicle, especially if he would make the payments. Faith filled out the paperwork, and in a couple of days, they drove the car off of the lot. Faith was glad that she could help out in any way she could, plus they wouldn't have to share a car anymore.

***

After a while, the kids got settled into their new schools. They were now going over to Kenny's every other weekend. Kenny's girlfriend seemed to treat Mark and Julie very well, and Faith appreciated it very much. Every time Kenny brought the kids back, he and Faith would argue. Faith begged Kenny to stop arguing when the kids could hear, but he never listened to her. He said things that didn't make any sense to Faith, and accused her of things that were not true. This stirred up a lot of commotion at Faith's house.

One time Kenny dropped the kids off and started in on Faith. Some of the neighbors were out, and Kenny yelled and caused a scene. He even reached over and took a swing at her. She jumped back and yelled at him, and then went inside to call the police. The police came, and Kenny continued to act like a fool. It had been almost a year, and Faith still couldn't get over how he was acting. He was a completely different man. She tried to keep things calm at the house, but the children would always side with their dad. This was because of their feelings towards Monty, which were getting worse.

Faith called the chief at the firehouse and told him how Kenny was acting in public, and that he needed to do something about his attitude, especially everyone knowing he was a firefighter. The Chief assured Faith that he would talk to Kenny. He called Kenny right away and told him to come in. Kenny was angry at Faith for calling his Chief, and she told him she had no other choice since he continued to act the way he did. After the Chief talked to Kenny, he settled down a little bit.

Anytime there was any upheaval, Faith checked her email. Once again, there was one from George which helped her every step of the way. It always brought some peace to her heart.

***

Monty and Faith were talking one night and thought it would be a good idea to have a gathering one weekend. Faith wanted loving people around her since there had been so much negativity lately. She wanted to invite Sylvia because she hadn't seen her in a while, although they kept in touch by phone. Faith couldn't wait to invite her to the gathering. They made all the necessary plans and learned that Sylvia and her daughter were coming. Several people who Monty and Faith knew through the ministry were also coming. That weekend was exactly what Faith needed.

It was a small gathering, and Faith couldn't be more excited. She fixed all kinds of food. It was an awesome spiritual time, and after Monty spoke, others shared what God was showing them. Faith could tell that Sylvia was hearing something spiritual.

Sylvia spoke up and said, "We think there are eight people here, but there are more. The room is jam-packed with spiritual beings. I saw them filling the living room, the den, and the kitchen, and all throughout," she said. "They were listening, too."

Faith felt chills as Sylvia spoke. Another lady shared that she had felt the presence of other beings as well. It was a beautiful time, and Faith was happy with how her first gathering turned out. Afterward, they all sat around and enjoyed all the wonderful food Faith had prepared. They talked and had a good time. Faith always hated to see Sylvia leave. She hugged her tight. Sylvia always had this look in her eye that Faith loved. She had such a big, loving heart, and she herself had been through so much. Faith could always feel her pain and had seen it in her eyes the very first day she met her.

Everyone said they had a good time before they left, and Monty drove Sylvia and her daughter back home. He would be gone for a few hours. As night came, Faith had another dream. She dreamed that she was sitting in a dark room lit only by candlelight. She was sitting on a small concrete bench beside a window with bars on it. She peered out and saw that she was at the very top of a big building, and it was dark inside. As she looked at the bars on the window and said to herself, *Wouldn't it be neat if I had my spiritual body?* As soon as she said that, she touched the bars and her hand went right through. She got excited and yelled, "I do have my spiritual body!" She floated out the window and circled around at the top of the building. She could see that her body was transparent and light.

Then she started flying around and headed toward an area that was lit. She found herself floating near the ceiling of a round room, and while she looked down and all around, she noticed that the place was some sort of private school for girls. She saw a young blonde girl, about fourteen years old, wearing a white shirt and a red and black plaid skirt. She hovered above her head and knew the girl was very upset. As she circled above her head, she gave the young girl a message. She reassured the girl that everything was going to be alright. Faith felt a sense of peace for herself and the girl, and then woke up.

The next day she couldn't wait to tell George and Monty about her dream. They were always good at interpreting them. The feeling that Faith had about this dream kept her on a high for over a month. That sense of having a spiritual body was exhilarating for Faith.

***

As the days went on in the new house, Faith saw that her money was dwindling. She had more bills than jobs, and it didn't help with Kenny's cutting the child support down. Monty seemed to be going on more ministry trips and wasn't helping Faith out with the bills. He just kept telling her that God has a plan for everything. There were many times that Faith felt like something wasn't right, and when she would tell George or Monty about it, they always said that God was doing things that she didn't understand right now. Faith had such a love and trust for God that she just listened to what George and Monty said. After all, they were ministers and much more experienced than she.

One morning while Faith was at the computer, Yahoo Messenger came up, and it was George. Faith's heart leaped with joy!

Hi George! she typed.

George typed a little more information about her and the ministry, and how mighty it was going to be. He told her that she would be prophesying over people, and the people would love her. She could hardly believe what she was hearing. She was so excited that she could hardly type back to George.

Then George told Faith that the people in the ministry were talking about how she and Monty lived in the same house, and rumors were spreading. *We cannot have this,* George told her. *This is what I'm hearing.* George said that during prayer time he heard that she and Monty need to get married to keep all the rumors at bay. Faith's heart hit the floor. She could hardly speak. She thought, *There is no way I would ever marry Monty. He's like a brother to her, and that is it.*

Faith told George to hold on for a moment, and went in the bathroom and threw up. Just the thought of the idea made her sick to her stomach. She came back to the computer and told George that she had to go for now and that she would talk with him later. She quickly turned the computer off. For the next few hours, Faith continued to throw up. Her head was spinning, and panicked thoughts flooded her mind. She did not want to do this. After a few hours, she got back on the computer to see if George was on. She waited about ten minutes, and then he was back on chat. Faith told George what happened and that she could not marry Monty, and that it made her sick to her stomach.

George explained that they would be going to an out-of-town meeting that would have three ministers in attendance. He told her that they would have a marriage ceremony at the gathering without ever getting a marriage license. It would stop the rumors and allow Faith to get serious with the ministry that God was creating for them. Faith felt relieved. George went on to say that she or Monty could not tell anyone that they were really not married until God told them that they could. Faith agreed because she knew it wasn't for real and because she wanted to have all the things that God wanted for her.

That weekend, Monty and Faith went to the gathering out of town, and sure enough, three ministers were present. Monty approached one of them early that morning and asked that he officiate the wedding. It would be a surprise to everyone. Faith was nervous. She didn't even like the thought of people thinking they were married. Her stomach remained queasy. She kept reminding herself that it was all for show, and nothing else.

Faith asked the lady of the house if she could check her email because she was waiting for an important message. She showed Faith where the computer was, and Faith saw a message from "Mom." Faith was excited again. *Maybe she'll say something different,* she thought. The words that Faith saw were almost the same thing that George had told her. Still, Faith's heart sank. "Mom" told Faith that she was not able to see the whole picture right now, and that was okay, and that was another reason why she and George were there to help.

You have to have trust, Faith, that God has a plan and you'll begin to see it soon. As soon as Faith started typing back, "Mom" was gone. Faith turned off the computer and wondered when she'd be able to hear things for herself.

***

After the gathering was over, the minister got up and said he had a special announcement. A wedding was about to take place, and all were invited. The people cheered and then asked who the couple was. The minister called Monty and Faith up front, and the people started clapping. Faith put on the best smile that she could, even though she still felt like throwing up. She kept telling herself over and over that this is what God wants, and she'd obey God. The minister started the ceremony, and Monty and Faith were married. Well, at least that is what the people thought. It was hard for Faith not to tell anyone the truth. She wanted to so badly. She did not want her children or anyone she knew believing that she married Monty, because they resented him. Once again, her heart was torn to pieces.

She cried out to God whenever she was alone, pleading, *Please get this over.*

She lay in bed at night, despite how bad things were, and with tearful eyes said, "I trust you, God." As she fell asleep, she had another spiritual dream. She dreamed that she was in a house and several people stood around. She didn't recognize any of them, and it seemed like they didn't even notice her there. Suddenly, she started floating towards the ceiling, then through the ceiling, and then through the roof. As she went through the roof, she was on her back with arms outstretched. Then she felt with a strong grip on her wrists, one by one, and a voice as loud as thunder said, "I've got you!" She awoke quickly. She knew it was a message from God telling her to remember that He had her through all of this. It made Faith feel better, and all of her worries dissipated at the time.

The next day she went on the computer and told George about her dream. He then confirmed to her that God has her, and she shouldn't worry about anything. She was to continue to trust as she had never trusted before. She was glad she had George to confide in, and couldn't wait to meet him in person after all of this was over. She very much wanted to be with George. He kept telling her that they had a little way to go and that there were more things God wanted to do. She knew that at the end of it, she'd finally meet George, marry him, and run a ministry together. She couldn't wait!

***

Faith slept in the following Saturday morning and woke to the birds chirping outside her window. It reminded her of times growing up when she listened to the birds. It seemed there were hundreds more at this house, and Faith didn't mind at all. After a lazy yawn, she got dressed and went to the kitchen to get a big breakfast started. The kids were stirring around, and after a while smelled the aroma of sausage cooking. It wasn't long before they were downstairs. After a late breakfast and a quick clean up, Faith checked her email. George had written, along with Mom!

Wow! Faith thought, and couldn't wait to read the emails. They were both pretty much saying the same thing, and it was urgent! As she read, George explained that a group from California was trying to find Monty, and were using astronomy and energy to locate him! These were not good people at all. They knew how big the ministry was going to get, and they were out to destroy it!

They are getting close to the area, so all you have to do is follow these instructions to the tee, his email said. George and Mom both told Faith to close all windows and lock all doors.

Make sure all the blinds are closed and the curtains drawn. No one can leave the house or even open a door or window. If anyone comes to your house, no matter who it is, you cannot answer the door. If a door is opened, these men will pick up on the energy and find Monty. These men are highly sensitive to energy and will find Monty if you don't follow these directions. I will not be able to write until this is all over. Monty will be able to pick up when this energy is over, but until then, please love, make sure everyone stays put and do not even step outside. I love you, George.

Faith gasped and put her hand over her mouth. She got up and went to find Monty. She told him to come here quickly and read the email from both George and Mom. Faith could see the concerned look on his face as he read the email. He turned around and told Faith to get the kids and explain to them what is going on.

"We need to do this now," Monty said. He told the kids what was happening, and they joined in helping to close all blinds and curtains, and make sure all doors were locked. Faith went back over everything to make sure everything was shut. Everyone sat in the living room for a while, and then the kids went about their business. They talked and played quietly. Monty and Faith stayed and prayed for a while. When they were done, Monty told Faith he kept seeing mountains.

"Spirit put me in the mountains, and I was walking as if I was really there. I feel like there will be something with mountains at some point."

Faith just looked at him and said, "Okay."

Later on that afternoon, Monty felt that the threat was over.

"I'm going to check my email," he said, "to see if George has written."

Monty got up and went into the other room. After a few minutes, he came back and said, "Nothing yet." He told Faith to check her email in a few minutes to see if she received anything. About ten minutes later Faith checked, and sure enough, George had written, telling her that the coast was clear and they could open everything back up.

You all did great! he said. *The men couldn't find Monty and are heading back to California.* Faith was happy to hear the news and told Monty and the kids.

***

Early Sunday morning, Faith got a call from Sylvia.

"Hi Mama," Faith said with excitement. She adored Sylvia and always loved talking to her. Sylvia's voice was serious as she asked Faith, "What the hell was happening yesterday?"

"What do you mean?" asked Faith.

Sylvia said that during meditation, she saw Faith's house with what looked like huge angel wings covering the whole house. A whirlwind surrounded that house.

"You all were being protected from something, and I want to know!" said Sylvia.

Faith told Sylvia what took place the day before, and how men had come to find Monty and destroy the ministry.

Sylvia said, "God was protecting you, and God showed me!"

Faith was in awe and said out loud, "Thank you, God, for protecting all of us!"

She and Sylvia talked for a little bit longer, and then said their goodbyes.

"I love you, Mama," Faith said.

"I love you too, baby," Sylvia said with her sweet voice. They hung up, and Faith went in to tell Monty what God showed Sylvia last night.

After dinner, the kids played on the PlayStation, and Faith and Monty sat out on the deck in the back. Monty sat in the chair that was up against the kitchen windows, and Faith sat across from him. They were chatting when Faith saw some sort of flash of light reflecting off the window. When her eyes looked at Monty's face, his mouth was wide open as he stared into the backyard pine trees.

Faith asked him quickly, "What's going on?"

Monty said, "I just saw a few orbs in the trees!"

Faith was exhilarated and quickly got up and sat in the chair beside him.

"I want to see them, I want to see them!" she exclaimed. Her heart was beating fast, but there was nothing. Suddenly Faith saw a beautiful orange transparent orb in the pine trees. Her eyes got big, and before she could speak, it disappeared. She jumped up in excitement and told Monty she saw it. Monty said he saw it too. Faith had never seen an orb before, and it thrilled her to no end! They sat out there for a while and chatted and then went in the house, still talking about the orbs.

***

Later that evening, Kenny's girlfriend, Janiah, called. She wanted to know if she could pick up the kids and take them out for ice cream. Faith told her that was okay, and that they had just finished dinner and would see her in a little while. Faith liked Janiah, who was always good to her kids. When she arrived, she asked Faith if she could talk to her privately, and the two went outside on the deck. Janiah told her that she and Kenny were not getting along at all. Kenny was upset because they couldn't afford another child.

Faith didn't know what to say, except that she was there for her in any way she could be. Janiah hugged Faith and thanked her. She was already eight months pregnant. Faith also told her not to believe everything that Kenny was telling her and that he lied about a lot of things. Janiah said that she could tell Faith was a good woman, and Faith thanked her. Faith yelled for the kids to go with Janiah for ice cream. They excitedly hopped in the car and left.

That Thanksgiving, Faith invited Janiah over for dinner, and she accepted. Faith fixed a wonderful meal, and for some reason, it tasted better than ever! Janiah had a good time, and the kids were glad to have her over because they really liked her. After Janiah left, Faith and the kids helped clean up the dishes and settled down for the evening. The kids went to their rooms to play.

As time went on, Kenny and Janiah's relationship ended. She already had two boys by her first marriage and was now expecting another baby. She told Kenny that she didn't want him in her life anymore, and was soon admitted to the hospital to have her baby. She called Faith and told her she'd keep her informed. A few days later, Janiah announced that she had given birth to a baby boy. Faith asked if she could come up to see her, and Janiah said yes. Faith had already bought a little outfit for the baby and a card for Janiah. She arrived just as they were getting ready to bring the baby into the room.

Janiah told the nurse to hand the baby to Faith. The nurse put the little baby boy in Faith's arms, and she cradled him with such love. She couldn't believe that she was in a hospital room with her ex-husband's girlfriend, holding his baby! Faith didn't care. This was a child, and she felt love for him. She thanked Janiah for letting her hold the baby, and then they talked for a while. Faith handed the baby back to Janiah and went home. Janiah had already informed Kenny that she was going to raise the child on her own.

***

It seemed like things were changing so fast, that it was hard to keep up with everything going on. After dinner one evening, Faith and Monty went in the living room to pray for a while. Monty was deep in meditation and whispered, "Yes, Lord, yes, Lord." Little tears streamed down his cheeks, and he continued saying, "Yes, Lord." Faith wondered what he was hearing from God.

After Monty finished praying, he wiped his eyes. Faith just looked at him with her questioning eyes. He was still silent.

Finally, Faith asked him what he heard from God.

"I'm not quite sure," Monty said. "Just that God is moving us along, and things are going to heat up a little."

Faith was excited because all she ever thought about was getting that much closer to being with George. She didn't even take into consideration that Monty had said that things were going to heat up a little. She went upstairs and hugged and kissed Mark and Julie good night, and then she went to bed. God gave her another dream. Faith saw herself and two men, one on each side of her, all with their spiritual bodies walking down a dusty street. There were rows of houses on either side of the street, and as they were walking, they could see everything, yet people could not see them. It was an amazing feeling.

Suddenly, Faith heard in her spirit a woman yelling for help. Faith knew exactly which house it was, and literally flew quickly to the house and up the staircase. She found an old woman on the floor who had fallen. Faith scooped the old woman up in her arms and put her on her bed. The woman could see her, and Faith told her she was sent by God to help her. The woman screamed with joy and started clapping, and then she got out of bed and started dancing and singing praises. Faith felt the most glorious feeling, and then she woke up.

As she awoke, she just smiled and thanked God for using her to help that woman. She soon fell back asleep. The next morning she got on the computer and sent George an email about her dream. When he responded, he told her that God was giving her confirmation after confirmation, and to keep trusting in Him. Faith said she would. She left for the one cleaning job she had that morning and was home before the kids arrived from school. She made homemade banana bread from an old family recipe because the kids loved it so much. She loved the looks on their faces when they came in and smelled the aroma all through the house. They ran into the kitchen to get their treat.

Chapter 34: Nowhere to Go

"We could never learn to be brave and patient, if there were only joy in the world."
~ Helen Keller

One day, Faith received an email from George telling her that something was about to happen and she needed to put her full trust in God. He told her that she was on a spiritual journey, and so was Monty. George wouldn't tell her what was going to take place at the moment but assured Faith that no matter what things looked like, God had a plan. Faith trusted George and what he was telling her.

There were many times Faith felt like she was leading a double life. She could not tell anyone what she was receiving from George and "Mom." She spilled the beans a bit to Mark and Julie and could tell by the look in their eyes that they probably thought their mom was a little crazy for believing all this, and that somehow their Nanny was "talking" to her. Faith didn't tell them all that had been told.

One morning after everyone was gone, Faith sat down at her computer. It felt good to have the house to herself. As she checked her email, "Mom" popped up on chat again. Faith's heart started pounding with excitement, wondering what Mom had to share with her this time. Faith always had questions and hoped her mom could answer.

Hello child, the chat started.

Hi Mom! Faith typed with excitement.

"Mom" told Faith about this time being a time of trust, no matter what things looked like.

Yes Mom, Faith typed. *I will trust.*

"Mom" told Faith that even though she was getting messages on chat, she was actually standing right beside her in spirit. Faith turned around to see.

You can't see me, Faith, Mom said. *I want to show you something,* she continued. *I can type these messages with my "fingers," or I can use a thought process, and the words will just be there. Like this.*

Suddenly, phrase after phrase popped up so fast that Faith could not keep up.

Faith hollered out, "Slow down, Mom! I can't read that fast!"

She read what was in front of her, and when she was finished "Mom" told her that she didn't have to type. All Faith had to do was speak because "Mom" could hear her and answer back.

"Really?" Faith said out loud.

The words came up on chat from "Mom" that said, *Yes, really.*

Faith was wide-eyed. She sat back in her chair and didn't type messages to Mom the rest of the conversation. She just spoke out loud, and Mom answered! Faith could hardly believe what was taking place! The conversation went on for about twenty minutes, Faith just speaking out loud and mom answering her questions. Faith told her mom how much she missed her, and Mom responded by saying that she never leaves Faith's side.

I'm with you more now than ever before, and God is using me to help you through these next few phases of ministry because you are going to need it.

Thank you, Mom, Faith said. *I don't think I can do this without you.*

The messages popped up, responding to every little thing Faith asked. Then "Mom" said she had to go for now, but would be in touch very soon because another thing was coming up that required Faith's full trust.

Yes, Mom, I will.

Then "Mom" was gone.

Faith just sat there in amazement and was convinced, more than ever, that her mom was there to help her. There was no other explanation as to what just took place other than her mom's spirit coming through. To Faith, this was proof. This is what kept her going through all that was in front of her, no matter how bad things looked. It didn't matter what Kenny, Brandi, or anyone else had to say. Faith just had a conversation with her mother by sitting in a chair and speaking, while getting answers from her mom on the chat! But she couldn't tell anyone about it. They would think she'd lost her mind! But she knew different!

***

A couple of weeks went by, and Faith had pocketed the little bit of money that she made from her jobs. The five months of rent she put down was used up. She did have some money put aside, but it wasn't enough for the full rent. She still didn't have enough jobs and started to worry. A few days later, George wrote her a long letter and asked Faith if she remembered him telling her that God was getting ready to do something and needed for her to trust Him. Faith wrote him back and said, "Yes." Faith told George that whatever it was, she'd obey what God had for her.

George told her not to pay the next two months' rent—that God had it covered. Faith was scared. She has always paid her mortgage payments and in twenty years at her old house was never late, not even once. Faith knew she didn't have all the money needed for the rent that was due in two weeks. When the rent was due, she called the office and told them that she was going to be late. They didn't like it much but told her to have it as soon as she could. Faith was nervous, but she still trusted that God knew what He was doing.

Over the next week, the office kept calling Faith, and she told them that she may not have the money now, but would the following month. She kept telling Monty that she didn't like missing rent payments, and he kept assuring her that it was going to be okay. With both Monty and George telling her this, she believed them, even though it made her nervous. They were great men of God, and she had seen it firsthand. She knew that they could hear from God and wished that she could be more like them. Her heart was always in the right place. Then she remembered her mom telling her that she would have to trust like never before. It was very hard, but she did.

When the next month came, Faith skipped the rent payment again, and by the end of the month found an eviction notice on her front door. She cried and cried. She was confused. She started yelling at God and telling Him that she thought He was going to take care of it. She didn't realize at the time that is not what He meant. She went to the computer and vented to George about the eviction notice. He kept telling her that there are things that he knew that he couldn't tell her yet and that she just really needed to trust. Faith thought the world of George and eventually calmed down.

When Monty got home, Faith told him of the eviction notice. She told him that they had to be out at the end of the month, which was only one week away. Monty told Faith that he was going to be in California, ministering all that week. Faith didn't know what to do. *Where am I supposed to go? What do I do with everything in the house?* Monty told her to get a storage unit and put everything in there for now. He left for California, and George sent Faith an email and told her to get everything moved out, and he'd have instructions for her later on. Faith had to rent a moving truck, and Mark, Julie and Monty's son Jack helped pack up and move everything in the house and put it in storage. She ended up getting two of the biggest storage units.

It was exceptionally cold that weekend, with ice and snow on the ground. However, time seemed to fly by as Faith, and the kids packed everything up over the weekend and got it all in storage. The kids did an awesome job helping, and Faith was so thankful for them and all the hard work they did. Mark went back to his dad's apartment on Sunday. Faith kept out a suitcase for her and a suitcase for Julie, and packed them as full as she could. She kept a couple of blankets so they could return to the house and sleep on the floor. They had to be out in the morning.

Faith called Monty and told him they would spend the last night at the house and was waiting on instructions from George. She kept her computer hooked up at the house. Faith could hardly sleep that night and kept checking over and over for messages from George. She also kept wondering how this is going to affect Mark and Julie. Once again, they were being ripped out of their home. Faith was deeply distraught. All night long she kept praying that the kid's hearts would be okay and asked that God please tell her where to go.

At the end of her prayers, she said, "I trust you, God."

When morning came, Faith, Julie, and Jack cleaned up the house and put their suitcases and the computer in the car. Faith locked up the house and left the key under the mat. They all got in the car and drove off. There were about four inches of snow on the ground, and Faith asked the kids what they wanted for breakfast. Without paying the rent for the past two months, Faith had saved up some money. The kids wanted to go to Hardees, so Faith drove there, and they all sat down and ate. Faith, still thinking that she would hear something from George very soon, knew the only way she would find out is when Monty called. They sat in Hardees taking their time. Faith tried to keep the children's spirits up by smiling and poking fun. She made sure that their tummies were full.

Then Faith just drove around aimlessly for a while. It was all she could do to keep from breaking down. She had to remain vigilant for her daughter. She didn't want Julie to notice any distress at all because she didn't want her to worry. It was now late afternoon, and Faith never heard a word from Monty. She knew he was ministering, but didn't know the schedule. She called a couple of times and left him messages, telling him that she and the kids were just driving around and didn't know where to go. It was now lunchtime, and she took Julie and Jack to get something to eat. They ate lunch in the car as Faith continued to drive around. She felt helpless, hopeless, and worried. She had to be strong for Julie, even though she was falling apart. She had nowhere to go. Everyone had turned against her and wasn't talking to her. There was no one to reach out to.

She pulled off into a shopping center and just sat there, stunned and with tear-filled eyes. All of her belongings were in storage. There she sat with two kids in the car and absolutely nowhere to go. She couldn't believe all that had just transpired. She felt like her world was crumbling around her. She thought of her old home and how everything fell apart, and now this. Thoughts of her children and what they must be going through made her heart hurt even more.

Little did she know as she stared out the window, that this was just the beginning of the next chapter in her life. Little did she know that her whole life as she knew it was about to be stripped away and torn apart, piece by piece. Everything she ever knew, or thought she knew, seemed doomed. It took everything that she had in her not to fall apart right then and there. Faith was an expert at holding things in, but she had to find real strength greater now than ever before. She didn't want to take the chance of Julie seeing her fall into total despair. She had to be strong for her daughter.

Now what? she thought, in the face of complete uncertainty. *Now what?*

Epilogue

As this story ends on a cliffhanger, you might wonder about Faith's plight. What became of her and her children? What became of those glorious promises of ministry? There is no possible way to capture all the details in just one book. Faith's journey carries on in a sequel—Book Two in The Awakening series entitled Journey to the Heart.

Faith eventually finds herself on an incredible path of joy, pain, and enlightenment—one she can't quite imagine. The turbulence of her life continues, but she goes beyond *surviving* the experiences. Along the way, she evolves as a person and as a healer, still wrestling with her own trauma while God prepares her to help others. Her awakening is on the horizon, and thousands will begin their own healing process with her help.

Follow along as more of her story unfolds in Journey to the Heart.

Book Two: Journey to the Heart
Available at www.ElizaAnneMcDaniel.com

Made in the USA
Middletown, DE
12 September 2021